SUE1

DIVUS AUGUSTUS

SUETONIUS
DIVUS AUGUSTUS

Edited with Introduction
and Commentary by
JOHN M. CARTER

Bristol Classical Press

Cover illustration: silver denarius of Augustus minted ca. 20 BC
(British Museum, London BMC 334). [Drawing by Jean Bees]

This impression 2003
First published in 1982 by
Bristol Classical Press
an imprint of
Gerald Duckworth & Co. Ltd.
61 Frith Street, London W1D 3JL
Tel: 020 7434 4242
Fax: 020 7434 4420
inquiries@duckworth-publishers.co.uk
www.ducknet.co.uk

A catalogue record for this book is available
from the British Library

ISBN 0 906515 55 6

Printed in Great Britain by
Antony Rowe Ltd, Eastbourne

FOR

RUTH, COLIN & JUDITH

Head of a statue of Augustus as *pontifex maximus*
from the Via Labicana; Museo delle Terme, Rome.
[Drawing by Jean Bees.]

CONTENTS

PREFACE

This edition of Suetonius' *Life of Augustus* is intended to be
of use to all who have an interest in the historical aspect of
the book. I have attempted on the one hand to incorporate
references to up-to-date scholarship, and on the other to make
the commentary intelligible to, and usable by, students of
history who may not be able to read Suetonius in the original.
It is for this reason that I have commented from time to time
on the Penguin translation of Robert Graves (revised by Michael
Grant) as being the version most likely to be in the hands of
such students. I have also assumed that readers will have to
hand the excellent commentary of P.A. Brunt and J.M. Moore on
Augustus' *Res Gestae*.

I am aware that to confine oneself in the main to one aspect
of an author's work is not an entirely satisfactory procedure.
I have therefore tried to compensate for commenting on Suetonius chiefly as a historical 'source' by saying something in
the Introduction on questions of genre, style, and composition,
although lack of space has forced me to be brief and dogmatic.
The scope of the edition and my own limitations have likewise
entailed a neglect of Suetonius' Latinity which is regrettable
but not I hope fatal to adequate interpretation.

It is usual, in writing about Augustus, to refer to him as
Octavian up to 27 B.C. and as Augustus thereafter. Suetonius'
treatment makes it impossible to follow this convention and I
have therefore used the name Augustus throughout.

As regards bibliography, I have in most cases thought it sufficient to cite recent works, through which the full range of
references can without difficulty be reached by those who wish
to pursue any topic in greater depth. Complete documentation
of all the views and information presented in the commentary
would swell it enormously and only marginally increase whatever usefulness it may possess. Many standard works do not
appear in these pages; but this need not mean that they have
been ignored.

In conclusion, it remains to express my thanks to the British
Academy and the Central Research Fund of London University
for making possible a period of study in Rome, and to the
Council of Royal Holloway College for granting me leave and
supporting the minor expenses of my research.

9th May 1981   J.M.C.

INTRODUCTION

Suetonius and the Sources for Augustan History

§1   Suetonius' *Life of Augustus* is, with the possible
exception of the emperor's own *Res Gestae,* the most important
single document concerning him which has come down to us. Of
the three other connected accounts of Augustus, two deal only
with the early years of his career: these are the fragment of
the biography written by his contemporary and acquaintance
Nicolaus of Damascus, court historian to Herod the Great; and
the latter part of the work of the 2nd century historian Appian
on Rome's *Civil Wars,* which ends in 35 B.C. The third account
is that of Dio Cassius, senator and twice consul in Severan
times, which has some gaps but survives in large part complete.
All three men came from the eastern half of the empire and
wrote in Greek, and their understanding of Roman institutions
at the time of Augustus is not always perfect. The loss of
most of Nicolaus' biography is not the tragedy it might seem,
since it was based on Augustus' own, doubtless highly tendentious, autobiography and in any case went no further than
25 B.C. Appian, though good and detailed, does not even reach
the battle of Actium, while Dio (not unnaturally, seeing that
he was writing a History of Rome) has large omissions and cannot be pressed on points of detail and chronology. Suetonius,
on the other hand, is free from all these criticisms. His
treatment is complete, he is far enough from Augustus and his
dynasty to be tolerably objective, and as an Italian and high
civil servant he has an understanding of things Roman which
sometimes eludes the others. By temperament a compiler, he
preserves many precious facts whose accuracy there is no
reason to question. His major defect, from the point of view
of the modern historian, is that he has no interest in chronology and thus obscures the processes of change at work in the
forty years of the first princeps' reign. He does, though,
understand the importance of evidence and is remarkable amongst
ancient historical writers for the range and quantity of what
he adduces. No doubt his work in the imperial secretariat
(see §18 below) was responsible for developing this trait.

§2   Suetonius and Dio are thus the bedrock of any narrative
of Augustus' reign. (For their relationship, see §12 below.)
Other important literary sources are the relevant chapters of
Velleius Paterculus' outline of Roman history, published in
A.D. 29 and particularly concerned to flatter Tiberius; the
epitome of Livy; some of Plutarch's *Lives,* especially that of
Antony; the letters and Philippics of Cicero (for the years
44-43 B.C.); and the Augustan poets, who reveal attitudes and
ideals (and sometimes even policies) which are of the greatest
importance for our comprehension of the more intangible aspects
of Augustus' regime. The Jewish historian Josephus is valuable

for the relations of Rome and the Jews, and the geographer
Strabo describes the empire as it was under Augustus. We also
have Tacitus, particularly the opening chapters of the *Annals,*
and a whole range of post-Augustan writers, notably the Elder
Pliny, who contribute diverse snippets of information (see
CAH 10.866-876).

§3   The composite picture thus obtained is controlled and
amplified by the evidence of excavation and all kinds of non-
literary material, amongst which pride of place must go to
Augustus' own enumeration of his achievements, the great
inscription from Ankara known as the *Res Gestae* or the
Monumentum Ancyranum. This is a copy of the text set up on
two bronze pillars outside the emperor's mausoleum in Rome.
(See Brunt & Moore 1967). Other inscriptions, the coinage -
astonishing in its range and diversity of types -, works of
art, buildings, religious monuments, and the outlines of
Augustan law still visible in Justinian's *Digest*, all add to
the body of evidence which can be used to understand the
Augustan principate. But none can replace the coherent
exposition of the literary artist; the other material may
illuminate, confirm or correct him, but on its own it remains
enigmatic and a little impersonal. The key to Augustan
history must remain the literary accounts: and of these the
best, in its own terms, is that of Suetonius.

The Character of Suetonian Biography

§4   Biography was a relative newcomer among the various
genres of literary composition practised by the Greeks and
Romans. It tended to retain strong links with rhetorical
encomium, whether of the living or the dead, and with memoirs
composed by followers, admirers, or friends of the subject - a
species of composition which goes back to the early fourth
century B.C. with Xenophon's Socratic writings and Isocrates'
panegyric of Evagoras. It was also heavily influenced by the
Peripatetic school of philosophy, which was interested in biography for two reasons: one ethical, since it was believed
that the study of individual character could lead a man to a
more accurate understanding of virtue and vice, and that an
individual revealed his character through his actions; and
the other more technical, because the development of an art
could be illustrated by a collection of Lives of its well-
known practitioners, as for example in Suetonius' own *Lives
of the Famous Grammarians.* Peripatetic biography thus tended
to have a more objective character and indeed its most famous
and successful exponent Plutarch (who was about 20 years older
than Suetonius) says: "Perhaps it is not a bad thing for me to
introduce one or two pairs of characters of reckless life and
conspicuous defects into my *Lives,* not to divert and entertain

my readers ... (but so that) we shall be more eager to observe and imitate the better lives if we do not leave unrecorded the bad and the blameworthy" (Plutarch, *Demetrius* 1.5-6). None the less, panegyric and ethical admiration are not far apart, and both kinds of biography are inevitably structured by the categories of moral approval and disapproval. Events are told not simply because they happened, but in order to bring out some aspect of the character of the individual. This is the basis of the distinction between biography and history of which the earliest Latin biographer, Cornelius Nepos (see 77n.) is well aware. Introducing Pelopidas, he says: "I am afraid that if I start on a systematic exposition of his achievements, I may appear to be writing history rather than giving an account of his life" (*Nepos* 16.1). Plutarch is even more specific in divorcing the two: "I am not writing history, but biography, and in the most famous deeds there is not always a revelation of virtue or vice. In fact a little thing like a saying or a joke often reveals character more clearly than murderous battles, or vast musterings of armies, or sieges of cities" (Plutarch, *Alexander* 1.2).

§5 But ancient biography not only forswears historical explanation. It also refuses to set a man against the context of his age. Partly this is because of the origins of the genre, as described above, in which the individual's actions, achievements, and character are the sole focus of attention. But it is also partly because of that tendency of ancient thought termed 'substantialism' by Collingwood to see a man's character as something fixed and 'given' at birth. What to us appears as change (and hence needing explanation) was, to the ancients, merely the progressive uncovering of qualities which, though always present, had not at first been revealed. Tacitus' comments on Tiberius (*Annals* 6.51.5-6) are a perfect instance of this mode of thought: "his character, too, had its various stages. So long as he was a private citizen or held commands under Augustus, his life and reputation were blameless; while Germanicus and Drusus still lived, he was devious and cunning in pretending to virtuous qualities; until the death of his mother he was a mixture of good and bad; while he favoured (or feared) Sejanus, his cruelty was detestable but his lusts concealed; and finally, when shame and fear meant nothing to him and he followed only the *dictates of his own nature,* he launched out upon criminal and obscene wrongdoing". Suetonius delivers a similar judgement (*Tiberius* 42.1): "but after he had acquired the freedom of seclusion away from the public gaze, all his vices, *long imperfectly concealed,* were at last indulged together".

§6 This conception of an underlying static character revealed by action was in harmony with yet a third strand present in the ancestry of Latin biography - the Roman funeral *laudatio* (see 8.1 n.). In this, as in Roman commemorative inscriptions, stress was laid above all on the deceased's achievements in

public life, and particularly in war. By great deeds a
prominent member of the community both increased the power
and prosperity of the Roman people, and justified the status
which that people had conferred on him and his family by
choosing him to be a magistrate and military commander. Thus
there existed a native Roman tradition, which sought to re-
member and judge men by their deeds, long before the influence
of Greek biography reached Italy. A splendid product of this
tradition is Tacitus' *Agricola,* written in Suetonius' own lifetime.

§7   Suetonius' *Lives of the Caesars* clearly combine the Roman
'documentary' approach, in which the facts narrated allow the
reader to draw the desired conclusion for himself, and the
Greek ethical approach, in which the material is consistently
given relevance by the moral framework within which it appears,
whether this is explicit, as in *Nero* 19.3, or implicit, as in
Augustus. The particular combination is unique, and in this
sense Suetonius can be said to be original. His own earlier
and much shorter biographies of grammarians, rhetoricians, and
poets belong by their subject-matter to the world of Greek
literature and by their focus of interest to the 'technical'
species of Peripatetic biography; while his only extant pre-
decessor in the genre in Latin, Cornelius Nepos, works on a
far smaller scale and his clear emphasis on illustrating
qualities of character keeps him much closer to the kind of
ethical biography composed by Plutarch. This illustrative
trend, which is so clear in Plutarch and Nepos, favours the
presentation of information analytically, by categories; and
given the static conception of individual character and the
desire not to trespass on the territory of History which has
been noted above, the result seems inevitable. Speaking of
Augustus, Suetonius says (ch. 9): "after laying out a sort of
summary of his life, I shall go through its parts one by one,
not in chronological order but by categories, so that they can
be more distinctly presented and understood." This is the
most precise statement anywhere in the *Lives* of Suetonius'
general principle of procedure (though the beginning of *Julius,*
which could well have contained similar remarks, is lost).
The main heads which he uses to order his material are, in
Augustus, military life and achievements (10-25), civil and
political adminstration (26-60), and private life and interests
(60-93). The last of these flows, by a skilful transition,
into the narrative of Augustus' last days and death, and the
first is prefaced by the usual account of ancestry and early
life which was a necessary part of any extended biography.
The general historical background, and much of the detail, is
taken for granted. This is the basic pattern which underlies
all the *Lives,* though it is varied and adapted to suit each
emperor's career. In *Julius,* for example, the chronologically
ordered section describing his rise to power is naturally of
considerable length, and the account of the events leading up
to his murder is full and approaches History; but the inter-

vening portion contains many of the same sub-heads as
Augustus (e.g. adornment of the city, personal appearance,
sexual behaviour, treatment of soldiers) but in a different
order and not clearly differentiated into 'public' and
'private' categories. It is perhaps true that Suetonius
was by nature a cataloguer, as the subjects of some of his
lost works suggest (amongst them a book on Greek games,
another on ill-omened phrases, one on *Signs used in Books*,
and two on games and spectacles of the Romans); but we must
not forget that the traditions (such as they were) of the
biographical genre made it difficult to adopt a different
approach and that he is anything but mechanical in the way
he presents his various subjects.

(For further discussion of Suetonian biography, see Steidle
1951, Townend 1967, Mouchova 1968.)

The 'Life of Augustus'

§8 The *Augustus* forms the second of the eight books in which
the Twelve Caesars were originally arranged. An analysis of
its structure and content may be found in the introductory
commentaries to chapters 1, 5, 9, 13, 17, 19, 20, 24, 26, 32,
35, 41, 46, 47, 51, 59, 61, 66, 68, 79, 84, 90, and 97 below.
These can be read consecutively for a general view of the work,
and should be interpreted in the light of what has been said
above on the character of Suetonian biography.

§9 *Augustus* is the longest of the *Lives* and is generally
reckoned one of the best, both for the sympathy with which
Suetonius treats his subject and for the fullness and quality
of the information given. In this latter respect, *Julius*
and *Augustus* are noticeably superior to the later *Lives*, and
it has been suggested, with some plausibility, that the decline
from *Tiberius* onwards may be connected with Suetonius' dis-
missal from his post in Hadrian's secretariat and his consequent loss of easy access to the documentary material of the
palace archives, including imperial letters. This, however,
is not the only possible explanation, and it could be that
Suetonius lost the interest necessary to treat all twelve
Caesars at the same high level, or that the recently published
historical works of Tacitus and biographies of Plutarch (which
included lives of all the emperors from Augustus to Vitellius,
amongst them the extant *Galba* and *Otho*) had made his subjects
less suitable for extended treatment.

§10 Whatever the reason for this difference in quality in
the later *Lives*, it is clear that Suetonius drew upon a wide
range of material in composing *Augustus*: the emperor's autobiography (2.3, 27.4, 85.1), edicts (28.2), and autograph

letters (71.2, 87.3, 88); decrees of the senate (5, 58.2);
letters of Antony (*passim*), Cicero (3.2), and Cassius of
Parma (4.2); several writers known only by his citations
(Aquilius Niger, 11; Julius Saturninus, 27.2; Julius Marathus,
79.2, 94.3; C. Drusus, 94.6); others like Cremutius Cordus
(35.2), Valerius Messalla (74), Cornelius Nepos (77), and
Asclepiades of Mendes (94.4), who are referred to elsewhere
although none of their writings on Augustus survive; the
evidence of dedications (57.1); and the *Res Gestae* (43.1,
unattributed, but almost a verbatim quotation). Ancient
authors do not on the whole name their authorities, and it
is unlikely that this is anything like a complete list of
Suetonius' sources. For example, he never cites Livy, whose
history came down to 9 B.C., and must have been known to him.
And surely he also used the works of Pollio, Cassius Severus,
Seneca, and the Elder Pliny, not to speak of more obscure
figures, all of whom he cites in connection with other
emperors.

§11 To what extent Suetonius knew these sources at first hand
and to what extent he drew his information from secondary
accounts seems a question impossible to answer, as the latter
(notably the writings of Cremutius Cordus and Plutarch's
Augustus) do not survive. Only in one case, that of the *Res
Gestae*, is it possible to check Suetonius against his source.
There are some ten or a dozen possible references, ranging
from near-verbatim quotation, through obvious echoes of
Augustus' phraseology, to information which although clearly
originating with the *Res Gestae* could equally well have been
obtained from an intermediate source. In my view, the near-
quotations and the fact that the text was a prominent feature
of one of the more remarkable sights of Rome make it fantastic
to suppose that Suetonius had not read it for himself, even
though he never names it. If this is so, it may seem surprising that there are three places where there is an obvious
discrepancy between Suetonius and the monument. The first is
in ch. 10, where Suetonius gives as a reason for all the civil
wars Augustus' desire to take vengeance on Caesar's murderers,
while Augustus himself speaks of "freeing the republic from
the tyranny of a faction"; but Augustus' statement is clearly
tendentious, and there was no reason for Suetonius to reproduce
it if he did not believe it. The second is at 27.5, where
Suetonius (like Dio) makes Augustus accept the *cura morum
legumque* which the emperor says he declined. The explanation
here may be that Augustus' denial is oblique: "I accepted no
magistracy that was not in accord with ancestral custom".
By Suetonius' day, the imperial censorship had become, in
practice, just such a general "oversight of laws and morals"
as had been offered to Augustus and he may have thought that
it was, in fact, in accord with Republican forms. The third
discrepancy, at 35.1, concerns the revisions of the roll of
the senate (*lectiones*) and I can offer no explanation except
to observe that ancient scholarship depended much more on

memory and less on checking than the modern variety, and
Suetonius may simply have become muddled. These three instances apart, Suetonius has reported Augustus faithfully;
but it is fairly clear that the *Res Gestae*, though useful,
was not a source of great importance for him, nor did its
bald paragraphs form the framework on which he erected his
Life.

§12 Suetonius' general accuracy is shown by his substantial
agreement with the considerably more detailed, though incomplete, chronological account of Books 45-56 of Dio. Dio was
writing a hundred years after Suetonius, and he practices
total reticence in the matter of his sources. Therefore the
fact that he does not mention Suetonius does not necessarily
mean that he did not use him. But use is unlikely, for two
reasons: first, Suetonius' analytical and summarising method
of presentation makes it impossible for a conventional historian to convert his material into a narrative; and second,
the way the two authors report the dream of Atia (94.4) makes
it certain that Dio did not take the story from Suetonius but
either direct from Asclepiades or via a different intermediary.
The thesis of Schwartz (*RE* 3.1716) that Tacitus, Dio, and
Suetonius all depend on an unknown 'annalist' (whose lack of
character is so complete that even the date from which he is
supposed to have begun his annals eludes identification) has
recently been restated by Manuwald (1979); but I cannot believe
that Suetonius' *Augustus,* with its topical arrangement, wide
range of reference, and diversity of material, depends on a
single 'main source'. A reading of, for example, chapters
45-56 of *Julius* will dispel any notion that Suetonius had not
read widely in the primary source-material or was incapable
of handling it critically. The following position thus
emerges: Dio's 'main source' (if he had one) is unknown;
Suetonius did not have a 'main source' at all; Dio did not
use Suetonius; and yet there exists a very large measure of
agreement between them.

§13 We may therefore feel reasonably confident about the
reliability of both authors. One can of course find errors
in Suetonius, but these are for the most part trivial (see
e.g. notes on 17.4, 30.2, 31.2, 101.2 below). Apart from the
question of the senatorial *lectiones* and the *cura morum*, discussed above, his only serious mistakes seem to be in reporting
the patrician status of the Octavii (2.1) and in garbling the
admittedly complicated and controversial events of 44-43 B.C.
(ch. 10). Even here, he does not really misrepresent
Augustus' political stance, and it might be argued in Suetonius' defence that it was not felt to be the business of
the ancient biographer to provide an accurate historical
background to the actions of his subject. Finally, there is
the chapter on omens and prodigies (94) - but such stories
are in a class of their own and belong to a very special sub-
genre which never considered the literal truth to be important.

(For fuller discussion of the composition and emphases of
Augustus, see Hanslik 1954, Gascou 1976, Cizek 1977.)

Suetonius' Style

§14 Suetonius writes taut, economical, matter-of-fact Latin,
in which every word tells; but he is no conscious stylist
like the Younger Pliny and no seeker after effect like
Tacitus. Although the present edition is directed specifically
towards the historical content of his work, one feature of
his writing deserves notice because it is important to a
correct understanding of the text.

§15 Suetonius occasionally spells out the pattern of organisation he proposes to apply to his subject (the so-called
divisiones); notable examples in *Augustus* are in chapters
9 and 61, and it is not difficult to relate the text to the
heads there set out. What is not always so apparent is that
he constantly uses the same technique on a much smaller scale,
within paragraphs and even within sentences. Most paragraphs
begin with a key word which announces the topic about to be
treated. Two or more aspects of this topic may immediately
be indicated, of which one will then be handled. This finished, Suetonius will switch without any transition or warning
to the second, and so on. A good example is chapters 26-27 of
which the first sentence runs: "he took magistracies and
offices both (a) before the legal age and (b) of a new sort
and (c) perpetual". The rest of ch. 26 then deals with (a),
Augustus' consulships, all of which except the last two were
held below the legal age established in the Republic; in
ch. 27 we meet the triumvirate, which is (b), though it is
easy to miss the connection; and at 27.5 we come to (c),
perpetual tribunician power and perpetual 'oversight of laws
and morals'. Thus (c) is not in fact the somewhat illogical
and disconnected addition to (b) which on a quick or partial
reading it would seem to be. Within a single sentence an
instance is 35.3: "so that those selected and approved should
perform their duties as senators with (a) more ceremony and
(b) less trouble, he enacted that (a) before he took his seat
each man should offer incense and wine at the altar of the god
in whose temple the session was being held, and (b) regular
meetings of the senate should take place no more than twice
a month ...". If this peculiarity of Suetonius' style is not
appreciated, the reader will be tempted to interpret examples
illustrating only one aspect of a topic as though they applied
to all the aspects mentioned; and in consequence Suetonius
will appear to be a far less precise writer than he is.

§16 One other remarkable feature, though it causes no difficulty,
is that Augustus is the (unexpressed) subject, or very occ-

asionally the object, of almost every sentence from ch. 5
to ch. 100. This is a demonstration of how personal biography
could impose a pattern of thought and expression. It also
contributes to a certain monotony in the writing.

Suetonius' Life

§17 We know from Suetonius himself (*Otho* 10) that his father,
Suetonius Laetus, served as military tribune in the Thirteenth
Legion in A.D. 69. He therefore possessed the requisite
property-census (400,000 HS) to be an *eques* ('knight') and
belonged to the comfortably-off upper class of the empire,
men who constituted the aristocracy of the provinces and of
Italy outside Rome. His son, C. Suetonius Tranquillus, was
born ca. A.D. 65-72 (*Nero* 57.2, *Domitian* 12.2) perhaps at Hippo
Regius (Bône) on the North African coast some 150 miles west
of Carthage. Suetonius was in Rome as a teenager (*adulescent-
ulus*, *Domitian* 12.2) in the 80's, doubtless completing his ed-
ucation in the capital in the normal manner of the sons of the
municipal aristocracy who had some kind of public career in
view. We next hear of him some ten to fifteen years later, in
the correspondence of the younger Pliny, consul in the year 100,
advocate, *littérateur*, and administrator, who became his patron
and secured a military tribunate for him (Pliny, *Epp.* 5.10, 9.34)
and when Pliny was sent to govern Bithynia in A.D. 109-111
Suetonius accompanied him as one of his entourage (*cohors amicorum*). Evidently he earned Pliny's gratitude, for Pliny
obtained for him from Trajan the *ius trium liberorum*, by which,
although childless, he was permitted to enjoy certain legal
advantages conferred on fathers of three children (Pliny, *Epp.*
10.94-95).

§18 Most of the rest of the story is given by a damaged inscription from Hippo (Smallwood 1966, no. 281; Townend 1961)
which shows that Suetonius, having already attained the respectable, but unremarkable, distinction of being enrolled as
a member of the metropolitan jury panels (*adlectus inter sel-
ectos iudices*), was appointed to a priesthood, probably in
the capital. If this last inference is correct, Suetonius
is revealed as a recipient of imperial patronage and his subsequent appearance in the upper echelons of the palace bureaucracy is not a sudden stroke of the emperor's favour - still
less so if the gap which exists in the inscription before the
post *a studiis* contained an administrative office rather than
an honour. The exact duties of the *a studiis* are unknown,
except that they must have been connected in some way with
literary, and possibly legal, matters. Suetonius passed on,
understandably, to the oversight of the imperial liberary, the
post he must have been holding when Trajan died in 117. The
new emperor Hadrian promoted him to be his chief secretary and

one is tempted to suppose that it was Suetonius' tenure of this
office which in some way prompted the Hippo inscription. His
duties included overseeing the emperor's correspondence with
provincial governors and drafting replies to petitions and
other important letters. He must have worked closely with the
emperor and had ample opportunity for influencing his decisions.
This was the summit of his official career. Only the great
prefectures, of Egypt, of the corn supply, of the praetorian
guard, remained for him to reach; but they were likely to be
for ever barred to him because of his lack of military experience.

§19 Suetonius' promotion under Hadrian is associated with
that of another friend of Pliny, Septicius Clarus, who became
Hadrian's praetorian prefect. It appears that on Pliny's
death Septicius took over the role of Suetonius' patron. They
rose and fell together, for both were dismissed, if we can
believe the writer of the *Life of Hadrian* (11.3) in the
Historia Augusta, for over familiarity with the empress Sabina.
The date apparently indicated for this event, A.D. 122, has
now been thrown into doubt by the discovery of a military
diploma (*AE* 1973, 459) which may date Septicius' appointment
to the praetorian prefecture after 10th August 123 (Gascou
1978; *contra* Alföldy 1979). This at least makes it possible
that both he and Suetonius were still in office in 128 when
Hadrian visited Africa, an occasion on which the emperor's
secretary could well have been honoured by the citizens of
Hippo if he had been instrumental in securing some favour for
the town. The date of Suetonius' death is unknown, but is
probably later than 129-132, since he makes a reference to
Domitian's widow Domitia Longina, who survived until then,
as though she were no longer alive (*Titus* 10.2).

Imperium, Auctoritas, and Tribunicia Potestas

§20 The basis of constitutional power at Rome was *imperium,*
'power of command'. This was conferred on the higher magistrates (praetors, consuls, dictator) after, or as a result of,
their election to office. There were two varieties, civil
(*imperium domi*) exercised within the *pomoerium,* the sacred
boundary of the city of Rome, and military (*imperium militiae*),
exercised outside it. These could be separated. For example,
censors, whose duties were civil and who exercised their office
entirely within the city, possessed only *imperium domi* (if
they possessed it at all; the question is disputed), while
proconsuls possessed only *imperium militiae,* which they assumed
at a special ceremony on leaving the city for their province
and had to lay down again on re-entering the *pomoerium.*

§21 *Imperium* was not an absolute power. It was limited ter-

ritorially by the sphere (province) to which the holder was
designated. It was limited in time, either by the (normally
annual) duration of an elective office or by the terms of the
senatorial decree or popular law appointing a man to a pro-
magistracy or special command. It was limited by the existence
of equal or greater *imperia,* whose holders could impose a veto
on colleague or subordinate. Thus the principle of collegiality
seen in all Roman magistracies except the dictatorship served
as a check on the misuse of power. And finally, it was limited
by the general requirement laid upon magistrates to observe
the laws, and by the right of the individual citizen, so long
as he was not on military service, to appeal to the tribunes
of the plebs or to other magistrates whose *imperium* allowed
them to interpose a veto. Neither could *imperium* be delegated
except by express authority of senate or people, since it was
personal to the holder.

§22 The ranking order of holders of *imperium* (dictator –
consul - proconsul - praetor) corresponded to no difference
in their actual powers. A praetor could give the same range
of commands, and expect the same obedience, as a consul.
The purpose of the ranking order was to eliminate conflicts
of authority (not always successfully, as the great disaster
at Orange in 105 B.C. showed). Thus the only difference
between a commander who was acting *pro consule,* i.e. with
'consular' *imperium,* and one who was acting *pro praetore,*
i.e. with 'praetorian' *imperium,* was that the former could
give orders to the latter. It is for this reason that the provincial governors to whom Augustus, who himself held consular
imperium, delegated the power, were invested with only praetorian *imperium* in spite of the fact that many of them had
held consulships and were commanding the most important armies
of the state; while the much less significant governorships
of senatorial provinces (see 47n.) carried, as they had always
done, the title of *proconsul* although the vast majority of
their holders had held no higher magistracy than the praetorship.

§23 In addition to executive and military authority, *imperium*
also included powers of jurisdiction (though such powers
were separable from *imperium* and could be held independently).
It was by virtue of these that the proconsul was the highest
judicial authority in a province, and the urban and peregrine
praetors dispensed civil justice at Rome. Consular jurisdiction was a rarity in the late Republic, but was resuscitated
under Augustus and his successors.

§24 The military and political necessities of the late
Republic and early Empire resulted in the creation of *imperium
maius,* 'overriding *imperium*' which prevented clashes (or
deadlock) between holders of equal *imperium* who might have
reason to exercise it in the same area (see Last 1947). In
the case of Augustus, it was needed after 23 B.C., when by
ceasing to be consul, but continuing to govern his provinces

as proconsul, he lost the clear precedence over other provincial governors which his simultaneous tenure of the
consulship had hitherto given him. After this, the conferment
of *imperium maius* (not necessarily over the whole empire)
became a recognised way of marking out an imperial successor.
This power is usually, but inaccurately, referred to in
modern discussion as *imperium maius proconsulare,* a term
unknown to the Romans of Augustus' day.

§25 There can, in my view, be little doubt that it was
Augustus' continuous tenure of *imperium*, first consular and
then *maius*, together with the direct control of the strongest
provinces of the empire, which was the constitutional foundation of his power. His concealment of this *imperium* in the
Res Gestae probably amounts to proof of the proposition. The
attempts of Magdelain (1947) and Grant (1946) to convert that
important but intangible quality of *auctoritas* (personal
authority) which Augustus undoubtedly possessed (cf. *Res Gestae*
34.3) into some form of specific constitutional authority have
not won much support. As to the tribunician power, this has
commonly been held to be an important constitutional prop
(so proving the success of Augustan propaganda on the matter);
the truth is different, as I have tried to show in my note to
27.5 below. Discussions of the 'essence' of the Augustan
principate are by their nature inconclusive and not particularly rewarding, but much of value may be found in Wickert
1954, Béranger 1953, and Grenade 1961 - works which emanate
from a continental tradition of scholarship very different
from that which produced Syme's pungent and magisterial
Roman Revolution (1939), still the best single book for
obtaining an insight into the politics and power struggles
of the dying Republic and nascent Empire.

CHRONOLOGICAL TABLE

The left hand column includes in brackets the dates of Augustus'
consulships. Large case numbers after events refer to the re-
levant chapter of Suetonius.

B.C. 63   *Sept. 23* Birth of Augustus - 5.

     49   Outbreak of civil war between Caesar and Pompey.

     48   Caesar defeats Pompey at Pharsalus. Flight and
                 death of Pompey.

     45   Defeat of Pompey's sons at Munda.

     44   *March* 15 Murder of Caesar; Augustus returns to
                 Italy, opposes the consul Antony, raises an
                 army, and allies himself with the senatorial
                 group led by Cicero.

     43   Augustus is given (*Jan. 7*) a grant of *imperium*
   (*cos*.I)   by the senate - 8 and 10. Siege and (*April*)
                 battles of Mutina; deaths of the consuls
                 Hirtius and Pansa - 10-11. Augustus seizes
                 (*Aug. 19*) his first consulship - 26. Form-
                 ation of triumvirate (*Nov. 27*); proscriptions
                 - 27.

     42   Julius Caesar officially deified (*Jan.*). Cam-
                 paign and battles (*Oct.- Nov.*) of Philippi - 13.

     41   Antony in the East, meets Cleopatra. Civil war in
                 Italy between L. Antonius and Augustus - 13 - 14.

     41-40   Parthians invade Syria and Asia Minor.

     40   Surrender of L.Antonius (*Feb.?*) at Perusia - 15.
                 Return of Antony from Alexandria. Augustus
                 marries Scribonia - 62. 'Treaty' of Brundisium
                 between Antony and Augustus (*Autumn*). Antony
                 marries Octavia.

     39   'Treaty' of Misenum between the triumvirs and
                 Sextus Pompeius. Augustus divorces Scribonia
                 (*Dec.?*) - 62.

     39-38   Antony's generals drive the Parthians out of Syria.

     38   Augustus marries Livia - 62 and starts war against
                 Sextus Pompeius - 16.

     37   Triumvirate renewed by 'Treaty' of Tarentum

	(*Summer*) between Augustus and Antony - 27 n. Antony leaves Octavia in Italy and joins Cleopatra.
36	Augustus and Agrippa defeat Sextus Pompeius; Lepidus bids for power but is eliminated - 16. Antony conducts his disastrous Parthian expedition. Augustus given sacrosanctity.
35	Sextus Pompeius killed in Asia.
35-34	Augustus conducts successful military operations in Illyria - 20.
34	Antony invades and annexes Armenia. 'Donations of Alexandria' (*late Autumn*).
33 (*cos*. II)	Aedileship of Agrippa. Sharp deterioration in relations between Antony and Augustus. Expiry of triumvirate (*Dec. 31*) - 27 n.
32	Flight of consuls and more than a third of the senate to Antony; Italy and the western provinces swear oath of allegiance to Augustus - 17. Both sides make open preparations for war. Antony divorces Octavia.
31 (*cos*.III)	Campaign and battle of Actium (*Sept. 2*); Antony and Cleopatra flee to Egypt - 17.
31-30	Parthians overrun Armenia.
30 (*cos*.IV)	Augustus captures Alexandria (*Aug. 1*); suicides of Antony and Cleopatra - 17.
29 (*cos*.V)	Augustus returns to Italy and celebrates (*Aug. 13-15*) his triple triumph - 22.
28 (*cos*.VI)	Constitutional normalisation, culminating in 'First Settlement'.
27 (*cos*.VII)	'First Settlement' (*Jan. 13* and *16*); Augustus receives the governorship of Spain, Gaul, Syria, Cyprus, and Egypt for 10 years and remains consul - 47 n. He takes the name 'Augustus' and leaves Rome for Gaul and Spain.
26-25 (*cos*.VIII-IX)	Augustus' Cantabrian war - 20.
25	Marriage of Julia to Marcellus (December?).
24 (*cos*.X)	Augustus returns to Rome from Spain.

23 (*cos*.XI)	Severe illness of Augustus, followed by 'Second Settlement': he resigns his consulship, is granted *imperium maius* everywhere outside Rome, and counts his years of tribunician power from June 27 of this year - 27 n. and 28. Death of Marcellus (*Autumn*).
22	Augustus refuses dictatorship (*ca. Feb.*) and perpetual consulship.
22-19	Augustus visits Sicily, Greece, and the East.
21	Agrippa marries Julia.
20	Tiberius places Roman nominee on Armenian throne and the Parthians return captured Roman prisoners and legionary standards.
19	Augustus returns to Rome and receives consular powers and insignia. Agrippa in Spain.
18	Augustus' *imperium maius* renewed for 10 years; Agrippa is granted the tribunician power for 5 years (? also *imperium maius*).
18-17	'Moral' legislation of Augustus - 34.
17	*Ludi Saeculares* - 31. Augustus adopts his grandsons Gaius and Lucius - 64.
16-13	Agrippa in the East; Augustus in Gaul supervising campaigns.
15	Campaigns of Tiberius and Drusus in the Alpine regions (as first steps towards annexing Germany).
13	Agrippa granted *imperium maius* and his tribunician power renewed.
12	Death of Agrippa. Augustus becomes Pontifex Maximus after Lepidus' death in 13.
12-9	Campaigns of Tiberius in Dalmatia; Drusus on the Rhine - 20-21.
11	Tiberius marries Julia - 63.
9	Death of Drusus.
8	Augustus' *imperium maius* renewed. Death of Maecenas.
8-7	Tiberius campaigns on the Rhine.

6	Tiberius given tribunician power, but then retires to Rhodes.
5 (*cos*.XII)	Gaius Caesar introduced to public life and designated consul for A.D. 1.
2 (*cos*. XIII)	Lucius Caesar introduced to public life and designated consul for A.D. 4. Dedication of Temple of Mars Ultor and Forum of Augustus - 29. Title of Pater Patriae officially conferred on Augustus - 58. Banishment of the elder Julia - 65.
1	Expiry of Tiberius' tribunician power.
A.D. 1-3	Gaius Caesar campaigns in the East.
2	Tiberius returns to Italy; death of Lucius Caesar - 65.
3	Augustus' *imperium maius* renewed.
4	Death of Gaius Caesar - 65. Augustus adopts Tiberius and Agrippa Postumus - 65 - and re-invests Tiberius with tribunician power (? also *imperium* equal to his own).
4-6	Tiberius brings most of Germany under Roman control.
6	Revolt in Pannonia and Dalmatia - 21.
7-8	Banishment of Agrippa Postumus and the younger Julia - 65.
7-9	Tiberius suppresses Pannonian and Dalmatian revolts.
9	The Germans annihilate 3 legions under Quintilius Varus - 23.
10-11	Tiberius and Germanicus hold the Rhine frontier and make a limited counter-attack.
13	Renewal of Augustus' *imperium maius* and Tiberius' tribunician power. Conferment of *imperium* equal to Augustus' on Tiberius (if not already given in A.D. 4).
14	Death of Augustus (*Aug. 19*) - 99-100.

Table I

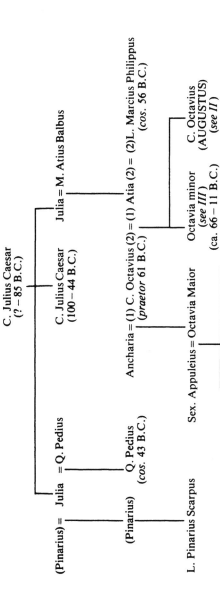

C. Julius Caesar
(? – 85 B.C.)

(Pinarius) = Julia = Q. Pedius

C. Julius Caesar
(100 – 44 B.C.)

Julia = M. Atius Balbus

(Pinarius)

Q. Pedius
(cos. 43 B.C.)

Ancharia = (1) C. Octavius (2) = (1) Atia (2) = (2)L. Marcius Philippus
(praetor 61 B.C.)   (cos. 56 B.C.)

L. Pinarius Scarpus

Sex. Appuleius = Octavia Maior

Octavia minor
(see III)
(ca. 66 – 11 B.C.)

C. Octavius
(AUGUSTUS)
(see II)

Sex. Appuleius
(cos. 29 B.C.)

M. Appuleius
(cos. 20 B.C.)

Table II

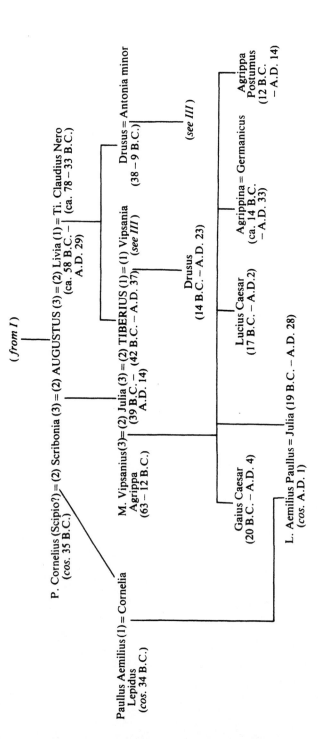

(*from I*)

P. Cornelius (Scipio?) = (2) Scribonia (3) = (2) AUGUSTUS (3) = (2) Livia (1) = Ti. Claudius Nero
(*cos.* 35 B.C.)   (ca. 58 B.C. –   (ca. 78 – 33 B.C.)
                                              A.D. 29)

Paullus Aemilius (1) = Cornelia
Lepidus
(*cos.* 34 B.C.)

M. Vipsanius (3) = (2) Julia (3) = (2) TIBERIUS (1) = (1) Vipsania
Agrippa   (39 B.C. –   (42 B.C. – A.D. 37)   (*see III*)
(63 – 12 B.C.)   A.D. 14)

Drusus = Antonia minor
(38 – 9 B.C.)

(*see III*)

Drusus
(14 B.C. – A.D. 23)

Gaius Caesar
(20 B.C. – A.D. 4)

Lucius Caesar
(17 B.C. – A.D.2)

Agrippina = Germanicus
(ca. 14 B.C.
– A.D. 33)

Agrippa
Postumus
(12 B.C.
– A.D. 14)

L. Aemilius Paullus = Julia (19 B.C. – A.D. 28)
(*cos.* A.D. 1)

(*see III*)

Table III

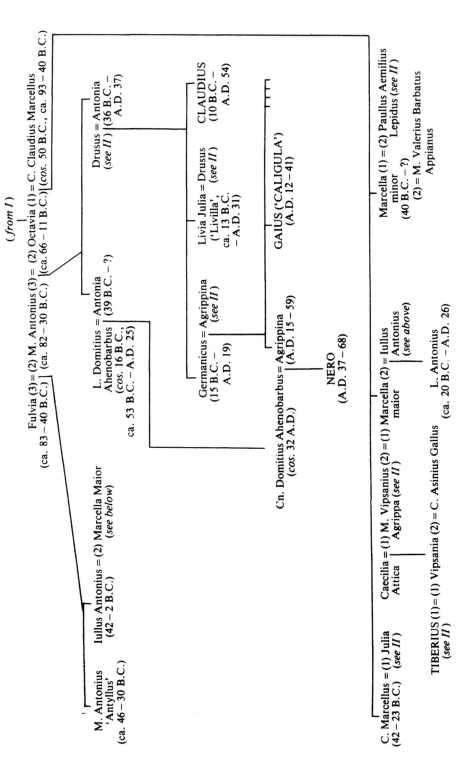

(from I)

Fulvia (3) = (2) M. Antonius (3) = (2) Octavia (1) = C. Claudius Marcellus
(ca. 83 – 40 B.C.) | (ca. 82 – 30 B.C.) | (ca. 66 – 11 B.C.) | (cos. 50 B.C., ca. 93 – 40 B.C.)

Drusus = Antonia
(see II) | (36 B.C. – A.D. 37)

L. Domitius = Antonia
Ahenobarbus | (39 B.C. – ?)
(cos. 16 B.C.,
ca. 53 B.C. – A.D. 25)

CLAUDIUS
(10 B.C. – A.D. 54)

Livia Julia = Drusus
('Livilla', | (see II)
ca. 13 B.C.
– A.D. 31)

GAIUS ('CALIGULA')
(A.D. 12 – 41)

Germanicus = Agrippina
(15 B.C. – | (see II)
A.D. 19)

Marcella (1) = (2) Paullus Aemilius
minor | Lepidus (see II)
(40 B.C. – ?)
(2) = M. Valerius Barbatus
Appianus

Cn. Domitius Ahenobarbus = Agrippina
(cos. 32 A.D.) | (A.D. 15 – 59)

NERO
(A.D. 37 – 68)

M. Antonius
'Antyllus'
(ca. 46 – 30 B.C.)

Iullus Antonius = (2) Marcella Maior
(42 – 2 B.C.) | (see below)

Marcella (2) = Iullus
maior | Antonius
(see above)

L. Antonius
(ca. 20 B.C. – A.D. 26)

Caecilia = (1) M. Vipsanius (2) = (1) Marcella
Attica | Agrippa (see II)

C. Marcellus = (1) Julia
(42 – 23 B.C.) | (see II)

TIBERIUS (1) = (1) Vipsania (2) = C. Asinius Gallus
(see II)

BIBLIOGRAPHY

I   Select list of modern editions and translations of
    Suetonius' and of Augustus' own writings (v)

(i) Text only (the *Twelve Caesars*):

ed. C.L. Roth, Leipzig (Teubner) 1857

ed. M. Ihm, Leipzig (Teubner) 1908

(ii) Text with commentary (*Divus Augustus* only):

ed. E.S. Shuckburgh, Cambridge 1896

ed. J.H. Westcott & E.M. Rankin, Boston 1918 (*with Divus
    Julius*)

ed. M. Adams, London 1939

ed. M.A. Levi, Florence 1951

(iii) Text with translation (the *Twelve Caesars*):

tr. (Eng.) J.C. Rolfe, 2 v. London (Loeb) 1914

tr. (Fr.) M. Rat, 2 v. Paris (Garnier) 1931

tr. (It.) G. Vitali, 2 v. Bologna 1951

tr. (Fr.) H. Ailloud, 3 v. Paris (Budé) 4th.ed. 1967

(iv) English translation only (the *Twelve Caesars*):

tr. Philemon Holland, London & New York (Broadway) 1923
    (repr. of ed. of 1606)

tr. A. Thomson, rev. T. Forester, London (Bohn) 1855.

tr. J. Gavorse, New York 1931

tr. R. Graves, rev. M. Grant, Harmondsworth (Penguin) 1979
    (first ed. 1959) - referred to as *GG* in notes

(v) Augustus' own writings:

Imperatoris Caesaris Augusti Operum Fragmenta, ed. H. Malcovati,

Turin (Paravia) 5th ed. 1969

Res Gestae Divi Augusti, with introduction and commentary,
P.A. Brunt & J.M. Moore, Oxford 1967 (omits Greek text; includes English translation)

[Numerous other editions of the *Res Gestae* (referred to as *RG*
in notes) exist; note especially those of T. Mommsen, 2nd ed.
Berlin 1883, and J. Gagé, 4th ed. Paris 1977. Both the Greek
and the Latin texts are available in Shuckburgh's *Augustus,*
see (ii) above, and in V. Ehrenberg and A.H.M. Jones, *Documents Illustrating the Reigns of Augustus and Tiberius,* 2nd
ed. Oxford 1976 - referred to as *E-J*³ in notes.]

II   Works referred to in the notes

*References are made by surname of the author(s) and date of
publication; for abbreviated periodical and other titles, see
list of abbreviations following this bibliography.*

Abbott F.F.   *Municipal Administration in the*
  & Johnson A.C. 1926   *Roman Empire* (Princeton, repr.
                               New York 1968)

Alföldi A. 1950-54   'Die Geburt der kaiserlichen
                               Bildsymbolik', *MH* 7 (1950) 1-13;
                               8 (1951) 190-215; 9 (1952) 204-
                               243; 10 (1953) 103-124; 11 (1954)
                               133-169

Alföldy G. 1979   'Marcius Turbo, Septicius Clarus,
                               Sueton, und die Historia Augusta',
                               ZPE 36 (1979) 233-253

Allison J.E.   'The *Lex Julia Maiestatis'*, *Latomus*
  & Cloud J.D. 1962   21 (1962) 711-731

Ashby T. 1935   *The Aqueducts of Ancient Rome* (ed.
                               I.A. Richmond, Oxford)

Astin A.E. 1963   'Augustus and *censoria potestas'*,
                               Latomus 22 (1963) 226-235

Baillie Reynolds P.K.   *The Vigiles of Imperial Rome*
  1926   (Oxford)

Bauman R.A. 1974   *The Crimen Maiestatis in the Roman*

	Republic and Augustan Principate (Johannesburg)
Bauman R.A. 1974	*Impietas in Principem* (Munich)
Béranger J. 1953	*Recherches sur l'Aspect Idéologique du Principat* (Basel)
Berchem D. van 1939	*Les Distributions de Blé et d'Argent à la Plèbe Romaine sous l'Empire* (Geneva)
Berchem D. van 1974	(Review of Rea 1972), *JRS* 64 (1974) 243-246
Bickerman E. 1972	*'Consecratio'* in W den Boer (ed.) *Le Culte des Souverains dans l'Empire romain* (Fondation Hardt, Entretiens XIX, Geneva-Vandoeuvres, 1972) 3-25
Bleicken J. 1962	*Senatsgericht und Kaisergericht* (Göttingen)
Boethius A. & Ward-Perkins J.B. 1970	*Etruscan and Roman Architecture* (Harmondsworth)
Bohec Y. le 1975	'Les centurions des chevaliers romains', *REA* 77 (1975) 108-123
Boucher J-P 1966	*Gaius Cornelius Gallus* (Paris)
Bowersock G. 1965	*Augustus and the Greek World* (Oxford)
Bringmann K. 1977	*'Imperium proconsulare* und Mitregenschaft im frühen Prinzipät', *Chiron* 7 (1977) 219-238
Brunt P.A. 1961	'The *lex Valeria Cornelia'*, *JRS* 51 (1961) 71-83
Brunt P.A. 1962	(Review of Jones 1960), *CR* 12 (1962) 70 f.
Brunt P.A. 1971	*Italian Manpower* (Oxford)
Brunt P.A. & Moore J.M. 1967	*Res Gestae Divi Augusti* (Oxford)
Buckland W.W. 1908	*The Roman Law of Slavery* (Cambridge)

Cadoux T.J. 1959   (Review of G. Vitucci, *Ricerche sulla praefectura urbi ...*), *JRS* 49 (1959) 152-160

Campbell B. 1978   'The marriage of soldiers under the Empire', *JRS* 68 (1978) 153-166

Carettoni G. 1967   'I problemi della zona augustea del Palatino alla luce dei recenti scavi', *Rendiconti della Pontificale Accademia di Archeologia* 39 (1966-7) 55-75

Carettoni G. 1978   'Roma - le costruzioni di Augusto e il tempio di Apollo sul Palatino', *Archeologia Laziale* (*Quaderni del Centro di Studio per l'Archeologia Etrusco-Italica* 1 (1978)) 72-74

Carter J.M. 1970   *The Battle of Actium* (London)

Carter J.M. 1977   'A new fragment of Octavian's inscription at Nicopolis', *ZPE* 24 (1977) 227-230

Chilver G.E.F. 1950   'Augustus and the Roman constitution', *Historia* 1 (1950) 408-435

Cizek E. 1977   *Structures et Idéologie dans les 'Vies des Douze Césars' de Suétone* (Paris)

Clarke M.L. 1953   *Rhetoric at Rome* (London)

Clavel M. & Lévêque P. 1971   *Villes et Structures Urbaines dans l'Occident Romain* (Paris)

Coarelli F. 1974   *Guida Archeologica di Roma* (Milan)

Combès R. 1966   *Imperator* (Paris)

Corbett P.E. 1930   *The Roman Law of Marriage* (Oxford)

Corbier M. 1974   *L'Aerarium Saturni et l'Aerarium Militare* (Rome)

Crawford M.H. 1974   *Roman Republican Coinage* (2 v., Cambridge)

Crook J.A. 1955   Consilium Principis: *Imperial Councils and Counsellors from Augustus to Diocletian* (Cambridge)

Crook J.A. 1967   *Law and Life of Rome* (London)

D'Arms J.H. 1977   'Proprietari et ville nel golfo di
                               Napoli' in *I Campi Flegrei nell'
                               Archeologia e nella Storia* (*Rome
                               4-7 May 1976*) 347-363

D'Arms J.H. 1970   *Romans on the Bay of Naples*
                               (Cambridge, Mass.)

Deininger J. 1965   *Die Provinziallandtage der
                               römischen Kaiserzeit* (Munich)

Deman E.B. van 1934   *The Building of the Roman Aqueducts*
                               (Washington)

Dudley D.R. 1967   *Urbs Roma* (London)

Durry M. 1938   *Les Cohortes Prétoriennes* (Paris)

Fishwick D. 1969   '*Genius* and *Numen*', HTR 62 (1969)
                               356-367

Freis H. 1967   *Die Cohortes Urbanae* (Bonner
                               Jahrbücher Beiheft 21)

Gagé J. 1936   'Actiaca', *MEFR* 53 (1936) 37-100

Gagé J. 1955   *Apollon Romain* (Paris)

Garnsey P.D.A. 1970   *Social Status and Legal Privilege
                               in the Roman Empire* (Oxford)

Garnsey P.D.A. 1966   'The *Lex Iulia* and appeal under
                               the empire', *JRS* 56 (1966) 167-189

Gascou J. 1976   'Suétone et l'ordre equestre', *REL*
                               54 (1976) 257-277

Gascou J. 1978   'Nouvelles données chronologiques
                               sur la carrière de Suétone',
                               Latomus 37 (1978) 436-444

Grant M. 1946   *From Imperium to Auctoritas: a
                               Historical Sudy of the Aes
                               Coinage of the Roman Empire 49 B.C.
                               - A.D. 14* (Cambridge)

Grenade P. 1961   *Essai sur les Origines du Principat*
                               (Paris)

Gros P. 1976   *Aurea Templa: Recherches sur l'
                               Architecture Religieuse de Rome*

	a l'Époque d'Auguste (Rome)
Habicht C. 1972	'Die augusteische Zeit' in W. den Boer ed. *Le Culte des Souverains dans l'Empire romaine* (*Fondation Hardt, Entretiens XIX, Geneva-Vandoeuvres,* 1972) 39-88
Hanslik R. 1954	'Die Augustusvita Suetons', *Wiener Studien* 67 (1954) 99-144
Harris H.A. 1972	*Sport in Greece and Rome* (London)
Heinen H. 1969	'Cäsar und Kaisarion', *Historia* 18 (1969) 185-203
Holloway R.R. 1966	'The tomb of Augustus and the princes of Troy', *AJA* 70 (1966) 171-173
Hopkins K. 1978	*Conquerors and Slaves* (Cambridge)
Instinsky H. 1962	*Die Siegel der Kaiser Augustus* (Baden-Baden)
Jameson S. 1969	'22 or 23?', *Historia* 18 (1969) 204-229
Jones A.H.M. 1960	*Studies in Roman Government and Law* (Oxford)
Kelly J.M. 1957	*Princeps Iudex* (Weimar)
Kelly J.M, 1976	*Studies in the Civil Judicature of the Roman Republic* (Oxford)
Kienast D. 1966	*Untersuchungen zu den Kriegsflotten der römischen Kaiserzeit* (Bonn)
Kloft H. 1970	*Liberalitas Principis* (Cologne & Vienna)
Kraft K. 1967a	'Zum Capricorn auf den Münzen des Augustus', *JNG* 17 (1967) 17-27
Kraft K. 1967b	'Der Sinn des Mausoleums des Augustus', *Historia* 16 (1967) 189-206
Kraft K. 1967c	'Zur Sueton *Divus Augustus* 69.2', *Hermes* 95 (1967) 496-499
Kunckel H. 1974	*Der Römische Genius* (Heidelberg)

26

Kunkel W. 1969 — 'Ueber die Entstehung des Senats-gerichts' *Sitz.ber. Bayr Akademie der Wissenschaften, Phil-hist. Kl.* (1969) Heft 2 (= *Kleine Schriften* Weimar 1974) 267-323

Lacey W.K. 1974 — 'Octavian in the Senate, January 27 B.C.', *JRS* 64 (1974) 176-184

Lacey W.K. 1979 — '*Summi fastigii vocabulum*: the story of a title', *JRS* 69 (1979) 28-34

Last H.M. 1947 — '*Imperium maius*: a note', *JRS* 37 (1947) 157-164

Last H.M. 1951 — 'On the tribunicia potestas of Augustus', *Rendiconti dell' Istituto Lombardo (Classe di Lettere, Scienze Morali e Storiche)* 84 (1951) 93-110

Levick B.M. 1972 — 'Abdication and Agrippa Postumus', *Historia* 21 (1972) 674-697

Levick B.M. 1976 — *Tiberius the Politician* (Rome)

Lewis M.W.H. 1955 — *The Official Priests of Rome under the Julio-Claudians* (Rome)

Lewis N. 1974 — *Greek Historical Documents: the Roman Principate 27 B.C. - A.D. 285* (Toronto)

Liebeschuetz J.W.H.G. 1979 — *Continuity and Change in Roman Religion* (Oxford)

Lintott A.W. 1968 — *Violence in Republican Rome* (Oxford)

Lugli G. 1952 - — *Fontes ad Topographiam veteris urbis Romae pertinentes* (Rome) - referred to as *Fontes*

McMullen R. 1974 — *Roman Social Relations 50 B.C. - A.D. 284* (New Haven)

Magdelain A. 1947 — *Auctoritas Principis* (Paris)

Manuwald B. 1979 — *Cassius Dio und Augustus* (Wiesbaden)

Mellor R. 1975 — ΘΕΑ ΡΩΜΗ: *The Worship of the Goddess Roma in the Greek World*

(Göttingen)

Michel D. 1967   *Alexander als Vorbild für Pompeius, Caesar, und M. Antonius* (Brussels)

Millar F.G.B. 1963   'The *fiscus* in the first two centuries', *JRS* 53 (1963) 28-42

Millar F.G.B. 1964a   *A Study of Cassius Dio* (Oxford)

Millar F.G.B. 1964b   'The *aerarium* and its officials under the empire', *JRS* 54 (1964) 33-40

Millar F.G.B. 1966   'The emperor, the senate, and the provinces', *JRS* 56 (1966) 156-166

Millar F.G.B. 1973   'Triumvirate and principate', *JRS* 63 (1973) 50-67

Millar F.G.B. 1977   *The Emperor in the Roman World* (London)

Momigliano A. 1942   'Terra marique', *JRS* 32 (1942) 52-64

Mouchova B. 1968   *Studien zur Kaiserbiographien Suetons* (Prague)

Nash E. 1961   *Pictorial Dictionary of Ancient Rome* (London)

Nicolet C. 1966   *L'Ordre Equestre a l'Époque Républicaine, I* (Paris)

Nicolet C. 1967   'Tribuni militum a populo', *MEFR* 79 (1967) 29-76

Nicolet C. 1976   'Le Cens senatorial sous la République et sous Auguste', *JRS* 66 (1976) 20-28

Nieblung G. 1956   'Laribus Augusti ministri primi', *Historia* 5 (1956) 303-331

North J.A. 1975   (Review of Weinstock 1970), *JRS* 65 (1975) 171-177

Oliver J.H. 1969   'Octavian's inscription at Nicopolis', *AJP* 90 (1969) 178-182

Paget R.F. 1968   'The ancient ports of Cumae', *JRS*

58 (1968) 159-169

Pani M. 1974   *Comitia e Senato* (Bari)

Pani M. 1972   *Roma e i Re d'Oriente da Augusto a Tiberio* (Bari)

Parker H.M.D. 1928   *The Roman Legions* (Oxford)

Pavis d'Escurac H. 1976   *La Préfecture de l'Annone* (Rome)

Piganiol A. 1923   *Recherches sur les Jeux Romains* (Strasbourg)

Quilici L. 1974   'La campagna romana come suburbio di Roma antica', *Parola di Passato* 108/9 (1974) 410-438

Rea J.R. 1972   (ed.) *Oxyrhynchus Papyri* XL (London)

Reynolds J.M. 1982   *Aphrodisias and Rome* (London)

Robert L. 1978   'Stèle funéraire de Nicomédie et séismes dans les inscriptions', *BCH* 102 (1978) 895-408

Robertis F. M. de   *Il Diritto Associativo Romano* (Bari)

Rowell H.T. 1940   'The forum and funeral *imagines* of Augustus', *MAAR* 17 (1940) 131-143

Ryberg I.S. 1955   *Rites of the State Religion in Roman Art* (Rome)

Saddington D.B. 1975   'The development of the Roman auxiliary forces from Augustus to Tiberius' in H. Temporini (ed.) *Aufstieg und Niedergang der Römischer Welt* II:3.176-201

Salmon E.T. 1969   *Roman Colonisation under the Republic* (London)

Sattler P. 1960   *Augustus und der Senat. Untersuchungen zur römischen Innenpolitik zwischen 30 und 17 v. Chr.* (Göttingen)

Schmitthenner W. 1952   *Octavian und das Testament Caesars* (Munich)

Schmitthenner W. 1958	'Octavians militärische Unterne-hmungen in den Jahren 35-33 v. Chr.', *Historia* 7 (1958) 189-236
Schmitthenner W. 1962	'Augustus spanische Feldzug und der Kampf um das Prinzipät', *Historia* 11 (1962) 29-85
Schmitthenner W. 1979	'Rome and India: aspects of uni-versal history during the Principate', *JRS* 69 (1979) 70-106
Shatzman I. 1972	'The Roman general's authority over booty', *Historia* 11 (1962) 177-205
Sherk R.K. 1969	*Roman Documents from the Greek East:* Senatus Consulta *and* Epistulae *to the Age of Augustus* (Baltimore)
Sherwin-White A.N. 1973	*The Roman Citizenship* (Oxford, 2nd. ed.)
Shipley F.W. 1931	'The chronology of the building operations in Rome from the death of Caesar to the death of Augustus', *MAAR* 9 (1931) 7-60
Smallwood E.M. 1966	*Documents illustrating the Prin-cipates of Nerva, Trajan and Hadrian* (Cambridge)
Smallwood E.M. 1967	*Documents illustrating the Prin-cipates of Gaius, Claudius, and Nero* (Cambridge)
Starr C.G. 1960	*The Roman Imperial Navy 31 B.C.-A.D. 324* (Cambridge)
Stavely E.S. 1972	*Greek and Roman Voting and Elections* (London)
Steidle W. 1963	*Sueton und die antike Biographie* (Munich, 2nd.ed.)
Stockton D. 1965	'Primus and Murena', *Historia* 14 (1965) 19-40
Sumner G.V. 1978	'Varrones Murenae', *HSCP* 82 (1978) 187-195

Swan M. 1966   'The consular *fasti* of 23 B.C. and the conspiracy of Varro and Murena', *HSCP* 71 (1966) 235-247

Syme R. 1933   'Some notes on the legions under Augustus', *JRS* 23 (1933) 14-33

Syme R. 1934   'The Spanish war of Augustus', *AJP* 55 (1934) 293-317

Syme R. 1939   *The Roman Revolution* (Oxford)

Syme R. 1958   'Imperator Caesar: a study in nomenclature', *Historia* 7 (1958) 175-188

Syme R. 1961   'Who was Vedius Pollio?', *JRS* 51 (1961) 23-30

Syme R. 1978   *History in Ovid* (Oxford)

Taylor L.R. 1931   *The Divinity of the Roman Emperor* (Middletown, Conn.)

Townend G.B. 1967   'Suetonius and his influence' in T.A. Dorey (ed.) *Latin Biography* (London)

Townend G.B. 1961   'The Hippo inscription and the career of Suetonius', *Historia* 10 (1961) 99-109

Treggiari S.M. 1969   *Roman Freedmen during the Late Republic* (Oxford)

Versnel H.S. 1970   Triumphus: *an Inquiry into the Origin, Development, and Meaning of the Roman Triumph* (Leiden)

Vessberg C. 1941   *Studien zur Kunstgeschichte der Römischen Republik* (2 v., Lund & Leipzig)

Watson G.R. 1969   *The Roman Soldier* (London)

Weaver P.R.C. 1972   *Familia Caesaris* (Cambridge)

Webster G. 1969   *The Roman Imperial Army of the First and Second Centuries A.D.* (London)

Weinstock S. 1971   *Divus Julius* (Oxford)

Weiss P. 1973	'Die "Säkularspiele" der Republik - ein annalistisches Fiktion?', *MDAI(R)* 80 (1973) 205-217
Wells C.M. 1972	*The German Policy of Augustus* (Oxford)
Wheeler R.E.M. 1955	*Rome beyond the Imperial Frontiers* (Harmondsworth)
Wickert L. 1954	'Princeps', *RE* 22.1998f.
Wiseman T.P. 1970	'The definition of *Eques Romanus* in the late Republic and early Empire', *Historia* 19 (1970) 67-83
Yavetz Z. 1969	*Plebs and Princeps* (Oxford)
Zadoks-Josephus-Jitta A.N. 1932	*Ancestral Portraiture in Rome and the Art of the Last Century of the Republic* (Amsterdam)
Zanker P. 1968	*Forum Augustum: das Bildprogramm* (Tübingen)
Zanker P. 1973	*Studien zu den Augustus-Porträts. 1: Der Actium-Typus* (Göttingen)

III   Abbreviations (by initial letters) used for books and periodicals

AE	L'Année Epigraphique
AJA	American Journal of Archaeology
AJP	American Journal of Philology
BCH	Bulletin de Correspondance Hellénique
BMC Aug	*The Coins of the Roman Empire in the British Museum* - vol.I, Augustus to Vitellius, by H. Mattingly (London, 1925)
CAH	*The Cambridge Ancient History*, ed. J.B. Bury, S.A. Cook, F.E. Adcock, and M.P. Charlesworth (12 vols., Cambridge, 1923-)
CIL	*Corpus Inscriptionum Latinarum* (Berlin, 1869-)
CR	The Classical Review

$E-J^3$ *Documents Illustrating the Reigns of Augustus and Tiberius*, 2nd enlarged ed. by V. Ehrenberg and A.H.M. Jones (Oxford, 1976)

FIRA   *Fontes Iuris Romani Anteiustiniani*, 2nd ed. by S. Riccobono (Florence, 1968)

GG   *Suetonius: Lives of the Twelve Caesars*, tr. by R. Graves, rev. by M. Grant (Harmondsworth, 1979)

HRFC   *A History of Rome through the Fifth Century*, by A.H.M. Jones, vol.I, The Republic (New York, 1968)

HSCP   Harvard Studies in Classical Philology

HTR   Harvard Theological Review

ILLRP   *Inscriptiones Latinae Liberae Rei Publicae*, 2nd ed. by A. Degrassi (2 vols., Florence, 1972)

Inscr It   *Inscriptiones Italiae*, vol.13, Fasti et Elogia, ed. by A. Degrassi (2 vols., Rome 1937 and 1963)

JNG   Jahrbuch für Numismatik und Geldgeschichte

JRS   Journal of Roman Studies

LR   *Roman Civilisation, Sourcebook*, vol.I, The Republic and II, The Empire, rev. ed. by N. Lewis and and M. Reinhold (New York, 1966)

MAAR   Memoirs of the American Academy in Rome

MDAI(R)   Mitteilungen des Deutschen Archaologischen Instituts (Römische Abteilung)

MEFR   Mélanges d'Archeologie et d'Histoire de l'École Francaise de Rome

MH   Museum Helveticum

Not Sc   Notizie degli Scavi di Antichità (Atti della Accademia Nazionale dei Lincei, Rome)

ORF^3 *Oratorum Romanorum Fragmenta*, 3rd ed. H. Malcovati (Paravia, 1966)

RE   *Realencyclopädie der klassicschen Altertumswissenschaft*, by A. Pauly, ed. by G. Wissowa (Stuttgart, 1893-)

REA   Revue des Études Anciennes

REL   Revue des Études Latines

ZPE   Zeitschift für Papyrologie und Epigraphik

Text

The following are the significant variations in this edition
from the Teubner text of M. Ihm (Stuttgart, 1908), with a note
of the source of those not appearing in Ihm's *apparatus crit-
icus*. Minor alterations of spelling (e.g. Messalla for
Messala) and punctuation, or expansions of abbreviations (e.g.
s(enatus) c(onsultum)) are not listed.

Reference	*Ihm*	*This edition*
10.2	translativum	tralaticium
17.2	T. Domitium	Cn. Domitium (*Shuckburgh*)
17.3	†ad desideria	desideria
17.5	Caesare patre	Caesare
31.5	ad illorum ⟨...⟩ velut ad exemplar	ad illorum velut exemplar
32.3	tricensimo	vicesimo quinto
38.2	virili toga	virili toga sumpta
40.5	circave	circove
41.2	undecimo	†undecimo (see 41.2 n.)
43.1	histriones ⟨...⟩ non in foro	histriones. ⟨Circensibus ludis gladiatoriisque muneribus frequentissime editis interiecit pler- umque bestiarum African- arum venationes⟩ non in foro
53.2	adoperta	adaperta
58.2	laeta huic	laeta huic ⟨urbi⟩
63.1	genero	generum (*Carter*)
67.2	ei fregit	effregit
69.2	uxor mea est	uxor mea est? (*Kraft*)
71.3	aleatorum	aleatorium
72.1	constat	fuisse constat
72.2	technyphion	τεχνόφυον
76.1	bibulum	bubulum
79.2	†etiam memoriam	et a memoria
83	†sestertio	segestri (*Carter*)
96.1	at ⟨que⟩ exitum praesagiente. ⟨...⟩ Philippos	et exitum praesagiente. Philippis
98.3	rerumque ⟨...⟩ missilia	rerumque ⟨omnium⟩ missilia
98.4	consueuerat	consuerat

C. SUETONI TRANQUILLI

DE VITA CAESARUM

LIBER II: DIVUS AUGUSTUS

1:1   Gentem Octaviam Velitris praecipuam olim fuisse multa
declarant. nam et vicus celeberrima parte oppidi iam
pridem Octavius vocabatur et ostendebatur ara Octavio consecrata, qui bello dux finitimo, cum forte Marti rem di-
vinam faceret, nuntiata repente hostis incursione, semi-
cruda exta rapta foco prosecuit, atque ita proelium
ingressus victor redit. decretum etiam publicum exstabat,
quo cavebatur ut in posterum quoque simili-modo exta
Marti redderentur, reliquiaeque ad Octavios referrentur.

2:1   ea gens a Tarquinio Prisco rege inter minores-gentis ad-
lecta in senatum, mox a Servio Tullio in patricias tra-
ducta, procedente tempore ad plebem se contulit, ac
rursus magno intervallo per Divum Iulium in patriciatum
redit. primus ex hac magistratum populi suffragio cepit

2:2   C. Rufus. is quaestorius Gnaeum et Gaium procreavit, a
quibus duplex Octaviorum familia defluxit condicione di-
versa, siquidem Gnaeus et deinceps ab eo reliqui omnes
functi sunt honoribus summis; at Gaius eiusque posteri,
seu fortuna seu voluntate, in equestri ordine constiterunt
usque ad Augusti patrem. proavus Augusti secundo Punico
bello stipendia in Sicilia tribunus militum fecit Aemilio
Papo imperatore. avus municipalibus magisteriis contentus
abundante patrimonio tranquillissime senuit.

2:3   sed haec alii; ipse Augustus nihil amplius quam equestri
familia ortum se scribit vetere ac locuplete, et in qua
primus senator pater suus fuerit. M. Antonius libertinum
ei proavum exprobrat, restionem e pago Thurino, avum argentarium. nec quicquam ultra de paternis Augusti maioribus

36

repperi.

3:1   C. Octavius pater a principio aetatis et re et existi-
matione magna fuit, ut equidem mirer hunc quoque a nonnullis argentarium atque etiam inter divisores operasque
campestris proditum; amplis enim innutritus opibus, honores et adeptus est facile et egregie administravit. ex
praetura Macedoniam sortitus, fugitivos, residuam Spartaci
et Catilinae manum, Thurinum agrum tenentis in itinere
3:2 delevit, negotio sibi in senatu extra ordinem dato. provinciae praefuit non minore iustitia quam fortitudine;
namque Bessis ac Thracibus magno proelio fusis, ita socios
tractavit, ut epistulae M. Ciceronis extent quibus Quintum
fratrem, eodem tempore parum secunda fama proconsulatum
Asiae administrantem, hortatur et monet, imitetur in pro-
4:1 merendis sociis vicinum suum Octavium. decedens Macedonia,
prius quam profiteri se candidatum consulatus posset, mortem obiit repentinam, superstitibus liberis Octavia maiore,
quam ex Ancharia, et Octavia minore item Augusto, quos
ex Atia tulerat. Atia M. Atio Balbo et Iulia, sorore C.
Caesaris, genita est. Balbus, paterna stirpe Aricinus,
multis in familia senatoriis imaginibus, a matre Magnum
Pompeium artissimo contingebat gradu functusque honore
praeturae inter vigintiviros agrum Campanum plebi Iulia
4:2 lege divisit. verum idem Antonius, despiciens etiam
maternam Augusti originem, proavum eius Afri generis
fuisse et modo unguentariam tabernam modo pistrinum Ariciae exercuisse obicit. Cassius quidem Parmensis quadam
epistula non tantum ut pistoris, sed etiam ut nummulari
nepotem sic taxat Augustum: 'materna tibi farina est ex
crudissimo Ariciae pistrino: hanc finxit manibus collybo
decoloratis Nerulonensis mensarius'.
5:1   natus est Augustus M. Tullio Cicerone C. Antonio coss.
IX Kal. Octob., paulo ante solis exortum, regione Palati,
ad Capita Bubula, ubi nunc sacrarium habet, aliquanto post
quam excessit constitutum. nam ut senatus actis continetur,

cum C. Laetorius, adulescens patricii generis, in deprecanda
graviore adulterii poena praeter aetatem atque natales hoc
quoque patribus-conscriptis allegaret, esse possessorem ac
velut aedituum soli, quod primum Divus Augustus nascens
attigisset, peteretque donari quasi proprio suo ac pecu-
liari deo, decretum est ut ea pars domus consecraretur.

6:1 nutrimentorum eius ostenditur adhuc locus in avito suburbano iuxta Velitras permodicus et cellae penuariae instar,
tenetque vicinitatem opinio tamquam et natus ibi sit. huc
introire nisi necessario et caste religio est, concepta
opinione veteri, quasi temere adeuntibus horror quidam et
metus obiciatur, sed et mox confirmata, nam cum possessor
villae novus seu forte seu temptandi causa cubitum se eo
contulisset, evenit ut post paucissimas noctis horas ex-
turbatus inde subita vi et incerta paene semianimis cum
strato simul ante fores inveniretur.

7:1 infanti cognomen Thurino inditum est, in memoriam maiorum originis, vel quod regione Thurina (recens eo nato)
pater Octavius adversus fugitivos rem prospere gesserat.
Thurinum cognominatum satis certa probatione tradiderim,
nactus puerilem imagunculam eius aeream veterem, ferreis
et paene iam exolescentibus litteris hoc nomine inscriptam,
quae dono a me principi data inter cubiculi Lares colitur.
sed et a M. Antonio in epistulis per contumeliam saepe
Thurinus appellatur, et ipse nihil amplius quam mirari se
7:2 rescribit, pro obprobrio sibi prius nomen obici. postea
Gai Caesaris et deinde Augusti cognomen assumpsit, alterum
testamento maioris avunculi, alterum Munati Planci sen-
tentia, cum, quibusdam censentibus Romulum appellari
oportere quasi et ipsum conditorem urbis, praevaluisset,
ut Augustus potius vocaretur, non tantum novo sed etiam
ampliore cognomine, quod loca quoque religiosa et in quibus augurato quid consecratur augusta dicantur, ab auctu
vel ab avium gestu gustuve, sicut etiam Ennius docet
scribens: augusto augurio postquam incluta condita Roma est.

8:1   quadrimus patrem amisit. duodecimum annum agens aviam
Iuliam defunctam pro contione laudavit. quadriennio post
virili toga sumpta, militaribus donis triumpho Caesaris
Africano donatus est, quanquam expers belli propter aetatem.
profectum mox avunculum in Hispanias adversus Cn. Pompei
liberos, vixdum firmus a gravi valitudine, per infestas
hostibus vias paucissimis comitibus (naufragio etiam facto)
subsecutus, magnopere demeruit, approbata cito etiam morum
indole super itineris industriam.

8:2   Caesare post receptas Hispanias expeditionem in Dacos
et inde in Parthos destinante, praemissus Apolloniam
studiis vacavit. utque primum occisum eum heredemque se
comperit, diu cunctatus an proximas legiones imploraret,
id quidem consilium ut praeceps inmaturumque omisit.
ceterum urbe repetita hereditatem adiit, dubitante matre,
vitrico vero Marcio Philippo consulari multum dissuadente.

8:3   atque ab eo tempore exercitibus comparatis primum cum M.
Antonio M.que Lepido, deinde tantum cum Antonio per duodecim fere annos, novissime per quattuor et quadraginta
solus rem publicam tenuit.

9:1   proposita vitae eius velut summa, partes singillatim
neque per tempora sed per species exsequar, quo distinctius
demonstrari cognoscique possint.

    bella civilia quinque gessit: Mutinense, Philippense,
Perusinum, Siculum, Actiacum; e quibus primum ac novissimum
adversus M. Antonium, secundum adversus Brutum et Cassium,
tertium adversus L. Antonium triumviri fratrem, quartum

10:1   adversus Sextum Pompeium Cn. filium. omnium bellorum
initium et causam hinc sumpsit: nihil convenientius ducens
quam necem avunculi vindicare tuerique acta, confestim ut
Apollonia rediit, Brutum Cassiumque et vi necopinantis et
(quia provisum periculum subterfugerant) legibus aggredi
reosque caedis absentis deferre statuit. ludos autem

victoriae Caesaris, non audentibus facere quibus optigerat

10:2 id munus, ipse edidit. et quo constantius cetera quoque

exequeretur, in locum tr. pl. (forte demortui) candidatum

se ostendit, quanquam patricius necdum senator. sed ad-

versante conatibus suis M. Antonio consule, quem vel prae-

cipuum adiutorem speraverat, ac ne publicum quidem et

tralaticium ius ulla in re sibi sine pactione gravissimae

mercedis impertiente, ad optimates se contulit, quibus

eum invisum sentiebat, maxime quod D. Brutum obsessum

Mutinae provincia a Caesare data et per senatum confirmata

10:3 expellere armis niteretur. hortantibus itaque nonnullis

percussores ei subornavit, ac fraude deprehensa periculum

in vicem metuens veteranos simul in suum ac rei publicae

auxilium (quanta potuit largitione) contraxit; iussusque

comparato exercitui pro praetore praeesse et cum Hirtio

ac Pansa, qui consulatum susceperant, D. Bruto opem ferre,

demandatum bellum tertio mense confecit duobus proeliis.

10:4 priore Antonius fugisse eum scribit ac sine paludamento

equoque post biduum demum apparuisse, sequenti satis con-

stat non modo ducis, sed etiam militis functum munere at-

que in media dimicatione, aquilifero legionis suae graviter

11:1 saucio, aquilam umeris subisse diuque portasse. hoc bello

cum Hirtius in acie, Pansa paulo post ex vulnere perissent,

rumor increbruit ambos opera eius occisos, ut Antonio fug-

ato, re publica consulibus orbata, solus victores exercitus

occuparet. Pansae quidem adeo suspecta mors fuit, ut Glyco

medicus custoditus sit, quasi venenum vulneri indidisset.

adicit his Aquilius Niger, alterum e consulibus Hirtium in

12:1 pugnae tumultu ab ipso interemptum. sed ut cognovit Anton-

ium post fugam a M. Lepido receptum ceterosque duces et ex-

ercitus consentire pro partibus, causam optimatium sine

cunctatione deseruit, ad praetextum mutatae voluntatis

dicta factaque quorundam calumniatus, quasi alii se puerum,

alii ornandum tollendumque iactassent, ne aut sibi aut

veteranis par gratia referretur. et quo magis paenitentiam

His Formz Ally

priors sectae approbaret, Nursinos grandi pecunia et quam
pendere nequirent multatos extorres oppido egit, quod Mutinensi acie interemptorum civium tumulo publice extructo
ascripserant, pro libertate eos occubuisse.

13:1   inita cum Antonio et Lepido societate, Philippense quoque bellum, quamquam invalidus atque aeger, duplici proelio
transegit, quorum priore castris exutus vix ad Antoni cornu
fuga evaserat. nec successum victoriae moderatus est, sed
capite Bruti Romam misso, ut statuae Caesaris subiceretur,
in splendidissimum quemque captivum non sine verborum con-
13:2   tumelia saevit, ut quidem uni suppliciter sepulturam pre-
canti respondisse dicatur iam istam volucrum fore potestatem; alios, patrem et filium, pro vita rogantis sortiri
vel micare iussisse, ut alterutri concederetur, ac spec-
tasse utrumque morientem, cum patre, quia se optulerat,
occiso filius quoque voluntariam occubuisset necem. quare
ceteri, in his M. Favonius ille Catonis aemulus, cum cate-
nati producerentur, imperatore Antonio honorifice salutato,
hunc foedissimo convicio coram prosciderunt.

13:3   partitis post victoriam officiis, cum Antonius Orientem
ordinandum, ipse veteranos in Italiam reducendos et municipalibus agris conlocandos recepisset, neque veteranorum
neque possessorum gratiam tenuit, alteris pelli se, alteris
14:1   non pro spe meritorum tractari querentibus. quo tempore
L. Antonium fiducia consulatus, quem gerebat, ac fraternae
potentiae res novas molientem confugere Perusiam coegit
et ad deditionem fame compulit, non tamen sine magnis suis
et ante bellum et in bello discriminibus. nam cum spectaculo ludorum gregarium militem in quattuordecim ordinibus
sedentem excitari per apparitorem iussisset, rumore ab ob-
trectatoribus dilato quasi eundem mox et discruciatum nec-
asset, minimum afuit quin periret concursu et indignatione
turbae militaris. saluti fuit, quod qui desiderabatur repente comparuit incolumis ac sine iniuria. circa Perusinum
autem murum sacrificans paene interceptus est a manu

15:1 gladiatorum, quae oppido eruperat. Perusia capta in plu-
rimos animadvertit, orare veniam vel excusare se conant-
ibus una voce occurrens moriendum esse. scribunt quidam, trecentos ex dediticiis electos utriusque ordinis ad
aram Divo Iulio extructam Idibus Martiis hostiarum more
mactatos. extiterunt qui traderent, conpecto eum ad arma
isse, ut occulti adversarii et quos metus magis quam vol-
untas contineret, facultate L. Antoni ducis praebita, de-
tegerentur devictisque is et confiscatis, promissa veteranis praemia persolverentur.

16:1 Siculum bellum incohavit in primis, sed diu traxit
intermissum saepius, modo reparandarum classium causa,
quas tempestatibus duplici naufragio et quidem per aes-
tatem amiserat, modo pace facta, flagitante populo ob
interclusos commeatus famemque ingravescentem; donec navi-
bus ex integro fabricatis ac viginti servorum milibus
manumissis et ad remum datis, portum Iulium apud Baias,
inmisso in Lucrinum et Avernum lacum mari, effecit. In
quo cum hieme tota copias exercuisset, Pompeium inter
Mylas et Naulochum superavit, sub horam pugnae tam arto
repente somno devinctus, ut ad dandum signum ab amicis

16:2 excitaretur. unde praebitam Antonio materiam putem ex-
probrandi ne rectis quidem oculis eum aspicere potuisse
instructam aciem, verum supinum, caelum intuentem, stu-
pidum cubuisse, nec prius surrexisse ac militibus in con-
spectum venisse quam a M. Agrippa fugatae sint hostium
naves. alii dictum factumque eius criminantur, quasi
classibus tempestate perditis exclamaverit etiam invito
Neptuno victoriam se adepturum, ac die circensium prox-

16:3 imo sollemni pompae simulacrum dei detraxerit. nec temere
plura ac maiora pericula ullo alio bello adiit. traiecto
in Siciliam exercitu, cum partem reliquam copiarum con-
tinenti repeteret, oppressus ex improviso a Demochare et
Apollophane praefectis Pompei, uno demum navigio aeger-
rime effugit. iterum cum praeter Locros Regium pedibus

42

iret et prospectis biremibus Pompeianis terram legentibus,
suas ratus, descendisset ad litus, paene exceptus est.
tunc etiam per devios tramites refugientem servus Aemili
Pauli comitis eius, dolens proscriptum olim ab eo patrem
Paulum et quasi occasione ultionis oblata, interficere
conatus est.

16:4   post Pompei fugam collegarum alterum M. Lepidum, quem
ex Africa in auxilium evocarat, superbientem viginti legionum fiducia summasque sibi partes terrore et minis vin-
dicantem spoliavit exercitu supplicemque concessa vita
Circeios in perpetuum relegavit.

17:1   M. Antonii societatem semper dubiam et incertam recon-
ciliationibusque variis male focilatam abrupit tandem, et
quo magis degenerasse eum a civili more approbaret, testamentum, quod is Romae, etiam de Cleopatra liberis inter
heredes nuncupatis, reliquerat, aperiundum recitandumque
17:2 pro contione curavit. remisit tamen hosti iudicato nec-
essitudines amicosque omnes, atque inter alios C. Sosium
et Cn. Domitium tunc adhuc consules. Bononiensibus quoque publice, quod in Antoniorum clientela antiquitus erant,
gratiam fecit coniurandi cum tota Italia pro partibus suis.
nec multo post navali proelio apud Actium vicit, in serum
dimicatione protracta, ut in nave victor pernoctaverit.

17:3 ab Actio cum Samum in hiberna se recepisset, turbatus nun-
tiis de seditione praemia et missionem poscentium, quos
ex omni numero confecta victoria Brundisium praemiserat,
repetita Italia, tempestate in traiectu bis conflictatus
(primo inter promuntoria Peloponnesi atque Aetoliae, rursus circa montes Ceraunios, utrubique parte liburnicarum
demersa, simul eius, in qua vehebatur, fusis armamentis
et gubernaculo diffracto) nec amplius quam septem et viginti dies, donec desideria militum ordinarentur, Brundisii
commoratus, Asiae Syriaeque circuitu Aegyptum petit ob-
sessaque Alexandrea, quo Antonius cum Cleopatra confugerat,
17:4 brevi potitus est. et Antonium quidem, seras condiciones

pacis temptantem, ad mortem adegit viditque mortuum.
Cleopatrae, quam servatam triumpho magnopere cupiebat,
etiam psyllos admovit, qui venenum ac virus exugerent,
quod perisse morsu aspidis putabatur. ambobus communem
sepulturae honorem tribuit ac tumulum ab ipsis incohatum

17:5 perfici iussit. Antonium iuvenem, maiorem de duobus
Fulvia genitis, simulacro Divi Iuli, ad quod post multas
et irritas preces confugerat, abreptum interemit. item
Caesarionem, quem ex Caesare Cleopatra concepisse prae-
dicabat, retractum e fuga supplicio adfecit. reliquos
Antonii reginaeque communes liberos non secus ac necessitudine iunctos sibi et conservavit et mox pro condicione

18:1 cuiusque sustinuit ac fovit. per idem tempus conditorium
et corpus Magni Alexandri, cum prolatum e penetrali sub-
iecisset oculis, corona aurea imposita ac floribus as-
persis veneratus est, consultusque, num et Ptolemaeum
inspicere vellet, regem se voluisse ait videre, non mor-

18:2 tuos. Aegyptum in provinciae formam redactam ut fera-
ciorem habilioremque annonae urbicae redderet, fossas omnis, in quas Nilus exaestuat, oblimatas longa vetustate
militari opere detersit. quoque Actiacae victoriae memoria
celebratior et in posterum esset, urbem Nicopolim apud Actium condidit ludosque illic quinquennales constituit et
ampliato vetere Apollinis templo locum castrorum, quibus
fuerat usus, exornatum navalibus spoliis Neptuno ac Marti
consecravit.

19:1 tumultus posthac et rerum novarum initia coniurationes-
que complures, prius quam invalescerent indicio detectas,
compressit alias alio tempore: Lepidi iuvenis, deinde
Varronis Murenae et Fanni Caepionis, mox M. Egnati, exin
Plauti Rufi Lucique Pauli progeneri sui, ac praeter has
L. Audasi, falsarum tabularum rei ac neque aetate neque
corpore integri, item Asini Epicadi ex gente Parthina
ibridae, ad extremum Telephi, mulieris servi nomencula-
toris. nam ne ultimae quidem sortis hominum conspiratione

44

19:2 et periculo caruit. Audasius atque Epicadus Iuliam filiam
et Agrippam nepotem ex insulis, quibus continebantur,
rapere ad exercitus, Telephus quasi debita sibi fato domi-
natione et ipsum et senatum adgredi destinarant. quin
etiam quondam iuxta cubiculum eius lixa quidam ex Illyrico
exercitu, ianitoribus deceptis, noctu deprehensus est
cultro venatorio cinctus, imposne mentis an simulata de-
mentia, incertum; nihil enim exprimi quaestione potuit.]

20:1 externa bella duo omnino per se gessit, Delmaticum
adulescens adhuc, et (Antonio devicto) Cantabricum. Delma-
tico etiam vulnera excepit, una acie dextrum genu lapide
ictus, altera et crus et utrumque brachium ruina pontis
consauciatus. reliqua per legatos administravit, ut tamen
quibusdam Pannonicis atque Germanicis aut interveniret aut
non longe abesset, Ravennam vel Mediolanium vel Aquileiam

21:1 usque ab urbe progrediens. domuit autem partim ductu
partim auspiciis suis Cantabriam, Aquitaniam, Pannoniam,
Delmatiam cum Illyrico omni, item Raetiam et Vindelicos
ac Salassos, gentes Inalpinas. coercuit et Dacorum incursiones, tribus eorum ducibus cum magna copia caesis, Germanosque ultra Albim fluvium summovit, ex quibus Suebos et
Sigambros dedentis se traduxit in Galliam atque in proximis
Rheno agris conlocavit. alias item nationes male quietas

21:2 ad obsequium redegit. nec ulli genti sine iustis et necessariis causis bellum intulit, tantumque afuit a cupiditate
quoquo modo imperium vel bellicam gloriam augendi, ut quorundam barbarorum principes in aede Martis Ultoris iurare
coegerit mansuros se in fide ac pace quam peterent, a quibusdam vero novum genus obsidum, feminas, exigere tempta-
verit, quod neglegere marum pignora sentiebat; et tamen
potestatem semper omnibus fecit, quotiens vellent, obsides
recipiendi. neque aut crebrius aut perfidiosius rebellan-
tis (graviore umquam ultus est poena, quam ut captivos sub
lege venundaret, ne in vicina regione servirent neve intra

21:3 tricensimum annum liberarentur. qua virtutis moderationisque

fama Indos etiam ac Scythas, auditu modo cognitos, pellexit
ad amicitiam suam populique Romani ultro per legatos peten-
dam. Parthi quoque et Armeniam vindicanti facile cesserunt
et signa militaria, quae M. Crasso et M. Antonio ademerant,
reposcenti reddiderunt obsidesque insuper optulerunt, denique, pluribus quondam de regno concertantibus, nonnisi ab
ipso electum probaverunt.

22:1   Ianum Quirinum, semel atque iterum a condita urbe ante
memoriam suam clausum, in multo breviore temporis spatio
terra marique pace parta ter clusit. bis ovans ingressus
est urbem, post Philippense et rursus post Siculum bellum.
curulis triumphos tris egit, Delmaticum, Actiacum, Alexan-
23:1   drinum, continuo triduo omnes. graves ignominias cladesque
duas omnino nec alibi quam in Germania accepit, Lollianam
et Varianam, sed Lollianam maioris infamiae quam detrimenti,
Varianam paene exitiabilem, tribus legionibus cum duce
legatisque et auxiliis omnibus caesis. hac nuntiata excubias per urbem indixit, ne quis tumultus existeret, et
praesidibus provinciarum propagavit imperium, ut a peritis
23:2   et assuetis socii continerentur. vovit et magnos ludos
Iovi Optimo Maximo, si res p. in meliorem statum vertisset:
quod factum Cimbrico Marsicoque bello erat. adeo denique
consternatum ferunt, ut per continuos menses barba capilloque summisso caput interdum foribus illideret, vociferans:
'Quintili Vare, legiones redde!' diemque cladis quotannis
maestum habuerit ac lugubrem.

24:1   in re militari et commutavit multa et instituit, atque
etiam ad antiquum morem nonnulla revocavit. disciplinam
severissime rexit: ne legatorum quidem cuiquam, nisi gravate
hibernisque demum mensibus, permisit uxorem intervisere.
equitem Romanum, quod duobus filiis adulescentibus causa
detrectandi sacramenti pollices amputasset, ipsum bonaque
subiecit hastae; quem tamen, quod inminere emptioni publicanos videbat, liberto suo addixit, ut relegatum in agros
24:2   pro libero esse sineret. decimam legionem contumacius

parentem cum ignominia totam dimisit, item alias immodeste
missionem postulantes citra commoda emeritorum-praemiorum
exauctoravit. cohortes, si quae cessissent loco, decimatas
hordeo pavit. centuriones statione deserta, itidem ut mani-
pulares, capitali animadversione puniit, pro cetero delic-
torum genere variis ignominis adfecit, ut stare per totum
diem iuberet ante praetorium, interdum tunicatos discinctos-
que, nonnumquam cum decempedis, vel etiam caespitem portan-
25:1 tes. neque post bella civilia aut in contione aut per
edictum ullos militum commilitones appellabat, sed milites,
ac ne a filiis quidem aut privignis suis imperio praeditis
aliter appellari passus est, ambitiosius id existimans,
quam aut ratio militaris aut temporum quies aut sua domus-
25:2 que suae maiestas postularet. libertino milite, praeterquam Romae incendiorum causa et si tumultus in graviore
annona metueretur, bis usus est: semel ad praesidium coloniarum Illyricum contingentium, iterum ad tutelam ripae
Rheni fluminis; eosque, servos adhuc viris feminisque pec-
uniosioribus indictos ac sine mora manumissos, sub priore
vexillo habuit, neque aut commixtos cum ingenuis aut eodem
modo armatos.
25:3 dona militaria, aliquanto facilius phaleras et torques,
quicquid auro argentoque constaret, quam vallares ac murales
coronas, quae honore praecellerent, dabat; has quam parcissime et sine ambitione ac saepe etiam caligatis tribuit.
M. Agrippam in Sicilia post navalem victoriam caeruleo vexillo donavit. solos triumphales, quamquam et socios exped-
itionum et participes victoriarum suarum, numquam donis im-
pertiendos putavit, quod ipsi quoque ius habuissent tribu-
25:4 endi ea quibus vellent. nihil autem minus perfecto duci
quam festinationem temeritatemque convenire arbitrabatur.
crebro itaque illa iactabat: σπεῦδε βραδέως, ἀσφαλὴς γὰρ
ἐστ' ἀμείνων ἢ θρασὺς στρατηλάτης; et 'sat celeriter fieri
quidquid fiat satis bene'. proelium quidem aut bellum
suscipiendum omnino negabat, nisi cum maior emolumenti spes

quam damni metus ostenderetur. nam minima commoda non
minimo sectantis discrimine similes aiebat esse aureo hamo
piscantibus cuius abrupti damnum nulla captura pensari
posset.

26:1   magistratus atque honores et ante tempus et quosdam
novi generis perpetuosque cepit. consulatum vicesimo
aetatis anno invasit, admotis hostiliter ad urbem legionibus, missisque qui sibi nomine exercitus deposcerent; cum
quidem cunctante senatu Cornelius centurio, princeps lega-
tionis, reiecto sagulo ostendens gladii capulum, non dubi-
tasset in curia dicere: 'hic faciet, si vos non feceritis'.

26:2 secundum consulatum post novem annos, tertium anno inter-
iecto gessit, sequentis usque ad undecimum continuavit,
multisque mox, cum deferrentur, recusatis duodecimum magno,
id est septemdecim annorum, intervallo et rursus tertium
decimum biennio post ultro petiit, ut Gaium et Lucium filios
amplissimo praeditus magistratu suo quemque tirocinio de-

26:3 duceret in forum. quinque medios consulatus a sexto ad
decimum annuos gessit, ceteros aut novem aut sex aut quattuor aut tribus mensibus, secundum vero paucissimis horis.
nam die Kal. Ian. cum mane pro aede Capitolini Iovis
paululum curuli sella praesedisset, honore abiit suffecto
alio in locum suum. nec omnes Romae, sed quartum consulatum in Asia, quintum in insula Samo, octavum et nonum
Tarracone iniit.

27:1 triumviratum rei p. constituendae per decem annos administravit; in quo restitit quidem aliquamdiu collegis
ne qua fieret proscriptio, sed inceptam utroque acerbius
exercuit. namque illis in multorum saepe personam per
gratiam et preces exorabilibus, solus magnopere contendit
ne cui parceretur, proscripsitque etiam C. Toranium tutorem
suum, eundem collegam patris sui Octavi in aedilitate.

27:2 Iulius Saturninus hoc amplius tradit, cum peracta proscrip-
tione M. Lepidus in senatu excusasset praeterita et spem
clementiae in posterum fecisset, quoniam satis poenarum

exactum esset, hunc e diverso professum ita modum se pro-
scribendi statuisse, ut omnia sibi reliquerit libera. in
cuius tamen pertinaciae paenitentiam postea T. Vinium Philo-
poemenem, quod patronum suum proscriptum celasse olim dic-
27:3 eretur, equestri dignitate honoravit. in eadem hac potestate
multiplici flagravit invidia. nam et Pinarium equitem R.,
cum contionante se admissa turba paganorum apud milites
subscribere quaedam animadvertisset, curiosum ac specula-
torem ratus, coram confodi imperavit; et Tedium Afrum con-
sulem designatum, quia factum quoddam suum maligno sermone
carpsisset, tantis conterruit minis, ut is se praecipit-
27:4 averit; et Quintum Gallium praetorem, in officio saluta-
tionis tabellas duplices veste tectas tenentem, suspicatus
gladium occulere, nec quidquam statim, ne aliud inveniretur,
ausus inquirere, paulo post per centuriones et milites
raptum e tribunali, servilem in modum torsit ac fatentem
nihil iussit occidi, prius oculis eius sua manu effossis;
quem tamen scribit conloquio petito insidiatum sibi con-
iectumque a se in custodiam, deinde urbe interdicta dimissum,
27:5 naufragio vel latronum insidiis perisse. tribuniciam potestatem perpetuam recepit, in qua semel atque iterum per
singula lustra collegam sibi cooptavit. recepit et morum
legumque regimen aeque perpetuum, quo iure, quamquam sine
censurae honore, censum tamen populi ter egit: primum ac
tertium cum collega, medium solus.

28:1 de reddenda re publica bis cogitavit: primum post op-
pressum statim Antonium, memor obiectum sibi ab eo saepius,
quasi per ipsum staret ne redderetur; ac rursus taedio diu-
turnae valitudinis, cum etiam magistratibus ac senatu domum
accitis rationarium imperii tradidit. sed reputans, et se
privatum non sine periculo fore et illam plurium arbitrio
temere committi, in retinenda perseveravit, dubium eventu
28:2 meliore an voluntate. quam voluntatem, cum prae se identidem ferret, quodam etiam edicto his verbis testatus est:
'ita mihi salvam ac sospitem rem publicam sistere in sua

PRIVELESS   REAS

sede liceat, atque eius rei fructum percipere, quem peto,
ut optimi status auctor dicar, et moriens ut feram mecum
spem, mansura in vestigio suo fundamenta rei publicae quae
iecero'. fecitque ipse se compotem voti, nisus omni modo,
ne quem novi status paeniteret.

28:3   urbem, neque pro maiestate imperii ornatam et inunda-
tionibus incendiisque obnoxiam, excoluit adeo, ut iure sit
gloriatus marmoream se relinquere, quam latericiam accep-
isset. tutam vero, quantum provideri humana ratione pot-
29:1   uit, etiam in posterum praestitit. publica opera plurima
extruxit, e quibus vel praecipua: forum cum aede Martis
Ultoris, templum Apollinis in Palatio, aedem Tonantis Iovis
in Capitolio. fori extruendi causa fuit hominum et iudi-
ciorum multitudo, quae videbatur non sufficientibus duobus
etiam tertio indigere; itaque festinatius necdum perfecta
Martis aede publicatum est, cautumque ut separatim in eo
29:2   publica iudicia et sortitiones iudicum fierent. aedem
Martis bello Philippensi, pro ultione paterna suscepto,
voverat; sanxit ergo, ut de bellis triumphisque hic con-
suleretur senatus, provincias cum imperio petituri hinc
deducerentur, quique victores redissent, huc insignia
29:3   triumphorum conferrent. templum Apollinis in ea parte
Palatinae domus excitavit, quam fulmine ictam desiderari
a deo haruspices pronuntiarant; addidit porticus cum
bibliotheca Latina Graecaque, quo loco iam senior saepe
etiam senatum habuit decuriasque iudicum recognovit. Tonanti Iovi aedem consecravit liberatus periculo, cum ex-
peditione Cantabrica per nocturnum iter lecticam eius
fulgur praestrinxisset servumque praelucentem exanimasset.
29:4   quaedam etiam opera sub nomine alieno, nepotum scilicet
et uxoris sororisque, fecit, ut porticum basilicamque Gai
et Luci, item porticus Liviae et Octaviae theatrumque
Marcelli. sed et ceteros principes viros saepe hortatus
est, ut pro facultate quisque monimentis vel novis vel
29:5   refectis et excultis urbem adornarent. multaque a multis

tunc extructa sunt, sicut a Marcio Philippo aedes Herculis
Musarum, a L. Cornificio aedes Dianae, ab Asinio Pollione
atrium Libertatis, a Munatio Planco aedes Saturni, a Cor-
nelio Balbo theatrum, a Statilio Tauro amphitheatrum, a
M. vero Agrippa complura et egregia.

30:1 spatium urbis in regiones vicosque divisit instituitque,
ut illas annui magistratus sortito tuerentur, hos magistri
e plebe cuiusque viciniae lecti. adversus incendia excubias
nocturnas vigilesque commentus est; ad coercendas inunda-
tiones alveum Tiberis laxavit ac repurgavit, completum olim
ruderibus et aedificiorum prolationibus coartatum. quo
autem facilius undique urbs adiretur, desumpta sibi Flaminia via Arimino tenus munienda, reliquas triumphalibus
viris ex manubiali pecunia sternendas distribuit.)

30:2 aedes sacras vetustate conlapsas aut incendio absumptas
refecit easque et ceteras opulentissimis donis adornavit,
ut qui in cellam Capitolini Iovis sedecim milia pondo auri
gemmasque ac margaritas quingenties sestertium una donatione

31:1 contulerit. postquam vero pontificatum maximum, quem numquam vivo Lepido auferre sustinuerat, mortuo demum suscepit,
quidquid fatidicorum librorum Graeci Latinique generis nullis vel parum idoneis auctoribus vulgo ferebatur, supra
duo milia contracta undique cremavit ac solos retinuit
Sibyllinos, hos quoque dilectu habito; condiditque duobus

31:2 forulis auratis sub Palatini Apollinis basi. annum a Divo
Iulio ordinatum, sed postea neglegentia conturbatum atque
confusum, rursus ad pristinam rationem redegit; in cuius
ordinatione Sextilem mensem e suo cognomine nuncupavit,
magis quam Septembrem quo erat natus, quod hoc sibi et
primus consulatus et insignes victoriae optigissent.

31:3 sacerdotum et numerum et dignitatem sed et commoda auxit,
praecipue Vestalium virginum. cumque in demortuae locum
aliam capi oporteret, ambirentque multi ne filias in sortem
darent, adiuravit, si cuiusquam neptium suarum competeret

31:4 aetas, oblaturum se fuisse eam. nonnulla etiam ex antiquis

caerimonis paulatim abolita restituit, ut Salutis augurium,
Diale flaminium, sacrum Lupercale, ludos saeculares et Compitalicios. Lupercalibus vetuit currere inberbes, item
saecularibus ludis iuvenes utriusque sexus prohibuit ullum
nocturnum spectaculum frequentare nisi cum aliquo maiore
natu propinquorum. Compitales Lares ornari bis anno instituit, vernis floribus et aestivis.

31:5   proximum a dis immortalibus honorem memoriae ducum praestitit, qui imperium populi Romani ex minimo maximum red-
didissent. itaque et opera cuiusque manentibus titulis
restituit et statuas omnium triumphali effigie in utraque
fori sui porticu dedicavit, professus edicto commentum id
se, ut ad illorum velut exemplar et ipse, dum viveret, et
insequentium aetatium principes exigerentur a civibus.
Pompei quoque statuam contra theatri eius regiam marmoreo
Iano superposuit, translatam e curia, in qua C. Caesar
fuerat occisus.

32:1   pleraque pessimi exempli in perniciem publicam aut ex
consuetudine licentiaque bellorum civilium duraverant aut
per pacem etiam extiterant; nam et grassatorum plurimi
palam se ferebant succincti ferro, quasi tuendi sui causa,
et rapti per agros viatores sine discrimine liberi servi-
que ergastulis possessorum supprimebantur, et plurimae
factiones titulo collegi novi ad nullius non facinoris
societatem coibant. igitur grassaturas dispositis per
opportuna loca stationibus inhibuit, ergastula recognovit,
32:2 collegia praeter antiqua et legitima dissolvit. tabulas
veterum aerari debitorum, vel praecipuam calumniandi materiam, exussit; loca in urbe publica iuris ambigui possessoribus adiudicavit; diuturnorum reorum et ex quorum
sordibus nihil aliud quam voluptas inimicis quaereretur
nomina abolevit, condicione proposita, ut si quem quis
repetere vellet, par periculum poenae subiret. ne quod
autem maleficium negotiumve inpunitate vel mora elaberetur,
triginta amplius dies, qui honoraris ludis occupabantur,

32:3 **actui** rerum accomodavit. ad tris iudicum decurias quartam
addidit ex inferiore censu, quae ducenariorum vocaretur iu-
dicaretque de levioribus summis. iudices a vicensimo quinto
aetatis anno adlegit, id est quinquennio maturius quam solebant. ac plerisque iudicandi munus detractantibus, vix concessit ut singulis decuriis per vices annua vacatio esset,
et ut solitae agi Novembri ac Decembri mense res omitteren-
33:1 tur. ipse ius dixit assidue et in noctem nonnumquam, si
parum corpore valeret, lectica pro tribunali collocata vel
etiam domi cubans. dixit autem ius non diligentia modo
summa sed et lenitate, siquidem manifesti parricidii reum,
ne culleo insueretur, quod nonnisi confessi adficiuntur hac
poena, ita fertur interrogasse 'certe patrem tuum non occi-
33:2 disti?'. et cum de falso testamento ageretur omnesque sig-
natores lege Cornelia tenerentur, non tantum duas tabellas,
damnatoriam et absolutoriam, simul cognoscentibus dedit,
sed tertiam quoque, qua ignosceretur iis, quos fraude ad
33:3 signandum vel errore inductos constitisset. appellationes
quotannis urbanorum quidem litigatorum praetori delegabat
urbano, ac provincialium consularibus viris, quos singulos
cuiusque provinciae negotiis praeposuisset.
34:1   leges retractavit et quasdam ex integro sanxit, ut sumptuariam et de adulteriis et de pudicitia, de ambitu, de
maritandis ordinibus. hanc cum aliquanto severius quam
ceteras emendasset, prae tumultu recusantium perferre non
potuit, nisi adempta demum lenitave parte poenarum et vaca-
34:2 tione trienni data auctisque praemiis. sic quoque abolitio-
nem eius publico spectaculo pertinaciter postulante equite,
accitos Germanici liberos receptosque partim ad se partim
in patris gremium ostentavit, manu vultuque significans ne
gravarentur imitari iuvenis exemplum. cumque etiam inmatur-
itate sponsarum et matrimoniorum crebra mutatione vim legis
eludi sentiret, tempus sponsas habendi coartavit, divortiis
modum imposuit.
35:1   senatorum affluentem numerum deformi et incondita turba

(erant enim super mille, et quidam indignissimi et post necem Caesaris per gratiam et praemium adlecti, quos or- civos vulgus vocabat) ad modum pristinum et splendorem re- degit duabus lectionibus: prima ipsorum arbitratu, quo vir virum legit, secunda suo et Agrippae; quo tempore existim- atur lorica sub veste munitus ferroque cinctus praesedisse, decem valentissimis senatorii ordinis amicis sellam suam

35:2 circumstantibus. Cordus Cremutius scribit, ne admissum quidem tunc quemquam senatorum nisi solum et praetemptato sinu. quosdam ad excusandi se verecundiam compulit serva- vitque etiam excusantibus insigne vestis et spectandi in

35:3 orchestra epulandique publice ius. quo autem lecti pro- batique et religiosius et minore molestia senatoria munera fungerentur, sanxit, ut prius quam consideret quisque ture ac mero supplicaret apud aram eius dei, in cuius templo coiretur, et ne plus quam bis in mense legitimus senatus ageretur, Kalendis et Idibus, neve Septembri Octo- brive mense ullos adesse alios necesse esset quam sorte ductos, per quorum numerum decreta confici possent; sibi- que instituit consilia sortiri semenstria, cum quibus de negotiis ad frequentem senatum referendis ante tractaret.

35:4 sententias de maiore negotio non more atque ordine sed prout libuisset perrogabat, ut perinde quisque animum in- tenderet ac si censendum magis quam adsentiendum esset.

36:1 auctor et aliarum rerum fuit, in quis: ne acta senatus publicarentur, ne magistratus deposito honore statim in provincias mitterentur, ut proconsulibus ad mulos et taber- nacula quae publice locari solebant certa pecunia consti- tueretur, ut cura aerari a quaestoribus urbanis ad praetor- ios praetoresve transiret, ut centumviralem hastam quam quaesturam functi consuerant cogere decemviri cogerent.

37:1 quoque plures partem administrandae rei publicae caperent, nova officia excogitavit: curam operum publicorum, viarum, aquarum, alvei Tiberis, frumenti populo dividundi, praefec- turam urbis, triumviratum legendi senatus, et alterum

recognoscendi turmas equitum, quotiensque opus esset. censores creari desitos longo intervallo creavit. numerum
praetorum auxit. exegit etiam, ut quotiens consulatus sibi
daretur, binos pro singulis collegas haberet, nec optinuit,
reclamantibus cunctis satis maiestatem eius imminui, quod
38:1 honorem eum non solus sed cum altero gereret. nec parcior
in bellica virtute honoranda, super triginta ducibus iustos
triumphos et aliquanto pluribus triumphalia ornamenta de-
cernenda curavit.

38:2 liberis senatorum, quo celerius rei publicae assuescerent,
protinus virili toga⟨sumpta⟩latum clavum induere et curiae
interesse permisit, militiamque auspicantibus non tribunatum
modo legionum, sed et praefecturas alarum dedit; ac ne qui
expers castrorum esset, binos plerumque laticlavios prae-
posuit singulis alis.

?8:3 equitum turmas frequenter recognovit, post longam inter-
capedinem reducto more travectionis. sed neque detrahi
quemquam in travehendo ab accusatore passus est, quod fieri
solebat, et senio vel aliqua corporis labe insignibus permisit, praemisso in ordine equo, ad respondendum quotiens
citarentur pedibus venire; mox reddendi equi gratiam fecit
eis, qui maiores annorum quinque et triginta retinere eum
39:1 nollent. impetratisque a senatu decem adiutoribus, unum
quemque equitum rationem vitae reddere coegit atque in ex-
probratis alios poena, alios ignominia notavit, plures ad-
monitione, sed varia. lenissimum genus admonitionis fuit
traditio coram pugillarium, quos taciti et ibidem statim
legerent; notavitque aliquos, quod pecunias levioribus
40:1 usuris mutuati graviore faenore collocassent. ac comitiis
tribuniciis si deessent candidati senatores, ex equitibus
R. creavit, ita ut potestate transacta, in utro vellent
ordine manerent. cum autem plerique equitum attrito bellis civilibus patrimonio spectare ludos e quattuordecim
non auderent metu poenae theatralis, pronuntiavit non
teneri ea, quibus ipsis parentibusve equester census umquam

fuisset.

40:2 populi recensum vicatim egit, ac ne plebs frumentationum causa frequentius ab negotiis avocaretur, ter in annum quaternum mensium tesseras dare destinavit; sed desideranti consuetudinem veterem concessit rursus, ut sui cuiusque mensis acciperet. comitiorum quoque pristinum ius reduxit ac multiplici poena coercito ambitu, Fabianis et Scaptiensibus tribulibus suis die comitiorum, ne quid a quoquam candidato desiderarent, singula milia nummum a se dividebat.

40:3 magni praeterea existimans sincerum atque ab omni colluvione peregrini ac servilis sanguinis incorruptum servare populum, et civitates Romanas parcissime dedit et manumittendi modum terminavit. Tiberio pro cliente Graeco petenti rescripsit, non aliter se daturum, quam si praesens sibi persuasisset, quam iustas petendi causas haberet; et Liviae pro quodam tributario Gallo roganti civitatem negavit, immunitatem optulit affirmans, facilius se passurum fisco detrahi aliquid, quam civitatis Romanae vulgari hon-

40:4 orem. servos non contentus multis difficultatibus a libertate et multo pluribus a libertate iusta removisse, cum et de numero et de conditione ac differentia eorum qui manumitterentur curiose cavisset, hoc quoque adiecit, ne vinctus umquam tortusve quis ullo libertatis genere civitatem adipisceretur.

40:5 etiam habitum vestitumque pristinum reducere studuit, ac visa quondam pro contione pullatorum turba, indignabundus et clamitans en Romanos, rerum dominos, gentemque togatam! negotium aedilibus dedit, ne quem posthac paterentur in foro circove nisi positis lacernis togatum consistere.

41:1 liberalitatem omnibus ordinibus per occasiones frequenter exhibuit. nam et invecta urbi Alexandrino triumpho regia gaza tantam copiam nummariae rei effecit, ut faenore deminuto plurimum agrorum pretiis accesserit, et postea quotiens ex damnatorum bonis pecunia superflueret, usum

eius gratuitum iis qui cavere in duplum possent ad certum
tempus indulsit. senatorum censum ampliavit ac pro octin-
gentorum milium summa quodecies sestertium taxavit, supple-
41:2 vitque non habentibus. congiaria populo frequenter dedit,
sed diversae fere summae: modo quadringenos, modo trecenos,
nonnumquam ducenos quinquagenosque nummos; ac ne minores
quidem pueros praeteriit, quamvis nonnisi ab undecimo
aetatis anno accipere consuessent. frumentum quoque in
annonae difficultatibus saepe levissimo, interdum nullo
pretio viritim admensus est tesserasque nummarias duplicavit.
42:1 sed ut salubrem magis quam ambitiosum principem scires,
querentem de inopia et caritate vini populum severissima
coercuit voce: satis provisum a genero suo Agrippa per-
42:2 ductis pluribus aquis, ne homines sitirent. eidem populo
promissum quidem congiarium reposcenti bonae se fidei
esse respondit; non promissum autem flagitanti turpitud-
inem et impudentiam edicto exprobravit affirmavitque non
daturum se quamvis dare destinaret. nec minore gravitate
atque constantia, cum proposito congiario multos manumissos
insertosque civium numero comperisset, negavit accepturos
quibus promissum non esset, ceterisque minus quam promiserat
42:3 dedit, ut destinata summa sufficeret. magna vero quondam
sterilitate ac difficili remedio, cum venalicias et lanis-
tarum familias peregrinosque omnes, exceptis medicis et
praeceptoribus, partimque servitiorum urbe expulisset, ut
tandem annona convaluit, impetum se cepisse scribit fru-
mentationes publicas in perpetuum abolendi, quod earum
fiducia cultura agrorum cessaret; neque tamen perseverasse,
quia certum haberet posse per ambitionem quandoque restitui.
atque ita posthac rem temperavit, ut non minorem aratorum
ac negotiantium quam populi rationem deduceret.
43:1 spectaculorum et assiduitate et varietate et magnificen-
tia omnes antecessit. fecisse se ludos ait suo nomine
quater, pro aliis magistratibus (qui aut abessent aut non
sufficerent) ter et vicies. fecitque nonnumquam vicatim

ac pluribus scaenis per omnium linguarum histriones; ⟨cir-
censibus ludis gladiatoriisque muneribus frequentissime
editis interiecit plerumque bestiarum Africanarum venationes⟩
non in foro modo, nec in amphitheatro, sed et in circo et
in Saeptis, et aliquando nihil praeter venationem edidit;
athletas quoque, extructis in campo Martio sedilibus lig-
neis; item navale proelium, circa Tiberim cavato solo, in
quo nunc Caesarum nemus est. quibus diebus custodes in
urbe disposuit, ne raritate remanentium grassatoribus ob-
43:2 noxia esset. in circo aurigas cursoresque et confectores
ferarum, et nonnumquam ex nobilissima iuventute, produxit.
sed et Troiae lusum edidit frequentissime maiorum minorum-
que puerorum, prisci decorique moris existimans, clarae
stirpis indolem sic notescere. in hoc ludicro Nonium
Asprenatem lapsu debilitatum aureo torque donavit passus-
que est ipsum posterosque Torquati ferre cognomen. mox
finem fecit talia edendi, Asinio Pollione oratore graviter
invidioseque in curia questo Aesernini nepotis sui casum,
qui et ipse crus fregerat.
43:3   ad scenicas quoque et gladiatorias operas et equitibus
Romanis aliquando usus est, verum prius quam senatus consulto interdiceretur. postea nihil sane praeterquam
adulescentulum Lycium honeste natum exhibuit, tantum ut
ostenderet; quod erat bipedali minor, librarum septemdecim
43:4 ac vocis immensae. quodam autem muneris die Parthorum obsides, tunc primum missos, per mediam arenam ad spectaculum
induxit superque se subsellio secundo collocavit. solebat
etiam citra spectaculorum dies, si quando quid invisitatum
dignumque cognitu advectum esset, id extra ordinem quolibet
loco publicare: ut rhinocerotem apud Saepta, tigrim in
scaena, anguem quinquaginta cubitorum pro comitio.
43:5   accidit votivis Circensibus, ut correptus valitudine
lectica cubans tensas deduceret; rursus commissione ludorum,
quibus theatrum Marcelli dedicabat, evenit ut laxatis
sellae curulis compagibus caderet supinus. nepotum quoque

suorum munere cum consternatum ruinae metu populum retinere
et confirmare nullo modo posset, transiit e loco suo atque
in ea parte consedit, quae suspecta maxime erat.

44:1   spectandi confusissimum ac solutissimum morem correxit
ordinavitque, motus iniuria senatoris, quem Puteolis per
celeberrimos ludos consessu frequenti nemo receperat. facto
igitur decreto patrum ut, quotiens quid spectaculi usquam
publice ederetur, primus subselliorum ordo vacaret senator-
ibus, Romae legatos liberarum sociarumque gentium vetuit
in orchestra sedere, cum quosdam etiam libertini generis

44:2 mitti deprendisset. militem secrevit a populo. maritis
e plebe proprios ordines assignavit, praetextatis cuneum
suum, et proximum paedagogis, sanxitque ne quis pullatorum
media cavea sederet. feminis ne gladiatores quidem, quos
promiscue spectari sollemne olim erat, nisi ex superiore

44:3 loco spectare concessit. solis virginibus Vestalibus
locum in theatro, separatim et contra praetoris tribunal,
dedit. athletarum vero spectaculo muliebre secus omnes
adeo summovit, ut pontificalibus ludis pugilum par postu-
latum distulerit in insequentis diei matutinum tempus,
edixeritque mulieres ante horam quintam venire in theatrum

45.1 non placere. ipse circenses ex amicorum fere libertorum-
que cenaculis spectabat, interdum ex pulvinari, et quidem
cum coniuge ac liberis sedens. spectaculo plurimas horas,
aliquando totos dies aberat, petita venia commendatisque
qui suam vicem praesidendo fungerentur. verum quotiens
adesset, nihil praeterea agebat, seu vitandi rumoris causa,
quo patrem Caesarem vulgo reprehensum commemorabat, quod
inter spectandum epistulis libellisque legendis aut re-
scribendis vacaret, seu studio spectandi ac voluptate,
qua teneri se neque dissimulavit umquam et saepe ingenue

45:2 professus est. itaque corollaria et praemia in alienis
quoque muneribus ac ludis et crebra et grandia de suo offer-
ebat, nullique Graeco certamini interfuit, quo non pro
merito quemque certantium honorarit. spectavit autem

studiosissime pugiles et maxime Latinos, non legitimos atque
ordinarios modo, quos etiam committere cum Graecis solebat,
sed et catervarios oppidanos, inter angustias vicorum pug-
45:3 nantis temere ac sine arte. universum denique genus operas
aliquas publico spectaculo praebentium etiam cura sua dig-
natus est: athletis et conservavit privilegia et ampliavit;
gladiatores sine missione edi prohibuit; coercitionem in
histriones magistratibus, omni tempore et loco lege vetere
45:4 permissam, ademit praeterquam ludis et scaena. nec tamen
eo minus aut xysticorum certationes aut gladiatorum pugnas
severissime semper exegit. nam histrionum licentiam adeo
compescuit, ut Stephanionem togatarium, cui in puerilem
habitum circumtonsam matronam ministrasse compererat, per
trina theatra virgis caesum relegaverit, Hylan pantomimum,
querente praetore, in atrio domus suae nemine excluso
flagellis verberarit, et Pyladen urbe atque Italia sum-
moverit, quod spectatorem, a quo exsibilabatur, demon-
strasset digito conspicuumque fecisset.

46:1 ad hunc modum urbe urbanisque rebus administratis,
Italiam duodetriginta coloniarum numero, deductarum ab se,
frequentavit operibusque ac vectigalibus publicis plurifariam instruxit, etiam iure ac dignatione urbi quodam
modo pro parte aliqua adaequavit, excogitato genere suffragiorum, quae de magistratibus urbicis decuriones colo-
nici in sua quisque colonia ferrent et sub die comitiorum
obsignata Romam mitterent. ac necubi aut honestorum
deficeret copia aut multitudinis suboles, equestrem militiam petentis etiam ex commendatione publica cuiusque
oppidi ordinabat; at iis, qui e plebe regiones sibi re-
visenti filios filiasve approbarent, singula nummorum
milia pro singulis dividebat.

47:1 provincias validiores et quas annuis magistratuum im-
periis regi nec facile nec tutum erat, ipse suscepit,
ceteras proconsulibus sortito permisit; et tamen nonnullas
commutavit interdum atque ex utroque genere plerasque

saepius adiit. urbium quasdam, foederatas sed ad exitium
licentia praecipites, libertate privavit, alias aut aere
alieno laborantis levavit, aut terrae motu subversas denuo
condidit, aut merita erga populum Romanum adlegantes Latini-
tate vel civitate donavit. nec est, ut opinor, provincia,
excepta dumtaxat Africa et Sardinia, quam non adierit. in
has fugato Sex. Pompeio traicere ex Sicilia apparantem con-
tinuae et immodicae tempestates inhibuerunt, nec mox occasio
aut causa traiciendi fuit.

48:1   regnorum quibus belli iure potitus est, praeter pauca,
aut isdem quibus ademerat reddidit, aut alienigenis con-
tribuit. reges socios etiam inter semet ipsos necessitudinibus mutuis iunxit, promptissimus affinitatis cuiusque
atque amicitiae conciliator et fautor; nec aliter universos
quam membra partisque imperii curae habuit, rectorem quoque
solitus apponere aetate parvis aut mente lapsis, donec
adulescerent aut resipiscerent; ac plurimorum liberos et
educavit simul cum suis et instituit.

49:1   ex militaribus copiis legiones et auxilia provinciatim
distribuit, classem Miseni et alteram Ravennae ad tutelam
Superi et Inferi maris conlocavit, ceterum numerum partim
in urbis partim in sui custodiam adlegit, dimissa Calagurritanorum manu, quam usque ad devictum Antonium, item Germanorum, quam usque ad cladem Varianam inter armigeros
circa se habuerat. neque tamen umquam plures quam tres
cohortes in urbe esse passus est easque sine castris; reliquas in hiberna et aestiva circa finitima oppida dimittere
49:2 assuerat. quidquid autem ubique militum esset, ad certam
stipendiorum praemiorumque formulam adstrinxit, definitis
pro gradu cuiusque et temporibus militiae et commodis
missionum, ne aut aetate aut inopia post missionem sollici-
tari ad res novas possent. utque perpetuo ac sine difficul-
tate sumptus ad tuendos eos prosequendosque suppeteret,
aerarium militare cum vectigalibus novis constituit.

49:3   et quo celerius ac sub manum adnuntiari cognoscique

posset, quid in provincia quaque gereretur, iuvenes primo
modicis intervallis per militaris vias, dehinc vehicula disposuit. commodius id visum est, ut qui a loco idem perferunt
litteras, interrogari quoque, si quid res exigant, possint.

50:1 in diplomatibus libellisque et epistulis signandis initio
sphinge usus est, mox imagine Magni Alexandri, novissime
sua, Dioscuridis manu sculpta, qua signare insecuti quoque
principes perseverarunt. ad epistulas omnis horarum quoque
momenta nec diei modo sed et noctis, quibus datae significa-
rentur, addebat.

51:1 clementiae civilitatisque eius multa et magna documenta
sunt. ne enumerem, quot et quos diversarum partium venia
et incolumitate donatos principem etiam in civitate locum
tenere passus sit: Iunium Novatum et Cassium Patavinum e
plebe homines alterum pecunia, alterum levi exilio punire
satis habuit, cum ille Agrippae iuvenis nomine asperrimam
de se epistulam in vulgus edidisset, hic convivio pleno
proclamasset, neque votum sibi neque animum deesse con-

51:2 fodiendi eum. quadam vero cognitione, cum Aemilio Aeliano
Cordubensi inter cetera crimina vel maxime obiceretur quod
male opinari de Caesare soleret, conversus ad accusatorem
commotoque similis 'velim,' inquit, 'hoc mihi probes; fac-
iam sciat Aelianus et me linguam habere, plura enim de eo
loquar'; nec quicquam ultra aut statim aut postea inquisiit.

51:3 Tiberio quoque de eadem re, sed violentius, apud se per
epistulam conquerenti ita rescripsit 'aetati tuae, mi
Tiberi, noli in hac re indulgere et nimium indignari quemquam esse, qui de me male loquatur; satis est enim, si hoc
habemus ne quis nobis male facere possit'.

52:1 templa, quamvis sciret etiam proconsulibus decerni solere,
in nulla tamen provincia nisi communi suo Romaeque nomine
recepit (nam in urbe quidem pertinacissime abstinuit hoc
honore) atque etiam argenteas statuas olim sibi positas
conflavit omnis exque iis aureas cortinas Apollini Palatino
dedicavit.

53:1   dictaturam magni vi offerente populo, genu nixus deicta
ab umeris toga nudo pectore deprecatus est. domini apella-
tionem ut maledictum et obprobrium semper exhorruit. cum,
spectante eo ludos, pronuntiatum esset in mimo 'o dominum
aequum et bonum!' et universi quasi de ipso dictum exul-
tantes comprobassent, et statim manu vultuque indecoras
adulationes repressit et insequenti die gravissimo cor-
ripuit edicto; dominumque se posthac appellari ne a liberis
quidem aut nepotibus suis vel serio vel ioco passus est, at-
53:2 que eius modi blanditias etiam inter ipsos prohibuit. non
temere urbe oppidove ullo egressus aut quoquam ingressus
est nisi vespera aut noctu, ne quem officii causa inquietaret. in consulatu pedibus fere, extra consulatum saepe
adaperta sella per publicum incessit. promiscuis salutationibus admittebat et plebem, tanta comitate adeuntium
desideria excipiens, ut quendam ioco corripuerit, quod sic
sibi libellum porrigere dubitaret, quasi elephanto stipem.
53:3 die senatus numquam patres nisi in curia salutavit et
quidem sedentis, ac nominatim singulos nullo submonente;
etiam discedens eodem modo sedentibus valere dicebat.
officia cum multis mutuo exercuit, nec prius dies cuiusque
sollemnes frequentare desiit, quam grandi iam natu et in
turba quondam sponsaliorum die vexatus. Gallum Cerrinium
senatorem minus sibi familiarem, sed captum repente oculis
et ob id inedia mori destinantem praesens consolando revocavit ad vitam.

54:1   in senatu verba facienti dictum est 'non intellexi,' et
ab alio 'contradicerem tibi, si locum haberem'. interdum
ob immodicas disceptantium altercationes e curia per iram
se proripienti quidam ingesserunt licere oportere senator-
ibus de re publica loqui. Antistius Labeo senatus lectione,
cum vir virum legeret, M. Lepidum hostem olim eius et tunc
exulantem legit, interrogatusque ab eo an essent alii dig-
55:1 niores, suum quemque iudicium habere respondit. nec
ideo libertas aut contumacia fraudi cuiquam fuit. etiam
sparsos de se in curia famosos libellos nec expavit et

magna cura redarguit, ac ne requisitis quidem auctoribus
id modo censuit, cognoscendum posthac de iis, qui libellos
aut carmina ad infamiam cuiuspiam sub alieno nomine edant.
56:1   iocis quoque quorundam invidiosis aut petulantibus lac-
essitus, contradixit edicto. et tamen ne de inhibenda
testamentorum licentia quicquam constitueretur, intercessit.
quotiens magistratuum comitiis interesset, tribus cum candidatis suis circuibat supplicabatque more sollemni. ferebat
et ipse suffragium in tribu, ut unus e populo. testem se
in iudiciis et interrogari et refelli aequissimo animo
56:2   patiebatur. forum angustius fecit, non ausus extorquere
possessoribus proximas domos. numquam filios suos populo
commendavit ut non adiceret 'si merebuntur'. eisdem praetextatis adhuc assurrectum ab universis in theatro et a
stantibus plausum gravissime questus est. amicos ita
magnos et potentes in civitate esse voluit, ut tamen pari
iure essent quo ceteri legibusque iudiciariis aeque tene-
56:3   rentur. cum Asprenas Nonius artius ei iunctus causam
veneficii, accusante Cassio Severo, diceret, consuluit
senatum quid officii sui putaret; cunctari enim se, ne
si superesset, eripere legibus reum, sin deesset, desti-
tuere ac praedamnare amicum existimaretur; et consentien-
tibus universis sedit in subselliis per aliquot horas,
verum tacitus et ne laudatione quidem iudiciali data.
56:4   affuit et clientibus, sicut Scutario cuidam, evocato quondam suo, qui postulabatur iniuriarum. unum omnino e
reorum numero, ac ne eum quidem nisi precibus eripuit,
exorato coram iudicibus accusatore, Castricium, per quem
de coniuratione Murenae cognoverat.
57:1   pro quibus meritis quantopere dilectus sit, facile est
aestimare. omitto senatus consulta, quia possunt videri
vel necessitate expressa vel verecundia. equites Romani
natalem eius sponte atque consensu biduo semper celebrarunt. omnes ordines in lacum Curti quotannis ex voto
pro salute eius stipem iaciebant, item Kal. Ian. strenam

in Capitolio, etiam absenti, ex qua summa pretiosissima deorum simulacra mercatus, vicatim dedicabat, ut Apollinem
57:2 Sandaliarium et Iovem Tragoedum aliaque. in restitutionem
Palatinae domus incendio absumptae veterani, decuriae,
tribus, atque etiam singillatim e cetero genere hominum
libentes ac pro facultate quisque pecunias contulerunt,
delibante tantum modo eo summarum acervos neque ex quoquam
plus denario auferente. revertentem ex provincia non
solum faustis ominibus, sed et modulatis carminibus pro-
sequebantur. observatum etiam est, ne quotiens introiret
58:1 urbem, supplicium de quoquam sumeretur. patris patriae
cognomen universi repentino maximoque consensu detulerunt
ei: prima plebs, legatione Antium missa; dein, quia non
recipiebat, ineunti Romae spectacula frequens et laureata;
mox in curia senatus, neque decreto neque adclamatione,
58:2 sed per Valerium Messallam. is mandantibus cunctis, 'quod
bonum,' inquit, 'faustumque sit tibi domuique tuae, Caesar
Auguste! sic enim nos perpetuam felicitatem rei publicae
et laeta huic ⟨urbi⟩ precari existimamus: senatus te con-
sentiens cum populo Romano consalutat patriae patrem'.
cui lacrimans respondit Augustus his verbis (ipsa enim,
sicut Messallae, posui) 'compos factus votorum meorum,
patres conscripti, quid habeo aliud deos immortales precari,
quam ut hunc consensum vestrum ad ultimum finem vitae mihi
perferre liceat?'
59:1   medico Antonio Musae, cuius opera ex ancipiti morbo
convaluerat, statuam aere conlato iuxta signum Aesculapi
statuerunt. nonnulli patrum familiarum testamento caverunt,
ut ab heredibus suis praelato titulo victimae in Capitolium
ducerentur votumque pro se solveretur, quod superstitem
Augustum reliquissent. quaedam Italiae civitates diem, quo
primum ad se venisset, initium anni fecerunt. provinciarum
pleraeque super templa et aras ludos quoque quinquennales
60:1 paene oppidatim constituerunt. reges amici atque socii et
singuli in suo quisque regno Caesareas urbes condiderunt et

cuncti simul aedem Iovis Olympii Athenis, antiquitus in-
cohatam, perficere communi sumptu destinaverunt Genioque
eius dedicare; ac saepe regnis relictis, non Romae modo
sed et provincias peragranti cotidiana officia togati ac
sine regio insigni more clientium praestiterunt.

61:1   quoniam qualis in imperis ac magistratibus regendaque
per terrarum orbem pace belloque re publica fuerit
posui, referam nunc interiorem ac familiarem eius vitam,
quibusque moribus atque fortuna domi et inter suos egerit
61:2 a iuventa usque ad supremum vitae diem. matrem amisit in
primo consulatu, sororem Octaviam quinquagensimum et quartum agens aetatis annum. utrique cum praecipua officia
vivae praestitisset, etiam defunctae honores maximos
tribuit.

62:1   sponsam habuerat adulescens P. Servili Isaurici filiam,
sed reconciliatus post primam discordiam Antonio, expos-
tulantibus utriusque militibus ut et necessitudine aliqua
iungerentur, privignam eius Claudiam, Fulviae ex P. Clodio
filiam, duxit uxorem vixdum nubilem, ac simultate cum
62:2 Fulvia socru orta dimisit intactam adhuc et virginem. mox
Scriboniam in matrimonium accepit, nuptam ante duobus consularibus, ex altero etiam matrem. cum hac quoque divor-
tium fecit, pertaesus, ut scribit, morum perversitatem
eius, ac statim Liviam Drusillam matrimonio Tiberi Neronis
et quidem praegnantem abduxit, dilexitque et probavit
unice ac perseveranter.

63:1   ex Scribonia Iuliam, ex Livia nihil liberorum tulit,
cum maxime cuperet. infans, qui conceptus erat, immaturus
est editus. Iuliam primum Marcello, Octaviae sororis suae
filio tantum quod pueritiam egresso, deinde, ut is obiit,
M. Agrippae nuptum dedit, exorata sorore, ut sibi generum
cederet; nam tunc Agrippa alteram Marcellarum habebat et
63.2 ex ea liberos. hoc quoque defuncto, multis ac diu, etiam
ex equestri ordine, circumspectis condicionibus, Tiberium
privignum suum elegit coegitque praegnantem uxorem, et ex

qua iam pater erat, dimittere. M. Antonius scribit, primum
eum Antonio filio suo despondisse Iuliam, dein Cotisoni
Getarum regi, quo tempore sibi quoque invicem filiam regis
in matrimonium petisset.

64:1   nepotes ex Agrippa et Iulia tres habuit Gaium et Lucium
et Agrippam, neptes duas Iuliam et Agrippinam. Iuliam L.
Paullo censoris filio, Agrippinam Germanico sororis suae
nepoti collocavit. Gaium et Lucium adoptavit domi per
assem et libram emptos a patre Agrippa, tenerosque adhuc
ad curam rei publicae admovit et consules designatos cir-
64:2 cum provincias exercitusque dimisit. filiam et neptes
ita instituit, ut etiam lanificio assuefaceret, vetaretque
loqui aut agere quicquam nisi propalam et quod in diurnos
commentarios referretur; extraneorum quidem coetu adeo
prohibuit, ut L. Vinicio, claro decoroque iuveni, scrip-
serit quondam parum modeste fecisse eum, quod filiam suam
64:3 Baias salutatum venisset. nepotes et litteras et natare
aliaque rudimenta per se plerumque docuit ac nihil aeque
elaboravit quam ut imitarentur chirographum suum; neque
cenavit una, nisi ut in imo lecto assiderent, neque iter
fecit nisi ut vehiculo anteirent aut circa adequitarent.
65:1 sed laetum eum atque fidentem et subole et disciplina
domus Fortuna destituit. Iulias, filiam et neptem, omnibus probris contaminatas relegavit; Gaium et Lucium in
duodeviginti mensium spatio amisit ambos, Gaio in Lycia,
Lucio Massiliae defunctis. Tertium nepotem Agrippam
simulque privignum Tiberium adoptavit in foro lege curiata;
ex quibus Agrippam brevi ob ingenium sordidum ac ferox
abdicavit seposuitque Surrentum.
65:2 aliquanto autem patientius mortem quam dedecora suorum
tulit. nam Gai Lucique casu non adeo fractus, de filia
absens ac libello per quaestorem recitato notum senatui
fecit abstinuitque congressu hominum diu prae pudore,
etiam de necanda deliberavit. certe cum sub idem tempus
una ex consciis liberta Phoebe suspendio vitam finisset

65:3 maluisse se ait Phoebes patrem fuisse. relegatae usum
vini omnemque delicatiorem cultum ademit neque adiri a
quopiam libero servove, nisi se consulto, permisit, et ita
ut certior fieret, qua is aetate, qua statura, quo colore
esset, etiam quibus corporis notis vel cicatricibus. post
quinquennium demum ex insula in continentem lenioribusque
paulo condicionibus transtulit eam. nam ut omnino revoc-
aret, exorari nullo modo potuit, deprecanti saepe populo
Romano et pertinacius instanti tales filias talesque con-
65:4 iuges pro contione inprecatus. ex nepte Iulia post dam-
nationem editum infantem adgnosci alique vetuit. Agrippam
nihilo tractabiliorem, immo in dies amentiorem, in insulam
transportavit saepsitque insuper custodia militum. cavit
etiam senatus consulto ut eodem loci in perpetuum contin-
eretur, atque ad omnem et eius et Iuliarum mentionem in-
gemiscens, proclamare etiam solebat:

Αἴθ᾽ ὄφελον ἄγαμός τ᾽ ἔμεναι ἄγονός τ᾽ ἀπολέσθαι!

nec aliter eos appellare, quam tris vomicas ac tria carcino-
mata sua.
66:1   amicitias neque facile admisit et constantissime retinuit, non tantum virtutes ac merita cuiusque digne prosecutus, sed vitia quoque et delicta, dum taxat modica,
perpessus. neque enim temere ex omni numero in amicitia
eius afflicti reperientur praeter Salvidienum Rufum, quem
ad consulatum usque, et Cornelium Gallum, quem ad prae-
fecturam Aegypti, ex infima utrumque fortuna provexerat.
66:2 quorum alterum res novas molientem damnandum senatui
tradidit, alteri ob ingratum et malivolum animum domo et
provinciis suis interdixit. sed Gallo quoque et accusa-
torum denuntiationibus et senatus consultis ad necem con-
pulso, laudavit quidem pietatem tantopere pro se indig-
nantium, ceterum et inlacrimavit et vicem suam conquestus
est quod sibi soli non liceret amicis, quatenus vellet.

66:3   **irasci.** reliqui potentia atque opibus ad finem vitae sui
quisque ordinis principes floruerunt, quanquam et offensis
intervenientibus. desideravit enim nonnumquam, ne de pluribus referam, et M. Agrippae patientiam et Maecenatis taciturnitatem, cum ille ex levi frigoris suspicione et quod
Marcellus sibi anteferretur, Mytilenas se relictis omnibus
contulisset, hic secretum de comperta Murenae coniuratione
uxori Terentiae prodidisset.

66:4   **exegit** et ipse in vicem ab amicis benivolentiam mutuam,
tam a defunctis quam a vivis. nam quamvis minime appeteret
hereditates, ut qui numquam ex ignoti testamento capere
quicquam sustinuerit, amicorum tamen suprema iudicia moros-
issime pensitavit, neque dolore dissimulato, si parcius
aut citra honorem verborum, neque gaudio, si grate pieque
quis se prosecutus fuisset. legata vel partes hereditatium,
a quibuscumque parentibus relicta sibi, aut statim liberis
eorum concedere, aut si pupillari aetate essent, die virilis
togae vel nuptiarum cum incremento restituere consuerat.

67:1   **patronus** dominusque non minus severus quam facilis et
clemens, multos libertorum in honore et usu maximo habuit,
ut Licinum et Celadum aliosque. Cosmum servum gravissime
de se opinantem non ultra quam compedibus coercuit. Diomeden dispensatorem, a quo simul ambulante incurrenti repente fero apro per metum obiectus est, maluit timiditatis
arguere quam noxae, remque non minimi periculi, quia tamen

67:2   **fraus** aberat, in iocum vertit. idem Polum ex acceptissimis
libertis mori coegit compertum adulterare matronas; Thallo
a manu, quod pro epistula prodita denarios quingentos ac-
cepisset, crura effregit; paedagogum ministrosque Gai fili,
per occasionem valitudinis mortisque eius superbe avareque
in provincia grassatos, oneratos gravi pondere cervicibus
praecipitavit in flumen.

68:1   **prima** iuventa variorum dedecorum infamiam subiit. Sextus
Pompeius ut effeminatum insectatus est; M. Antonius adop-
tionem avunculi stupro meritum; item Lucius Marci frater

quasi pudicitiam, delibatam a Caesare, Aulo etiam Hirtio
in Hispania trecentis milibus nummum substraverit, solitus-
que sit crura suburere nuce ardenti, quo mollior pilus
surgeret. sed et populus quondam universus ludorum die
et accepit in contumeliam eius et adsensu maximo conpro-
bavit versum in scaena pronuntiatum de gallo Matris deum
tympanizante 'videsne, ut cinaedus orbem digito temperat?'.
69:1 adulteria quidem exercuisse ne amici quidem negant, ex-
cusantes sane non libidine, sed ratione commissa, quo
facilius consilia adversariorum per cuiusque mulieres ex-
quireret. M. Antonius super festinatas Liviae nuptias
obiecit et feminam consularem e triclinio viri coram in
cubiculum abductam, rursus in convivium rubentibus auri-
culis incomptiore capillo reductam; dimissam Scriboniam,
quia liberius doluisset nimiam potentiam paelicis; condiciones quaesitas per amicos, qui matres familias et
adultas aetate virgines denudarent atque perspicerent,
69:2 tamquam Toranio mangone vendente. scribit etiam ad ipsum
haec, familiariter adhuc necdum plane inimicus aut hostis
'quid te mutavit? quod reginam ineo? uxor mea est? nunc
coepi, an abhinc annos novem? tu deinde solam Drusillam
inis? ita valeas, uti tu, hanc epistulam cum leges, non
inieris Tertullam aut Terentillam aut Rufillam aut Salviam
Titiseniam aut omnes. an refert, ubi et in qua arrigas?'
70:1 cena quoque eius secretior in fabulis fuit, quae vulgo
δωδεκάθεος vocabatur; in qua deorum dearumque habitu dis-
cubuisse convivas et ipsum pro Apolline ornatum, non Antoni
modo epistulae singulorum nomina amarissime enumerantis
exprobrant, sed et sine auctore notissimi versus:

> Cum primum istorum conduxit mensa choragum,
>   sexque deos vidit Mallia sexque deas;
> impia dum Phoebi Caesar mendacia .udit,
>   ‹dum nova divorum cenat adulteria:
> omnia se a terris tunc numina declinarunt,
>   fugit et auratos Iuppiter ipse thronos.

70:2   auxit cenae rumorem summa tunc in civitate penuria ac
fames, adclamatumque est postridie omne frumentum deos
comedisse et Caesarem esse plane Apollinem, sed Tortorem:
quo cognomine is deus quadam in parte urbis colebatur.
notatus est et ut pretiosae supellectilis Corinthiorumque
praecupidus, et aleae indulgens. nam et proscriptionis
tempore ad statuam eius ascriptum est:

> pater argentarius, ego Corinthiarius,

cum existimaretur quosdam propter vasa Corinthia inter pro-
scriptos curasse referendos; et deinde bello Siciliensi
epigramma vulgatum est:

> postquam bis classe victus naves perdidit,
> aliquando ut vincat, ludit assidue aleam.

71:1   ex quibus sive criminibus sive maledictis infamiam im-
pudicitiae facillime refutavit et praesentis et posterae
vitae castitate; item lautitiarum invidiam, cum et Alexandria capta nihil sibi praeter unum murrinum calicem ex
instrumento regio retinuerit, et mox vasa aurea assidu-
issimi usus conflaverit omnia. circa libidines haesit;
postea quoque, ut ferunt, ad vitiandas virgines promptior,
quae sibi undique etiam ab uxore conquirerentur. aleae
rumorem nullo modo expavit, lusitque simpliciter et palam
oblectamenti causa etiam senex, ac, praeterquam Decembri
71:2 mense, aliis quoque festis et profestis diebus. nec id
dubium est. autographa quadam epistula 'cenavi,' ait,
'mi Tiberi, cum isdem; accesserunt convivae Vinicius et
Silius pater. inter cenam lusimus geronticos et heri et
hodie, talis enim iactatis, ut quisque canem aut seniónem
miserat, in singulos talos singulos denarios in medium
conferebat, quos tollebat universos, qui Venerem iecerat'.
71:3 et rursus aliis litteris 'nos, mi Tiberi, quinquatrus

satis iucunde egimus; lusimus enim per omnis dies forumque
aleatorium calfecimus. frater tuus magnis clamoribus rem
gessit; ad summam tamen perdidit non multum, sed ex magnis
detrimentis praeter spem paulatim retractum est. ego per-
didi viginti milia nummum meo nomine, sed cum effuse in
lusu liberalis fuissem, ut soleo plerumque. nam si quas
manus remisi cuique exegissem, aut retinuissem quod cuique donavi, vicissem vel quinquaginta milia. sed hoc
malo; benignitas enim mea me ad caelestem gloriam ef-
71:4 feret'. scribit ad filiam 'misi tibi denarios ducentos
quinquaginta, quos singulis convivis dederam, si vellent
inter se inter cenam vel talis vel par impar ludere'.
72:1 in ceteris partibus vitae continentissimum fuisse con-
stat ac sine suspicione ullius vitii. habitavit primo
iuxta Romanum forum, supra scalas anularias, in domo quae
Calvi oratoris fuerat; postea in Palatio, sed nihilo minus
aedibus modicis Hortensianis, et neque laxitate neque cultu
conspicuis, ut in quibus porticus breves essent Albanarum
columnarum, et sine marmore ullo aut insigni pavimento con-
clavia. ac per annos amplius quadraginta eodem cubiculo
hieme et aestate mansit, quamvis parum salubrem valitudini
suae urbem hieme experiretur assidueque in urbe hiemaret.
72:2 si quando quid secreto aut sine interpellatione agere pro-
posuisset, erat illi locus in edito singularis, quem Syracusas et τεχνόφυον vocabat: huc transibat, aut in alicuius
libertorum suburbanum; aeger autem in domo Maecenatis cubabat. ex secessibus praecipue frequentavit maritima insulas-
que Campaniae, aut proxima urbi oppida, Lanuvium, Praeneste,
Tibur, ubi etiam in porticibus Herculis templi persaepe ius
72:3 dixit. ampla et operosa praetoria gravabatur, et neptis
quidem suae Iuliae, profuse ab ea extructa, etiam diruit
ad solum, sua vero quamvis modica non tam statuarum tabu-
larumque pictarum ornatu, quam xystis et nemoribus excoluit
rebusque vetustate ac raritate notabilibus: qualia sunt

Capreis immanium beluarum ferarumque membra praegrandia,
73:1 quae dicuntur gigantum ossa et arma heroum. instrumenti
eius et supellectilis parsimonia apparet etiam nunc residuis lectis atque mensis, quorum pleraque vix privatae
elegantiae sint. ne toro quidem cubuisse aiunt nisi
humili et modice instrato. veste non temere alia quam
domestica usus est, ab sorore et uxore et filia neptibus-
que confecta; togis neque restrictis neque fusis, clavo
nec lato nec angusto, calciamentis altiusculis, ut pro-
cerior quam erat videretur. et forensia autem et calceos
numquam non intra cubiculum habuit ad subitos repentinos-
que casus parata.

74:1   convivabatur assidue nec umquam nisi recta, non sine
magno ordinum hominumque dilectu. Valerius Messalla tradit,
neminem umquam libertinorum adhibitum ab eo cenae excepto
Mena, sed asserto in ingenuitatem post proditam Sexti
Pompei classem. ipse scribit, invitasse se quondam, in
cuius villa maneret, qui speculator suus olim fuisset.
convivia nonnumquam et serius inibat et maturius relin-
quebat, cum convivae et cenare inciperent prius quam
ille discumberet, et permanerent digresso eo. cenam
ternis ferculis, aut cum abundantissime senis praebebat,
ut non nimio sumptu, ita summa comitate. nam et ad com-
munionem sermonis tacentis vel summissim fabulantis pro-
vocabat, et aut acroamata et histriones aut etiam triviales ex circo ludios interponebat ac frequentius aretalogos.

75:1   festos et sollemnes dies profusissime, nonnumquam tantum ioculariter celebrabat. Saturnalibus, et si quando
alias libuisset, modo munera dividebat, vestem et aurum
et argentum, modo nummos omnis notae, etiam veteres regios
ac peregrinos, interdum nihil praeter cilicia et spongias
et rutabula et forpices atque alia id genus, titulis ob-
scuris et ambiguis. solebat et inaequalissimarum rerum
sortes et aversas tabularum picturas in convivio venditare

incertoque casu spem mercantium vel frustrari vel explere,
ita ut per singulos lectos licitatio fieret et seu iactura
76:1 seu lucrum communicaretur. cibi (nam ne haec quidem omi-
serim) minimi erat atque vulgaris fere. secundarium panem
et pisciculos minutos et caseum bubulum manu pressum et
ficos virides biferas maxime appetebat; vescebaturque et
ante cenam quocumque tempore et loco, quo stomachus desider-
asset. verba ipsius ex expistulis sunt 'nos in essedo panem
76:2 et palmulas gustavimus'. et iterum 'dum lectica ex regia
domum redeo, panis unciam cum paucis acinis uvae duracinae
comedi'. et rursus 'ne Iudaeus quidem, mi Tiberi, tam dil-
igenter sabbatis ieiunium servat quam ego hodie servavi,
qui in balineo demum post horam primam noctis duas buccas
manducavi prius quam ungui inciperem'. ex hac inobservantia
nonnumque vel ante initum vel post dimissum convivium solus
77:1 cenitabat, cum pleno convivio nihil tangeret. vini quoque
natura parcissimus erat. non amplius ter bibere eum sol-
itum super cenam in castris apud Mutinam, Cornelius Nepos
tradit. postea quotiens largissime se invitaret, senos
sextantes non excessit, aut si excessisset, reiciebat. et
maxime delectatus est Raetico, neque temere interdiu bibit.
pro potione sumebat perfusum aqua frigida panem, aut cuc-
umeris frustum vel lactuculae thyrsum, aut recens aridumve
pomum suci vinosioris.
78:1 post cibum meridianum, ita ut vestitus calciatusque erat,
retectis pedibus paulisper conquiescebat, opposita ad oculos manu. a cena in lecticulam se lucubratoriam recipiebat;
ibi, donec residua diurni actus aut omnia aut ex maxima
parte conficeret, ad multam noctem permanebat. in lectum
inde transgressus, non amplius cum plurimum quam septem
horas dormiebat, ac ne eas quidem continuas, sed ut in illo
78:2 temporis spatio ter aut quater expergisceretur. si inter-
ruptum somnum reciperare, ut evenit, non posset, lectoribus
aut fabulatoribus arcessitis resumebat, producebatque ultra
primam saepe lucem. nec in tenebris vigilavit umquam nisi

assidente aliquo. matutina vigilia offendebatur; ac si
vel officii vel sacri causa maturius evigilandum esset, ne
id contra commodum faceret, in proximo cuiuscumque domes-
ticorum cenaculo manebat. sic quoque saepe indigens
somni, et dum per vicos deportaretur et deposita lectica
inter aliquas moras condormiebat.

79:1   forma fuit eximia et per omnes aetatis gradus venustis-
sima; quamquam et omnis lenocinii neglegens et in capite
comendo tam incuriosus, ut raptim compluribus simul tonsor-
ibus operam daret, ac modo tonderet modo raderet barbam,
eoque ipso tempore aut legeret aliquid aut etiam scriberet.
vultu erat vel in sermone vel tacitus adeo tranquillo
serenoque, ut quidam e primoribus Galliarum confessus
sit inter suos, eo se inhibitum ac remollitum, quo minus,
ut destinarat, in transitu Alpium per simulationem con-
79:2   loquii propius admissus in praecipitium propelleret. oculos habuit claros ac nitidos, quibus etiam existimari vol-
ebat inesse quiddam divini vigoris, gaudebatque, si qui
sibi acrius contuenti quasi ad fulgorem solis vultum sum-
mitteret; sed in senecta sinistro minus vidit; dentes
raros et exiguos et scabros; capillum leviter inflexum
et subflavum; supercilia coniuncta; mediocres aures;
nasum et a summo eminentiorem et ab imo deductiorem;
colorem inter aquilum candidumque; staturam brevem (quam
tamen Iulius Marathus, libertus et a memoria eius, quinque
pedum et dodrantis fuisse tradit), sed quae commoditate
et aequitate membrorum occuleretur, ut nonnisi ex compara-
tione astantis alicuius procerioris intellegi posset.

80:1   corpore traditur maculoso, dispersis per pectus atque alvum
genetivis notis in modum et ordinem ac numerum stellarum
caelestis ursae, sed et callis quibusdam, ex prurigine corporis adsiduoque et vehementi strigilis usu plurifariam
concretis ad impetiginis formam. coxendice et femore et
crure sinistro non perinde valebat, ut saepe etiam

inclaudicaret; sed remedio harenarum atque harundinum con-
firmabatur. dextrae quoque manus digitum salutarem tam
imbecillum interdum sentiebat, ut torpentem contractumque
frigore vix cornei circuli supplemento scripturae admoveret.
questus est et de vesica, cuius dolore calculis demum per
urinam eiectis levabatur.

81:1   graves et periculosas valitudines per omnem vitam aliquot expertus est; praecipue Cantabria domita, cum etiam
destillationibus iocinere vitiato ad desperationem redactus
contrariam et ancipitem rationem medendi necessario subiit:
quia calida fomenta non proderant, frigidis curari coactus
81:2   auctore Antonio Musa. quasdam et anniversarias ac tempore
certo recurrentes experiebatur; nam sub natalem suum plerumque languebat; et initio veris praecordiorum inflatione
temptabatur, austrinis autem tempestatibus gravedine. quare
quassato corpore, neque frigora neque aestus facile tolera-
82:1   bat. hieme quaternis cum pingui toga tunicis et subucula
et thorace laneo et feminalibus et tibialibus muniebatur,
aestate apertis cubiculi foribus, ac saepe in peristylo
saliente aqua atque etiam ventilante aliquo cubabat. solis
vero ne hiberni quidem patiens, domi quoque nonnisi petasa-
tus sub divo spatiabatur. itinera lectica et noctibus
fere, eaque lenta ac minuta faciebat, ut Praeneste vel
Tibur biduo procederet; ac si quo pervenire mari posset,
82:2   potius navigabat. verum tantam infirmitatem magna cura
tuebatur, in primis lavandi raritate; unguebatur enim
saepius, aut sudabat ad flammam, deinde perfundebatur
egelida aqua vel sole multo tepefacta. quotiens nervoᵣum
causa marinis Albulisque calidis utendum esset, contentus
hoc erat ut insidens ligneo solio, quod ipse Hispanico
verbo duretam vocabat, manus ac pedes alternis iactaret.

83:1   exercitationes campestres equorum et armorum statim
post civilia bella omisit et ad pilam primo folliculumque
transiit, mox nihil aliud quam vectabatur et deambulabat,
ita ut in extremis spatiis subsultim decurreret, segestri

vel lodicula involutus. animi laxanui causa moao pisca-
batur hamo, modo taljs aut ocellatis nucibusque luaebat
cum pueris minutis, quos facie et garrulitate amabilis
undique conquirebat, praecipue Mauros et Syros. nam pum-
ilos atque distortos et omnis generis eiusdem ut ludibria
naturae malique ominis abhorrebat.

84:1 eloquentiam studiaque liberalia ab aetate prima et
cupide et laboriosissime exercuit. Mutinensi bello in
tanta mole rerum et legisse et scripsisse et declamasse
cotidie traditur. nam deinceps neque in senatu neque apud
populum neque apud miljtes locutus est umquam nisi medi-
tata et composita oratione, quamvis non deficeretur ad
84:2 subita extemporali facultate. ac ne periculum memoriae
adiret aut in ediscendo tempus absumeret, instituit re-
citare omnia. sermones quoque cum singulis atque etiam
cum Livia sua graviores nonnisi scriptos et e libello
habebat, ne plus minusve loqueretur ex tempore. pronun-
tiabat dulci et proprio quodam oris sono, dabatque assiaue
phonasco operam; sed nonnumquam infirmatis faucibus, prae-
conis voce ad populum contionatus est.

85:1 multa varii generis prosa oratione composuit, ex quibus
nonnulla in coetu familiarium velut in auditorio recitavit,
sicut rescripta Bruto de Catone, quae volumina cum iam
senior ex magna parte legisset, fatigatus Tiberio tradidit
perlegenda; item hortationes ad philosophiam, et aliqua
de vita sua, quam tredecim libris Cantabrico tenus bello
85:2 nec ultra exposuit. poetica summatim attigit. unus liber
extat, scriptus ab eo hexametris versibus, cuius et argu-
mentum et titulus est Sicilia; extat alter aeque modicus
epigrammatum, quae fere tempore balinei meditabatur. nam
tragoediam magno impetu exorsus, non succedenti stilo,
abolevit quaerentibusque amicis, quidnam Aiax ageret, respondit, Aiacem suum in spongiam incubuisse.

86:1 genus eloquendi secutus est elegans et temperatum,
vitatis sententiarum ineptiis atque concinnitate et

'reconditorum verborum', ut ipse dicit, 'fetoribus'; prae-
cipuamque curam duxit sensum animi quam apertissime ex-
primere. quod quo facilius efficeret aut necubi lectorem
vel auditorem obturbaret ac moraretur, neque praepositiones
urbibus addere neque coniunctiones saepius iterare dubi-
tavit, quae detractae afferunt aliquid obscuritatis, etsi
86:2 gratiam augent. cacozelos et antiquarios, ut diverso
genere vitiosos, pari fastidio sprevit, exagitabatque
nonnumquam; in primis Maecenatem suum, cuius 'myrobrechis',
ut ait, 'cincinnos' usque quaque persequitur et imitando
per iocum irridet. sed nec Tiberio parcit et exoletas
interdum et reconditas voces aucupanti. M. quidem Antonium
ut insanum increpat, quasi ea scribentem, quae mirentur
potius homines quam intellegant; deinde ludens malum et
inconstans in eligendo genere dicendi ingenium eius, addit
86:3 haec 'tuque dubitas, Cimberne Annius an Veranius Flaccus
imitandi sint tibi, ita ut verbis, quae Crispus Sallustius
excerpsit ex Originibus Catonis, utaris? an potius Asiaticorum oratorum inanis sententiis verborum volubilitas in
nostrum sermonem transferenda?' et quadam epistula Agrip-
pinae neptis ingenium conlaudans 'sed opus est,' inquit,
'dare te operam, ne moleste scribas et loquaris'.
87:1   cotidiano sermone quaedam frequentius et notabiliter
usurpasse eum, litterae ipsius autographae ostentant, in
quibus identidem, cum aliquos numquam soluturos significare
vult, ad Kalendas Graecas soluturos ait; et cum hortatur
ferenda esse praesentia, qualiacumque sint 'contenti simus
hoc Catone'; et ad exprimendam festinatae rei velocitatem
87:2 'celerius quam asparagi cocuntur'; ponit assidue et pro
stulto 'baceolum', et pro pullo 'pulleiaceum', et pro cer-
rito 'vacerrosum', et 'vapide' se habere pro male, et 'betizare' pro languere, quod vulgo 'lachanizare' dicitur;
item 'simus' pro sumus, et 'domos' genitivo casu singulari
pro domuos. nec umquam aliter haec duo, ne quis mendam
magis quam consuetudinem putet.

87:3   notavi et in chirographo eius illa praecipue: non dividit
verba nec ab extrema parte versuum abundantis litteras in
alterum transfert, sea ibidem statim subicit circumducitque.

88:1 orthographiam, id est formulam rationemque scribendi a gram-
maticis institutam, non adeo custodit ac videtur eorum potius sequi opinionem, qui perinde scribendum ac loquamur
existiment. nam quod saepe non litteras modo sed syllabas
aut permutat aut praeterit, communis hominum error est.
nec ego id notarem, nisi mihi mirum videretur tradidisse
aliquos, legato eum consulari successorem dedisse ut rudi
et indocto, cuius manu 'ixi' pro 'ipsi' scriptum animad-
verterit. quotiens autem per notas scribit, B pro A, C
pro B ac deinceps eadem ratione sequentis litteras ponit;
pro X autem duplex A.

89:1   ne Graecarum quidem disciplinarum leviore studio tene-
batur. in quibus et ipsis praestabat largiter, magistro
dicendi usus Apollodoro Pergameno, quem iam grandem natu
Apolloniam quoque secum ab urbe iuvenis adhuc eduxerat,
deinde eruditione etiam varia repletus per Arei philosophi
filiorumque eius Dionysi et Nicanoris contubernium; non
tamen ut aut loqueretur expedite aut componere aliquid
auderet; nam et si quid res exigeret, Latine formabat
vertendumque alii dabat. sed plane poematum quoque non
imperitus, delectabatur etiam comoedia veteri et saepe

89:2 eam exhibuit spectaculis publicis. in evolvendis utriusque linguae auctoribus nihil aeque sectabatur, quam prae-
cepta et exempla publice vel privatim salubria, eaque ad
verbum excerpta aut ad domesticos aut ad exercituum pro-
vinciarumque rectores aut ad urbis magistratus plerumque
mittebat, prout quique monitione indigerent. etiam libros
totos et senatui recitavit et populo notos per edictum
saepe fecit, ut orationes Q. Metelli *de prole augenda* et
Rutili *de modo aedificiorum*, quo magis persuaderet utram-
que rem non ab se primo animadversam, sed antiquis iam
tunc curae fuisse.

89:3   ingenia saeculi sui omnibus modis fovit; recitantis et
benigne et patienter audiit, nec tantum carmina et histo-
rias, sed et orationes et dialogos. componi tamen aliquid
de se nisi et serio et a praestantissimis offendebatur, ad-
monebatque praetores, ne paterentur nomen suum commissionibus obsolefieri.

90:1   circa religiones talem accepimus. tonitrua et fulgura
paulo infirmius expavescebat, ut semper et ubique pellem
vituli marini circumferret pro remedio, atque ad omnem
maioris tempestatis suspicionem in abditum et concamaratum
locum se reciperet, consternatus olim per nocturnum iter
transcursu fulguris, ut praediximus.

91:1   somnia neque sua neque aliena de se neglegebat. Philippensi acie quamvis statuisset non egredi tabernaculo propter valitudinem, egressus est tamen amici somnio monitus;
cessitque res prospere, quando captis castris lectica eius,
quasi ibi cubans remansisset, concursu hostium confossa atque lacerata est. ipse per omne ver plurima et formidulos-
issima et vana et irrita videbat, reliquo tempore rariora
91:2 et minus vana. cum dedicatam in Capitolio aedem Tonanti
Iovi assidue frequentaret, somniavit, queri Capitolinum
Iovem cultores sibi abduci, seque respondisse, Tonantem
pro ianitore ei appositum; ideoque mox tintinnabulis fastigium aedis redimiit, quod ea fere ianuis dependebant.
ex nocturno visu etiam stipem quotannis die certo emendi-
cabat a populo, cavam manum asses porrigentibus praebens.

92:1   auspicia et omina quaedam pro certissimis observabat;
si mane sibi calceus perperam ac sinister pro dextro in-
duceretur, ut dirum; si terra marive ingrediente se longin-
quam profectionem forte rorasset, ut laetum maturique et
prosperi reditus. sed et ostentis praecipue movebatur.
enatam inter iuncturas lapidum ante domum suam palmam in
compluvium deorum Penatium transtulit, utque coalesceret
92:2 magno opere curavit. apud insulam Capreas veterrimae ilicis
demissos iam ad terram languentisque ramos convaluisse

adventu suo, adeo laetatus est, ut eas cum re publica Nea-
politanorum permutaverit, Aenaria data. observabat et
dies quosdam, ne aut postridie nundinas quoquam proficis-
ceretur, aut Nonis quicquam rei seriae incoharet; nihil in
hoc quidem aliud devitans, ut ad Tiberium scribit, quam
δυσφημίαν nominis.

93:1   peregrinarum caerimoniarum sicut veteres ac praeceptas
reverentissime coluit, ita ceteras contemptui habuit. namque Athenis initiatus, cum postea Romae pro tribunali de
privilegio sacerdotum Atticae Cereris cognosceret et quaedam secretiora proponerentur, dimisso consilio et corona
circumstantium solus audiit disceptantes. at contra non
modo in peragranda Aegypto paulo deflectere ad visendum
Apin supersedit, sed et Gaium nepotem, quod Iudaeam praeter-
vehens apud Hierosolyma non supplicasset, conlaudavit.

94:1   et quoniam ad haec ventum est, non ab re fuerit sub-
texere, quae ei prius quam nasceretur et ipso natali die
ac deinceps evenerint, quibus futura magnitudo eius et
perpetua felicitas sperari animadvertique posset.

94:2   Velitris antiquitus tacta de caelo parte muri, responsum
est eius oppidi civem quandoque rerum potiturum; qua fiducia Veliterni et tunc statim et postea saepius paene ad
exitium sui cum populo Romano belligeraverant; sero tandem
documentis apparuit, ostentum illud Augusti potentiam por-
tendisse.

94:3   auctor est Iulius Marathus, ante paucos quam nasceretur
menses prodigium Romae factum publice, quo denuntiabatur,
regem populo Romano naturam parturire; senatum exterritum
censuisse, ne quis illo anno genitus educaretur; eos qui
gravidas uxores haberent, quod ad se quisque spem traheret,
curasse ne senatus consultum ad aerarium deferretur.

94:4   in Asclepiadis Mendetis θεολογουμένων libris lego, Atiam,
cum ad sollemne Apollinis sacrum media nocte venisset,
posita in templo lectica, dum ceterae matronae dormirent,
obdormisse; draconem repente irrepsisse ad eam pauloque

post egressum; illam expergefactam quasi a concubitu mariti
purificasse se; et statim in corpore eius extitisse maculam
velut picti draconis, nec potuisse unquam exigi, adeo ut
mox publicis balineis perpetuo abstinuerit; Augustum natum
mense decimo et ob hoc Apollinis filium existimatum. eadem
Atia prius quam pareret somniavit, intestina sua ferri ad
sidera explicarique per omnem terrarum et caeli ambitum.
somniavit et pater Octavius, utero Atiae iubar solis exortum.

94:5   quo natus est die, cum de Catilinae coniuratione ageretur
in curia et Octavius ob uxoris puerperium serius affuisset,
nota ac vulgata res est P. Nigidium, comperta morae causa,
ut horam quoque partus acceperit, affirmasse dominum terrarum orbi natum. Octavio postea, cum per secreta Thraciae
exercitum duceret, in Liberi patris luco barbara caerimonia
de filio consulenti, idem affirmatum est a sacerdotibus,
quod infuso super altaria mero tantum flammae emicuisset,
ut supergressa fastigium templi ad caelum usque ferretur,
unique omnino Magno Alexandro apud easdem aras sacrificanti
94:6 simile provenisset ostentum. atque etiam sequenti statim
nocte videre visus est filium mortali specie ampliorem, cum
fulmine et sceptro exuviisque Iovis Optimi Maximi ac radi-
ata corona, super laureatum currum, bis senis equis candore
eximio trahentibus. infans adhuc, ut scriptum apud C.
Drusum extat, repositus vespere in cunas a nutricula loco
plano, postera luce non comparuit, diuque quaesitus tandem
in altissima turri repertus est, iacens contra solis
exortum.

94:7   cum primum fari coepisset, in avito suburbano obstre-
pentis forte ranas silere iussit, atque ex eo negantur ibi
ranae coaxare. ad quartum lapidem Campanae viae in nemore
prandenti ex inproviso aquila panem ei e manu rapuit, et
cum altissime evolasset, rursus ex inproviso leniter de-
lapsa reddidit.

94:8   Q. Catulus post dedicatum Capitolium duabus continuis
noctibus somniavit: prima, Iovem Optimum Maximum e prae-

textatis compluribus circum aram ludentibus unum secrevisse,
atque in eius sinum signum rei publicae quam manu gestaret
reposuisse, at insequenti, animadvertisse se in gremio Capitolini Iovis eundem puerum, quem cum detrahi iussisset,
prohibitum monitu dei, tanquam is ad tutelam rei publicae
educaretur; ac die proximo obvium sibi Augustum, cum in-
cognitum alias haberet, non sine admiratione contuitus,
simillimum dixit puero, de quo somniasset. quidam prius
somnium Catuli aliter exponunt, quasi Iuppiter compluribus
praetextatis tutorem a se poscentibus, unum ex eis demon-
strasset ad quem omnia desideria sua referrent, eiusque
osculum delibatum digitis ad os suum rettulisset.

94:9   M. Cicero C. Caesarem in Capitolium prosecutus, somnium
pristinae noctis familiaribus forte narrabat: puerum facie
liberali, demissum e caelo catena aurea, ad fores Capitoli
constitisse eique Iovem flagellum tradidisse; deinde repente Augusto viso, quem ignotum plerisque adhuc avunculus
Caesar ad sacrificandum acciverat, affirmavit ipsum esse,
cuius imago secundum quietem sibi obversata sit.

94:10   sumenti virilem togam tunica lati clavi, resuta ex utraque parte, ad pedes decidit. fuerunt qui interpretarentur,
non aliud significare, quam ut is ordo cuius insigne id
esset quandoque ei subiceretur.

94:11   apud Mundam Divus Iulius, castris locum capiens cum sil-
vam caederet, arborem palmae repertam conservari ut omen
victoriae iussit; ex ea continuo enata suboles adeo in
paucis diebus adolevit, ut non aequiperaret modo matricem,
verum et obtegeret frequentareturque columbarum nidis,
quamvis id avium genus duram et asperam frondem maxime
vitet. illo et praecipue ostento motum Caesarem ferunt,
ne quem alium sibi succedere quam sororis nepotem vellet.

94:12   in secessu Apolloniae Theogenis mathematici pergulam
comite Agrippa ascenderat; cum Agrippae, qui prior con-
sulebat, magna et paene incredibilia praedicerentur, re-
ticere ipse genituram suam nec velle edere perseverabat,

metu ac pudore, ne minor inveniretur. qua tamen post multas adhortationes vix et cunctanter edita, exilivit Theo-
genes adoravitque eum. tantam mox fiduciam fati Augustus
habuit, ut thema suum vulgaverit nummumque argenteum nota
sideris Capricorni, quo natus est, percusserit.

95:1   post necem Caesaris reverso ab Apollonia et ingrediente
eo urbem, repente liquido ac puro sereno circulus ad spe-
ciem caelestis arcus orbem solis ambiit, ac subinde Iuliae
Caesaris filiae monimentum fulmine ictum est. primo autem
consulatu et augurium capienti duodecim se vultures ut
Romulo ostenderunt, et immolanti omnium victimarum iocinera
replicata intrinsecus ab ima fibra paruerunt, nemine peri-
torum aliter coiectante quam laeta per haec et magna por-
tendi.

96:1   quin et bellorum omnium eventus ante praesensit. con-
tractis ad Bononiam triumvirorum copiis, aquila tentorio
eius supersedens duos corvos hinc et inde infestantis af-
flixit et ad terram dedit; notante omni exercitu, futuram
quandoque inter collegas discordiam talem qualis secuta
est, et exitum praesagiente. Philippis Thessalus quidam
de futura victoria nuntiavit auctore Divo Caesare, cuius
sibi species itinere avio occurrisset.

96:2   circa Perusiam, sacrificio non litanti cum augeri hos-
tias imperasset, ac subita eruptione hostes omnem rei di-
vinae apparatum abstulissent, constitit inter haruspices,
quae periculosa et adversa sacrificanti denuntiata essent,
cuncta in ipsos recasura qui exta haberent, neque aliter
evenit. pridie quam Siciliensem pugnam classe committeret,
deambulanti in litore piscis e mari exilivit et ad pedes
iacuit. apud Actium descendenti in aciem asellus cum asi-
nario occurrit: homini Eutychus, bestiae Nicon erat nomen;
utriusque simulacrum aeneum victor posuit in templo, in
quod castrorum suorum locum vertit.

97:1   mors quoque eius, de qua hinc dicam, divinitasque post
mortem evidentissimis ostentis praecognita est. cum

lustrum in campo Martio magna populi frequentia conderet,
aquila eum saepius circumvolavit transgressaque in vicinam
aedem super nomen Agrippae ad primam litteram sedit; quo
animadverso vota, quae in proximum lustrum suscipi mos est,
collegam suum Tiberium nuncupare iussit: nam se, quanquam
conscriptis paratisque iam tabulis, negavit suscepturum

97:2 quae non esset soluturus. sub idem tempus ictu fulminis
ex inscriptione statuae eius prima nominis littera efflu-
xit; responsum est, centum solos dies posthac victurum,
quem numerum C littera notaret, futurumque ut inter deos
referretur, quod aesar, id est reliqua pars e Caesaris
nomine, Etrusca lingua deus vocaretur.

97:3 Tiberium igitur in Illyricum dimissurus et Beneventum
usque prosecuturus, cum interpellatores aliis atque aliis
causis in iure dicendo detinerent, exclamavit, quod et
ipsum mox inter omina relatum est, non, si omnia moraren-
tur, amplius se posthac Romae futurum, atque itinere
incohato Asturam perrexit, et inde, praeter consuetudinem
de nocte, ad occasionem aurae evectus, causam valitudinis

98:1 contraxit ex profluvio alvi. tunc Campaniae ora proximis-
que insulis circuitis, Caprearum quoque secessui quadri-
duum impendit, remississimo ad otium et ad omnem comitatem
animo.

98:2 forte Puteolanum sinum praetervehenti vectores nautaeque de navi Alexandrina, quae tantum quod appulerat, candidati coronatique et tura libantes fausta omina et eximias
laudes congesserant: per illum se vivere, per illum navi-
gare, libertate atque fortunis per illum frui. qua re
admodum exhilaratus, quadragenos aureos comitibus divisit
iusque iurandum et cautionem exegit a singulis, non alio
datam summam quam in emptionem Alexandrinarum mercium ab-

98:3 sumpturos. sed et ceteros continuos dies inter varia
munuscula togas insuper ac pallia distribuit, lege proposita ut Romani Graeco, Graeci Romano habitu et sermone
uterentur. spectavit assidue exercentes ephebos, quorum

aliqua adhuc copia ex vetere instituto Capreis erat; isdem
etiam epulum in conspectu suo praebuit, permissa, immo ex-
acta iocandi licentia diripiendique pomorum et obsoniorum
rerumque ⟨omnium⟩ missilia. nullo denique genere hilari-
tatis abstinuit.

98:4   vicinam Capreis insulam Apragopolim appellabat, a de-
sidia secedentium illuc e comitatu suo. sed ex dilectis
unum, Masgaban nomine, quasi conditorem insulae κτίστην
vocare consuerat. huius Masgabae ante annum defuncti
tumulum cum e triclinio animadvertisset magna turba multisque luminibus frequentari, versum compositum ex tempore
clare pronuntiavit:

Κτίστου δὲ τύμβον εἰσορῶ πυρούμενον·

conversus ad Thrasyllum Tiberi comitem, contra accubantem
et ignarum rei, interrogavit cuiusnam poetae putaret esse;
quo haesitante, subiecit alium:

'Ορᾶς φάεσσι Μασγάβαν τιμώμενον;

ac de hoc quoque consuluit. cum ille nihil aliud respon-
deret quam, cuiuscumque essent optimos esse, cachinnum
98:5   sustulit atque in iocos effusus est. mox Neapolim trai-
ecit, quanquam etiam tum infirmis intestinis morbo var-
iante; tamen et quinquennale certamen gymnicum honori suo
institutum perspectavit et cum Tiberio ad destinatum locum
contendit. sed in redeundo adgravata valitudine, tandem
Nolae succubuit revocatumque ex itinere Tiberium diu secreto sermone detinuit, neque post ulli maiori negotio
animum accommodavit.

99:1   supremo die identidem exquirens, an iam de se tumultus
foris esset, petito speculo, capillum sibi comi ac malas
labantes corrigi praecepit, et admissos amicos percontatus
ecquid iis videretur mimum vitae commode transegisse

adiecit et clausulam:

ἐπεὶ δὲ πάνυ καλῶς πέπαισται, δότε κρότον
καὶ πάντες ἡμᾶς μετὰ χαρᾶς προπέμψατε.

omnibus deinde dimissis, dum advenientes ab urbe de Drusi
filia aegra interrogat, repente in osculis Liviae et in
hac voce defecit 'Livia, nostri coniugi memor vive, ac
vale!', sortitus exitum facilem et qualem semper optaverat.

99:2 nam fere quotiens audisset cito ac nullo cruciatu defunc-
tum quempiam, sibi et suis εὐθανασίαν similem (hoc enim
et verbo uti solebat) precabatur. unum omnino ante effla-
tam animam signum alienatae mentis ostendit, quod subito
pavefactus a quadraginta se iuvenibus abripi questus est.
id quoque magis praesagium quam mentis deminutio fuit,
siquidem totidem milites praetoriani extulerunt eum in
publicum.

100:1 obiit in cubiculo eodem, quo pater Octavius, duobus
Sextis, Pompeio et Appuleio, coss. XIV Kal. Septemb. hora
diei nona, septuagesimo et sexto aetatis anno, diebus V
et XXX minus.

100:2 corpus decuriones municipiorum et coloniarum a Nola
Bovillas usque deportarunt, noctibus propter anni tempus,
cum interdiu in basilica cuiusque oppidi vel in aedium
sacrarum maxima reponeretur. a Bovillis equester ordo
suscepit, urbique intulit atque in vestibulo domus conlocavit. senatus et in funere ornando et in memoria honoranda eo studio certatim progressus est, ut inter alia
complura censuerint quidam, funus triumphali porta ducen-
dum, praecedente Victoria quae est in curia, canentibus
neniam principum liberis utriusque sexus; alii, exequiarum
die ponendos anulos aureos ferreosque sumendos; nonnulli,

100:3 ossa legenda per sacerdotes summorum collegiorum. fuit et
qui suaderet, appellationem mensis Augusti in Septembrem
transferendam, quod hoc genitus Augustus, illo defunctus

esset; alius, ut omne tempus a primo die natali ad **exitum**
eius saeculum Augustum appellaretur et ita in fastos referretur.   verum adhibito honoribus modo, bifariam lauda-
tus est, pro aede Divi Iuli a Tiberio et pro rostris
veteribus a Druso Tiberi filio, ac senatorum umeris de-
100:4 latus in Campum crematusque.   nec defuit vir praetorius,
qui se effigiem cremati euntem in caelum vidisse iuraret.
reliquias legerunt primores equestris ordinis, tunicati
et discincti pedibusque nudis, ac Mausoleo condiderunt.
id opus inter Flaminiam viam ripamque Tiberis sexto suo
consulatu extruxerat circumiectasque silvas et ambulatio-
nes in usum populi iam tum publicarat.
101:1   testamentum L. Planco C. Silio coss. III Non. Apriles,
ante annum et quattuor menses quam decederet, factum ab
eo ac duobus codicibus partim ipsius partim libertorum
Polybi et Hilarionis manu scriptum depositumque apud se
virgines Vestales cum tribus signatis aeque voluminibus
101:2 protulerunt.   quae omnia in senatu aperta atque recitata
sunt.   heredes instituit primos, Tiberium ex parte dimidia
et sextante, Liviam ex parte tertia, quos et ferre nomen
suum iussit; secundos, Drusum Tiberi filium ex triente,
ex partibus reliquis Germanicum liberosque eius tres **sexus**
virilis; tertio gradu, propinquos amicosque compluris.
legavit populo Romano quadringenties, tribubus tricies
quinquies sestertium, praetorianis militibus singula milia
nummorum, cohortibus urbanis quingenos, legionaris trecenos nummos.   quam summam repraesentari iussit, nam et
101:3 confiscatam semper repositamque habuerat.   reliqua legata
varie dedit perduxitque quaedam ad vicies sestertium, quibus solvendis annuum diem finiit, excusata rei familiaris
mediocritate, nec plus perventurum ad heredes suos quam
milies et quingenties professus, quamvis viginti proximis
annis quaterdecies milies ex testamentis amicorum perce-
pisset, quod paene omne cum duobus paternis patrimoniis
ceterisque hereditatibus in rem publicam absumpsisset.

Iulias filiam neptemque, si quid iis accidisset, vetuit

101:4 sepulcro suo inferri. tribus voluminibus, uno mandata
de funere suo complexus est, altero indicem rerum a se
gestarum, quem vellet incidi in aeneis tabulis, quae
ante Mausoleum statuerentur, tertio breviarium totius
imperii, quantum militum sub signis ubique esset, quantum
pecuniae in aerario et fiscis et vectigaliorum residuis.
adiecit et libertorum servorumque nomina, a quibus ratio
exigi posset.

COMMENTARY

Modern books and articles are referred to by name of author,
year of publication, and page number where appropriate; a few
works are abbreviated by initial letters, as are the titles of
many periodicals. Full details of all will be found in the
Bibliography (p. 20). *Ancient authors* and their works are
either spelled out in full or cited in the conventional way
(a list may be found in Lewis and Short's *Latin Dictionary*).
An exception is *RG*, which means Augustus' *Res Gestae* (or
Monumentum Ancyranum). Figures in bold type refer to chapters
of the *Divus Augustus;* other *Lives* of Suetonius are cited by
the Emperor's name alone (or its standard abbreviation - *DJ*
etc.) without mention of Suetonius. Other abbreviations are:-

ch.	chapter	
HS	sestertius	(the normal unit of account, 4 to the denarius)
m.	metre	
MS	manuscript	
n.	note	

COMMENTARY

1-4 AUGUSTUS' ANCESTRY

Suetonius begins the *Life*, as is his habit, with his subject's ancestors. The hostile items are not contradicted or disproved, but presented without comment in such a way that they discredit not Augustus, but their authors.

1   Velitris: Velitrae is the modern Velletri, about 20 miles south-east of Rome.
ara Octavio consecrata: this altar was probably a private one, dedicated to the use of Octavius and his family; hence the dative *Octavio*.

2.1   ea gens a Tarquinio Prisco ... in patriciatum redit: the origin of the patriciate is obscure and controversial. In my view there can be little doubt that the patrician families of the early Republic in some sense owed their status to the kings, though it is not certain whether the caste distinction between plebeian and patrician predates the end of the monarchy. The extant Roman historians purvey a detailed (but not unanimous) tradition that Romulus had chosen the original patricians, the *gentes maiores*, and that the elder Tarquin, for whom Tacitus (*Ann.* 11.25.3) substitutes L. Brutus (!), added some more families, the *gentes minores*, to this body. Livy leaves us with the strong impression that only patricians could be senators. Suetonius here credits Servius Tullius with an action nowhere else recorded of him, speaks as though there could be non-patrician senators under the kings, and indulges in a patent anachronism by making a whole gens 'join the plebs' - a process which was possible for an individual by due ceremony in the late Republic, but highly unlikely for a family collectively in much earlier times. The single apparently reliable item in this farrago is the statement that Julius Caesar conferred the patriciate on Augustus, perhaps in 48 B.C. (Dio 45.2.7), more probably in 46 or 45 B.C., when he was empowered by a *lex Cassia* to add to the shrunken number of patrician families (Dio 43.47.3; Tacitus, *Ann.* 11.25. 3); but problems remain concerning Augustus' reported candidature for the tribunate of the plebs in 44 B.C. (see 10.1-4 n.).
Divus Iulius: Julius Caesar, murdered for aiming at monarchy and divinity in his lifetime, was officially deified, to the political advantage of his adopted son, in January 42 B.C. (Dio 47.18.4ff., *ILLRP* 409). On Caesar's divinity, see Weinstock 1971, North 1975, and 52 n.
C. Rufus: some have held Suetonius (or his MSS) to be in error over Rufus' praenomen: the consul of 165 B.C. was Cn.f(ilius) *Cn*.n(epos), but since we do not know when Rufus was quaestor we cannot assume the consul to have been his grandson. The date of ca. 230 B.C. for Rufus' quaestorship is based on the assumption that he was the father of the praetor of 205 B.C. (see below), and that the latter was the father of the consul of 165 B.C.; but in both cases an intervening generation may perfectly well be supposed (see Münzer in *RE* s.v. Octavius, no.79).

2.2 honoribus summis: the 'curule offices' of curule aedile, praetor, and consul: Cn. Octavius, the quaestor's elder son (or grandson, see above), did not progress beyond his praetorship of 205 B.C., though after this the family produced consuls in every generation (consuls of 165, 126, 87, 76 and 75 B.C.).

proavus Augusti ... in Sicilia: fixed by the reference to Aemilius Papus to 205 B.C. (Livy 25.38.13). It seems that *proavus* is to be taken, not in its technical sense of great-grandfather, but more loosely of a remote male ancestor (cf. Antony's insults, 2.3 & 4.2). Augustus' father, born 105-100 B.C., can only have been grandson of the military tribune if his father and grandfather <u>both</u> sired their sons when they were sixty or more. And if the *tessera nummularia* mentioned below (n. on *libertinum proavum*) is to be referred to Augustus' grandfather, he was still active as a banker in 53 B.C. and his father must have sired him when approaching 100 years of age!

2.3   ipse Augustus scribit: presumably in his lost autobiography which went down to 25 B.C. (85.1). The partially surviving *Life of Augustus* by Nicolaus of Damascus, a contemporary and admirer of the emperor, which is thought to have been largely based on this tendentious work, is similarly reticent about Augustus' forebears. The adoptive son of Julius Caesar, owing everything to that name, had no great desire to stress his municipal extraction.

M. Antonius: Antony's aspersions on Augustus' lineage belong either to the period late 44 - early 43 B.C., before and during the war of Mutina, or more probably to the war of words from 34-32 B.C. which preceded the final breach and armed struggle (see Scott 1933).

libertinum ... proavum ... avum argentarium: such fanciful abuse was part of the stock-in-trade of Republican politics (see Cicero, *in Pisonem* and Appendix VI in R.G. Nisbet's ed.) and shows little but the social prejudices of the upper class. It is possible that Augustus' grandfather did indeed practise banking: one C. Octavius certified a bag of money on a tag (*tessera nummularia*) dated June 13th 53 B.C. (*CIL* I^2 2663c = *ILLRP* 1046), but in view of the commonness of the name it is difficult to share Degrassi's confidence that this man is actually the grandfather of Augustus. A graffito of the time of the proscriptions averred that the father of Augustus was an *argentarius* (70.2), but Suetonius repudiates any such suggestion in 3.

3   The (fairly typical) career of Augustus' father is known in full from the *elogium* from the base of his statue (*ILS* 47 = *Inscr It* 13.3, no. 75). He was military tribune twice (the 70s B.C. were turbulent), quaestor, plebeian aedile, and president of a court before becoming praetor in 61 B.C. He was returned first in the poll (Velleius 2.59.2), the result doubt-less of his own considerable abilities and his marriage con-nection not only with the Iulii but also with Pompey (see 4). His appointment to the proconsulship of Macedonia followed the usual Republican procedure (see 47n.). The commission to mop up the remnant of the runaway slaves who had lent their support to the risings of the revolutionary aristocrat Catiline in 63 B.C. and the escaped gladiator Spartacus in 72 B.C. had to be given specially, because although a proconsul assumed his

imperium (see Introduction §20-25) on leaving Rome, he was not permitted to exercise it until he entered his province. By entrusting Octavius with this task, the Senate avoided the need to send one of the consuls or praetors of 60 B.C. on military operations during their year of office. Thurii was a Greek foundation on the west side of the Gulf of Tarentum; its mountainous hinterland is difficult to police even nowadays and has long afforded sanctuary to bandits and outlaws. Runaway slaves had no incentive to surrender in the Roman world, being liable to such punishments as mutilation or crucifixion. For his successful operations against the Thracian tribes, Octavius received a salutation from his troops as victorious general (*imperator*) which gave him *prima facie* grounds for claiming a triumph on his return to Rome (Velleius 2.59.2; *CIL* I², p.199). It appears that he died (at Nola - see 100.1) on the journey back from his province in the spring or early summer of 58 B.C.: Cicero's letter to his brother (see below) is dated Nov./Dec. 59 B.C. and his successor was one of the praetors of 59 B.C., L. Appuleius Saturninus.

3   divisores operasque campestris: agents who distributed bribes and organised intimidation or defences against it at election time (cf. n. on *decuriae*, 57.2).
epistulae M. Ciceronis: one reference survives - *ad Quintum Fratrem* 1.2.7. (*Ibid.* 1.1.21, where the MSS hesitate between C. and Cn. Octavius, has been shown - Lintott 1968, 129 - to refer to Cn. Octavius, praetor 79 B.C.).

4   Octavia maiore: by mistaking this lady for her younger half-sister, Plutarch (*Antony* 31.1-2) has caused needless confusion and even thrown her existence into doubt. She was in fact married to one Sextus Appuleius who became high priest of the deified Caesar (*flamen Iulialis*) and was accorded a public funeral some time after 30 B.C. (*ILS* 8963). Their sons were Sextus, consul 29 B.C. and Marcus, consul 20 B.C. (*ILS* 8783).
Octavia minore: born not later than 65 B.C., she was already married to C. Claudius Marcellus (consul 50 B.C.) in 53 when her great-uncle Julius Caesar offered to transfer her to Pompey on the death of Caesar's daughter Julia in childbirth (*DJ* 27.1): Roman girls were considered nubile at 12. She bore Marcellus two girls and a boy (see 63.1) and after his death in 41 B.C. she was married to Antony to seal the peace arranged at Brundisium in late 40 between her brother and her new husband. She had two more girls by him before he left her for Cleopatra. She loyally brought up in his house in Rome not only her own children, but also Antony's two sons by his previous marriage to Fulvia. Antony did not divorce her until 32 B.C. and she never remarried. She died in 11 B.C. (Dio 54.35.4).
C. Caesaris: the man we call Julius Caesar. The Republican aristocracy were usually known by *cognomen* alone (thus Cicero, Brutus, Caesar), or by *praenomen* and ⌐ognomen, as here, for greater formality or precision. The full form C. Iulius Caesar would only be used 'for the record'. If a man did not have a *cognomen*, the family name was used in the same way

(thus Octavius, Antonius). The conjunction of *nomen* and *cognomen* (without *praenomen*) in either order appears to have been colloquial in Cicero's day, but gradually became less so; the order *cognomen - nomen* occasionally found in Cicero becomes frequent in later writers. The only satisfactory explanation of these facts must be that the *cognomen* was originally felt to be not so much an additional as an alternative name. (See on Cicero, *ad Atticum* 2.24.3 in D.R. Shackleton-Bailey's ed.).

Aricinus: Aricia was an old Latin municipality about 15 miles south of Rome on the Via Appia.

imaginibus: the reference is to the practice of Roman families of displaying images of their ancestors in their houses. The Roman reverence for dead ancestors is not easy to separate from the cult of the *Lares familiares,* the household spirits. One should surely interpret Cicero's information (*in Verrem* II 5.36, *pro Rabirio Postumo* 16) that, by attaining the aedileship, he acquired the right of 'perpetuating his likeness' as referring to a right not of having ancestor-portraits on display at home, but of erecting a statue of himself in a public place (cf. elder Pliny *NH* 34.30). Whether or not it was controlled by law, the custom of exhibiting the images of ancestors at funerals so vividly described by Polybius (6.53.4-6) was in practice restricted to the aristocracy, who alone enjoyed such public burial. (See Zadoks-Jitta 1932 97ff.; Vessberg 1941 107f.).

inter vigintiviros ... Iulia lege divisit: Julius Caesar, as consul 59 B.C., carried a bill to divide up and distribute to 20,000 Roman citizens with 3 or more children state land in Campania currently leased to a variety of holders. (*DJ* 20.3). The administration of the scheme was entrusted to a commission of 20, amongst whom was Pompey.

Cassius Parmensis: C. Cassius from Parma, so called to distinguish him from his namesake C. Cassius Longinus who jointly led the conspiracy to kill Caesar in which both men took part. After Philippi, he eventually joined Sex. Pompeius in Sicily, then accompanied him on his flight to Asia after the battle of Naulochus (see 16.1), and went over to Antony in 35 B.C. He met his end after Actium (Valerius Maximus 1.7.7), the last of Caesar's murderers to die, if Velleius can be believed (2.87.3 but *cf.* Dio 51.8.2 on D. Turullius).

Nerulonensis mensarius: 'a money-changer from Nerulum', a place in Lucania. Cassius has improved on the insult of Antony (2.3) by giving this surely fictitious grandfather, in addition to his socially suspect calling, dirty hands and a small, remote, and scarcely Roman town to live in.

5-8 The second half of Suetonius' introduction deals with Augustus' birth, early childhood, and debut in public life in the shadow of his great-uncle Caesar. These were the years of the final breakdown of the Republican political system, culminating in the civil war of 49-45 B.C.; but ancient biography was not interested in making the connection between the acts and attitudes of a mature man and the experiences and impressions of his formative years, and Suetonius pays scant attention to Augustus' youth. It is almost *en passant* that we learn (8.2) that his mother had married again, and the character of L. Marcius Philippus, surely an important influence on his young stepson, is passed over in total silence. On the other hand, what Suetonius does emphasise in 5-7 is the numinous, so that by the time we reach 8 the idea that Augustus had a special connection with the divine is firmly established.

5   M. Tullio Cicerone C. Antonio coss.:   *i.e.* 63 B.C.

Capita Bubula: perhaps one of the *vici* (*see* 30.1), certainly a sub-division of the Palatine region. (Cf. *Domit.* 1.1.)

sacrarium: Augustus was not officially deified until after his death, so such a shrine could hardly be dedicated while he was still alive.

senatus actis: the minutes of the senate, first published at Julius' Caesar's behest in 59 B.C. (*DJ* 20.1), but suppressed under Augustus (36). They con+inued to be kept and were available to privileged persons such as Suetonius, and may possibly have again been published under Tiberius (*Tib.* 73; Dio 57.23.2).

adulterii poena: the penalty for adultery was severe, involving rele-gation to an island and forfeiture of property. Ironically, it had been made a criminal offence by the very God Augustus in whose name C. Laetorius was begging mercy. (See 34.1 n.)

6   tamquam et natus ibi sit ... quasi temere ... obiciatur: Suetonius habitually employs *tamquam* and *quasi,* with verbs in the sub-junctive, to introduce reported statements, without any implication that the alleged fact is untrue. Translate by 'that' - 'the opinion is pre-valent in the neighbourhood that he was born there.'

7   AUGUSTUS' NAMES

7.1 infanti cognomen Thurino ...:   the true reason for this abandoned *cognomen* must be the second offered by Suetonius (see 3.1). That Augustus did actually bear the name is put beyond doubt by his reply just below to Antony's mocking use of it. Suetonius' 'little image of him as a boy' with tne name in inset iron letters was almost certainly a learned fake made much later, probably after the emperor's death. In the late Republic, portrait-busts and statues were either funerary, to commemorate the dead, or honorific, to confirm status and reward achievement. For neither reason was the young Augustus likely to have his portrait made. The maker of the statuette (or miniature portrait?) knew some history and produced a bogus antique. It was convincing enough to fool Hadrian - it is not surprising that it appealed to his recondite and antiquarian tastes - and be placed amongst the cult images (former emperors, ancestors, and *Lares familiares*) in the emperor's own chamber. Augustus kept a likeness of a great-grandson who died in childhood among these *Lares cubiculi* (*Calig.* 7).

7.2 postea C. Caesaris et deinde Augusti cognomen: Augustus was instituted principal heir and 'adopted into his house and name' by Caesar in his will (*DJ* 83.2). The precise mechanism of a posthumous adoption is unclear, and some scholars (*e.g.* Schmitthenner 1952) deny that such an adoption could have legal validity and hold that all Caesar could do in his will was to sanction the use of his name by his young great-

nephew. In the popular eye, the difference was at first technical,
because in either case Augustus bore the name of C. Iulius Caesar and was
heir to ¼ of Caesar's estate. However, after the deification of Caesar
in 42 B.C., Augustus found himself 'Son of a God' and from 40 B.C. onwards
this was his recognised filiation. His adoption, whether or not strictly
legal, had become an accepted fact by then (and it must be said that in
the ancient sources there is no serious evidence that it had ever been
otherwise). The name of Caesar was of crucial importance to him in the
savage struggles of the civil wars; thanks to it, he was able to present
himself as the natural leader of the Caesarian party and the rightful
focus of the demand to take vengeance on his new father's murderers. He
could also claim the loyalty of all Caesar's troops, serving or veteran.
Any reference to his natural parentage undermined this position, based
as it was on a legal fiction. He therefore never used the form C. Iulius
Caesar Octavianus, which would have been the regular way of indicating
that he was a Caesar by adoption and an Octavius by birth; but Cicero,
along with others, like Brutus, who were less than enthusiastic about his
pretensions, did so for a while. Modern historians call him Octavian to
avoid confusion with his great-uncle during the period before he became
Augustus.

Suetonius does not allude to a remarkable stage in the development of
Augustus' nomenclature: this was his adoption of the word *imperator* as
a virtual *praenomen*. Hitherto it had been used after a man's name to
indicate that as commander he had been hailed victorious by his troops (*e.g.*
ILS 877 - CN POMPEIO CN F MAGNO IMP[eratori] COS TER PATRONO PUBLICE).
Between 43 and 38 B.C. Augustus' nomenclature moved from C. Iulius C.
f[ilius] Imp[erator] to Imperator Caesar Divi f[ilius]. He thus laid claim
to a permanent quality of successful generalship, and also, surprisingly,
dropped the name Iulius. This startling change is almost certainly connected with the titles used by his rivals in these years: Sextus Pompeius
styled himself Son of Neptune and turned his father's *cognomen* into a
praenomen to become Magnus (Pompeius) Pius, while Antony was venerated
in the East as the New Dionysus. (For full discussion and references, see
Syme 1958b; Combès 1966.)

By comparison, the final addition of 'Augustus' as a fresh *cognomen*
filling the gap left by the metamorphosis of Caesar into a family name,
is quite straightforward. To be the new Romulus, second founder of Rome,
might seem attractive, but not everyone would forget that the first
Romulus had killed his brother and become a king. For the victor of a
civil war, the name was a shade too apt. *Augustus*, splendid, reverend,
and faintly archaic, was a brilliant stroke, and Plancus' motion, carried
on Jan. 16th 27 B.C., set the seal on a new age. Henceforth the ruler of
the Roman world was *Imperator Caesar Divi f*[*ilius*] *Augustus*. The passing
of the Republic could hardly have been better symbolised.

Munati Planci: L. Munatius Plancus was one of the most distinguished,
astute, and unprincipled survivors of the civil wars. Velleius, who
valued loyalty, called him 'diseased with desertion' (2.83.1 *cf.* 2.76.1).
Caesar's appointee as governor of Transalpine Gaul in 44-43 B.C., he
professed loyalty to Cicero and the senate during the war of Mutina, but
remained in communication with Antony and ultimately joined him. During
these negotiations he took care to keep in with Augustus, and when the
triumvirate was formed he secured the consulship of 42 B.C. to which
Caesar had designated him. As one of the Antonian generals with troops

in Italy in the winter of 41-40 B.C. he had the opportunity to join Pollio
and Ventidius in saving Antony's brother Lucius, then besieged in Perusia
by Augustus and Agrippa; but again he temporised and prevented decisive
action by Antonian forces which in combination were certainly strong
enough to have crushed the opposition. Later he governed Asia, then Syria,
in Antony's interest, but deserted him for Augustus in 32 B.C., when
Antony's divorce of Octavia signalled that all hope of reconciliation was
gone. In the new era which his proposal inaugurated, his distinction was
confirmed by his appointment as one of the last pair of non-imperial
censors in 22 B.C. His great circular mausoleum still stands on the out-
skirts of Gaeta (ancient Caieta) on the seacoast south of Rome; the
epitaph (*E-J*³ no. 187 = *ILS* 886) is a stirring roll-call of the high
honours of the vanished Republic.

ab auctu: the correct etymology, from the root *aug-*, 'increase'.

Ennius: Q. Ennius, 239-169 B.C., the greatest Roman epic poet before
Virgil. A South Italian, he fought with the Romans against Carthage in
the Hannibalic war and wrote, inter alia, the *Annales,* an epic poem in
18 books which, using the hexameter metre for the first time in Latin,
brought the history of Rome down to 171 B.C. Some 550 lines, about 4% of
the whole, survive, thanks to quotation by other authors.

8.1 quadrimus: the word would normally mean 'in his fourth year';
here, unless Suetonius has simply made a mistake, it must signify 'after
his fourth birthday' or 'when he was four', since Augustus' father died
in late 59, or early 58 B.C. (see 3n.).

duodecimum annum ... aviam Iuliam: the aunt was Julius Caesar's
sister, the year 52-51 B.C. The *laudatio* (encomium) of the dead was a
central part of the funeral of a member of the nobility. The procession
halted in the Forum and the *laudatio* was delivered by one of the family or
a close friend to the assembled people. It was liable to contain much historically dubious material (*cf.* Cicero, *Brutus* 61-62). For an instance of
the kind of imaginary descent that could be claimed, see Julius Caesar's
laudatio of his aunt (*DJ* 6). Nicolaus of Damascus (*Vita Augusti* 3)
alleges that Augustus was only nine at the time, but Quintilian (12.6.1)
agrees with Suetonius.

quadriennio post: (*i.e.* 48-47 B.C.) dates only Augustus' assumption of
the *toga virilis,* his official entry upon public life. Caesar's African
triumph took place in Sept. 46 B.C., the month when Augustus celebrated
his seventeenth birthday and became qualified for military service.

profectum mox avunculum in Hispanias: in Nov. or Dec. 46 B.C. Caesar
decided to go into Spain (plural in the Latin because it was divided into
two provinces) to deal with serious resistance being offered to his
commanders there by the Pompeian survivors, led by Pompey's two sons
Gnaeus and Sextus. The campaign was decided by his victory at Munda,
March 17th 45 B.C. Augustus eventually joined him a few weeks later.

gravi valetudine: Augustus was plagued by ill-health all his life; see
13.1, 28.1, 43.5 and 83.

8.2 expeditionem in Dacos et inde in Parthos ...: The Romans
had never avenged the defeat of Crassus at Carrhae in 53 B.C., and
currently the Parthian prince Pacorus was lending effective support to
Caecilius Bassus, a Pompeian who was holding out in Apamea against Caesar's
legate Antistius Vetus. The Dacian king Burebista had made inroads into
the Roman province of Macedonia, and Caesar judged that he could be conveniently dealt with en route for Syria.

praemissus Apolloniam ...: Apollonia was north of modern Valona, on
the Illyrian coast some 60 miles north of Corfu. It was the terminus of

the southern fork of the Via Egnatia which led across to Thessalonica
and on towards the Hellespont and Asia. By the spring of 44 B.C. six
legions were awaiting Caesar, some nearby, some elsewhere in the province
(Appian *BC* 3.24). The dictator had designated Augustus his Master of
Horse (*magister equitum*) or second-in-command in succession to M. Aemilius
Lepidus, who was then holding the office but would resign it when he and
Caesar went their different ways on leaving Rome (Dio 43.51.7; *Inscr It*
13.1.58f., 134). This was an extraordinary honour for an unproven 18-
year old and it is strange that Suetonius does not mention it.

hereditatem adiit ...: Cicero (*ad Atticum* 14.10.3) uses the same
phrase, an abbreviated version of the formula *hereditatem adeo cernoque*
which the heir had to use to signify his formal acceptance (Gaius 2.165-6
cf. Cicero *ad Atticum* 11.2.1; younger Pliny *Epp.* 10.75.2). Under Roman
law, an heir (provided that he were neither a *suus heres*, *i.e.* a person
who became *sui iuris* on the death of the testator, nor a freedman) had
the option of refusing to accept if he thought the inheritance not worth
taking for any reason. No doubt the prudent Philippus considered the
legacy of Caesar's name to be political dynamite (see Cicero, *ad Atticum*
14.12.2), but a more practical reason for rejecting the inheritance was
Caesar's bequest of 300 sestertii a head to 'the people' (*DJ* 83.2), by
which presumably those receiving the corn dole in Rome are meant - a
number reduced by Caesar himself from 320,000 to 150,000 (*DJ* 41.3), but
still entailing an immediate outlay of 45m. HS, or roughly the pay of an
army of five legions for two years. Caesar was a wealthy man; but
where the money was, whether Augustus could get his hands on it, and how
far it would go when distributed on this scale, were all questions impossible to answer at the time.

Marcio Philippo ...: Augustus' stepfather L. Marcius Philippus was
of a family which counted consuls back to the early third century. He
himself had held the consulship in 56 B.C. and managed to remain neutral
in the civil war, as befitted a man whose wife was Caesar's niece while
his daughter (by a previous marriage) was Cato's wife. (See Syme 1939
128.)

8.3 atque ab eo tempore ...: this sentence, dividing up as it does
the whole of the rest of Augustus' life into three periods, signals the
end of the introduction: from the date of the new Caesar's decision to
take up his inheritance, his history was the political and military
history of Rome. Suetonius' generalisation is not absolutely accurate, in
that Augustus did not become master of the state with Antony and Lepidus
until Nov. 43 B.C.; but in the context it may pass, especially as
Suetonius gives some account of the period April 44 to Nov. 43 B.C. in
10-12 below. The twelve years are counted from 43-31 B.C., the forty-
four from 31 B.C.- A.D. 14.

9-25 AUGUSTUS' MILITARY ACHIEVEMENTS

**The Romans divided public life into two spheres, civil (*domi*)
and military (*militiae*). *Imperium* (see Introduction §20-25) in
the one field was not necessarily valid in the other. Suetonius
applies this traditional distinction to order his account of
Augustus as a public figure: 9-25 deal with his military record;**

26-60 with his civil.

Chapters 9-25 are themselves divided by category into civil
wars (9-18); insurrections and plots (19); foreign wars (20-21);
and a final section on generalities - triumphs, honours and
disasters, discipline, and rewards (22-25). Suetonius is not,
of course, writing a narrative history. His account of the
civil war period (44-30 B.C.) compresses or omits the causes,
course, and results of the wars, and neglects events not directly
connected with those wars. Suetonius emphasises throughout
material which shows Augustus in a personal light: in danger,
cruel, vengeful, impious, generous, brave, treacherous, resource-
ful, unscrupulous. On the whole the picture is unflattering,
yet there are enough gleams of light not to contradict the
impression, given by the opening chapters, of a man favoured by
the gods.

Chapter 9 itself serves as an introduction to i) the arrangement
of the rest of the work and ii) the period of the civil wars
elaborated in 10-18.

i) Suetonius habitually treats his subject by topics, unless
there is a strong chronological bias, as for example at the
beginning and end of a *Life*. This practice obscures change
and development of character and views, and presents the individual as a static conglomerate. We are given endless glimpses
of Augustus, but it is difficult to feel that we know him as
a person, except in the concluding chapters where Suetonius
writes a genuine narrative with the anecdotal material sub-
ordinated to a wider theme. (See Introduction §4-7).

ii) Suetonius includes the war of Actium in his list of civil
wars. In this he is more honest than Appian, who omitted it,
doubtless on the grounds which Augustan propaganda was at pains
to emphasise, that it was fought against a foreign foe, the
Queen of Egypt. (For an account of the period 44-30 B.C., see
Syme 1939 (chapters 7-21); Carter 1970.).

10-12 44-43 B.C. AND THE WAR OF MUTINA

Suetonius' opening statement, that Augustus' pretext for all
the wars was the need to avenge Caesar and safeguard his political acts, is certainly not true of the Perusine and Actian
wars and only doubtfully true of the war of Mutina. In this
last case the two reasons stated were incompatible, for the
governor of Cisalpine Gaul, whom Antony (illegally, according
to the party of Cicero but legally, according to modern opinion)
was trying to evict from the province, was Decimus Brutus, one
of Caesar's assassins; yet Decimus had been appointed governor
by Caesar. In helping him against Antony, Augustus could perhaps claim to be upholding Caesar's political acts (not that
there is any evidence that he made such a claim). The ostensible

ground for his support of Decimus was his loyalty to constitutional government and to a Republic menaced by the military
despotism of Antony. The real ground was his continuing
struggle with Antony for the leadership of the Caesarian party,
and to this any thoughts of avenging Caesar had, for the moment,
to remain subordinate. As to the other wars, that of Philippi
was undertaken precisely to take vengeance for Caesar (cf.
29.2), while Sextus Pompeius was a focus of resistance for all
anti-Caesarians and counted Caesar's assassin Cassius of Parma
among his followers. However, the immediate cause of the war
was Sextus' harassment of the Italian coast and his demands
for greater recognition from the triumvirs. Caesar's acts
are something of a red herring, as the senate itself had res-
olved, on Antony's own proposal only two days after the murder,
that all Caesar's acts and decrees should be confirmed (the
other side of the bargain being an amnesty for the murderers).
Augustus himself in the masterly opening sentences of *RG* makes
no mention of any desire to uphold his 'father's' acts. Rather,
he professes concern for the freedom of the Republic, and
stresses the legitimacy of his vengeance on the murderers: at
the age of nineteen on my own initiative and at my own expense I raised an
army, with which I set free the state when it was labouring under the
tyranny of a faction ... I drove into exile the men who butchered my father,
taking vengeance for their crime by proper process of law; and afterwards,
when they made war against the state, I defeated them twice in battle.

10.1-4 Suetonius confuses the order of the various items preceding the war of Mutina. In fact, Augustus did not prosecute
Caesar's murderers until after he had become triumvir in late
43 B.C. When he returned to Rome about the end of April his
chief concern was to enter on Caesar's heritage, both financially
by getting his hands on Ceasar's property so that he could discharge the legacies to the Roman *plebs*, and politically by ad-
vertising his filial piety and turning to his own account the
wave of public feeling which regarded the amnesty for the
murderers, arrived at in the senate on March 17th, as mean-
spirited and shabby.

The attempt to recover Caesar's property led him into litigation,
where the acting urban praetor, Antony's brother C. Antonius,
obstructed him, and into disputes with the consul himself who
in any case considered that he, not Augustus, was the rightful
leader of the Caesarian party and thought that the policy of
compromise was the right one. Augustus also wished to have his
adoption confirmed by the necessary *lex curiata* (see n. on
Agrippam 65.1), which should have been no more than a formality,
but was blocked. Unless the unanimous tradition that Caesar
had made him a patrician is wrong, his candidacy for the tribunate of the *plebs*, reported also by Plutarch (*Antony* 16.2)
and Dio (45.6.2), requires some explanation. The version of
Appian, whose account at this point is far superior to that of
both these two or Suetonius, says that Augustus supported one

Flaminius (Chilo?) for the vacant tribunate (like Suetonius,
he makes no mention of Helvius Cinna, the tribune who was killed
almost immediately after the death of Caesar), and that 'the
people', thinking that he refrained from standing himself
because he was under age (nothing being said about patrician
status, which should have constituted a permanent bar), proposed to vote for him none the less. At this point Antony
interposed his edict, to the effect that Augustus should do
nothing contrary to the laws, or be prepared to suffer for it
(Appian, BC 3.31). It is, of course, possible that Augustus
took the view that the sovereign people could elect whom they
liked, young or old, patrician or plebeian, to guard their
interests; but Appian's account has a ring of truth about it,
and makes Augustus' position not unlike that of Scipio
Aemilianus a hundred years previously when that worthy, in spite
of being under age and unqualified, was 'drafted' to the
consulship of 147 B.C. by popular pressure.

Augustus' staging (through Caesar's friend C. Matius) of the
games for the Victory of Caesar (i.e. at Pharsalus), from
July 20th to 30th was a notable demonstration of piety in face
of the reluctance of the officially constituted special
priestly college to hold them. It was during these games
that Augustus paid Caesar's legacy to the people and the comet
appeared which was instantly believed to be the spirit of
Caesar received into heaven.

Meanwhile Antony found himself on untenable middle ground
between Augustus' Caesarianism on the one hand and Cicero's
anti-Caesarianism on the other. He had in June prepared his
position by transferring the province of Cisalpine Gaul from
Decimus Brutus, one of Caesar's assassains, to himself for six
years. By early Oct. he and Augustus were open enemies and it
is to this stage that Augustus' alleged attempt to assassinate
him belongs. Whatever the truth of the matter, Suetonius is
certainly wrong to make this relatively trivial episode the
reason for Augustus to raise an illegal private army from
Caesar's veterans in Campania. He did this because Antony,
finding himself worsted in the political field, had gone to
Brindisi to collect legions recalled from Macedonia. He would
thus be equipped to deal forcibly with any opposition before
marching north to take over his province, and another army,
from Decimus Brutus.

In the event, Augustus induced two of the legions to desert
to him, forcing Antony to retire to Cisalpine Gaul sooner than
he had intended. And so Augustus, at the head of an illegal
army, and Cicero, the leader of the conservative senatorial
opposition to Antony (optimates) found they had a common enemy
and could profitably combine. Decimus Brutus refused to hand
over his province, claiming that Antony's law of June was
illegal, and was besieged in Mutina (Modena) about the end of
Dec. Cicero managed to legalise Augustus' position by securing

for him a special grant of propraetorian *imperium* and a mandate
to operate with the new consuls of 43 B.C., A. Hirtius and
C. Vibius Pansa, against Antony. Skirmishing began about the
end of Jan., but diplomatic activity continued and it was not
until about mid-March that military operations began in earnest.
The siege was finally raised after the two battles of Forum
Gallorum and Mutina, on April 14th and 21st. In fact Antony
won the second, but decided to withdraw westwards to Provence.

11   Hirtius was killed in the second battle, Pansa had been
wounded in the first (of which there survives the eye-witness
account of Ser. Galba, Cicero *ad Familiares* 10.30). The deaths
of both consuls were so convenient for Augustus that suspicion
was perhaps inevitable, and lasted long (*e.g.* Tacitus *Ann.*
1.10.1), but the honourable M. Brutus at least refused to believe that Glyco could have been guilty (Cicero, *Epp. ad Brutum*
14.2). Augustus took over control of both consular armies, and
when Decimus Brutus, who had unrealistically but inevitably
been appointed commander of all the Republican forces at Mutina,
asked him to hand over his legions, he refused, alleging that
his men would not serve under one of Caesar's murderers. Nor
did he co-operate with Decimus in the latter's forlorn pursuit
of Antony with his siege-weakened troops.

12   The governor of Gallia Narbonensis and Nearer Spain was
M. Lepidus, who professed resistance to Antony and obedience
to the constitutional government for a brief while before the
Caesarian veterans in both their armies reconciled the two men.
L. Munatius Plancus (see 7.2 n.), governor of Further Gaul,
and C. Asinius Pollio (see 43.2 n.), governor of Further Spain,
joined them by July; both owed loyalty to Caesar's memory, nor
would their troops have fought those of Antony and Lepidus.
Decimus Brutus realised he could do nothing against them and
attempted to join M. Brutus in Macedonia, but was killed by an
Alpine chieftain on the way.

Thus Augustus, the arch-Caesarian of them all, remained in
Cisalpine Gaul, the sole commander nominally loyal to the senate
in the provinces of the west. The outcome was inevitable.
Cicero and his allies (Suetonius' *optimates*) refused to take
Augustus seriously and thought he could be discarded, now that
Antony was out of Italy and M. Brutus and Cassius had armies
in the east to deal with the Caesarian alliance. Cicero certainly called him a 'boy' (*e.g.* *Epp. ad Brutum* 23.7) and is
likely, though he never admitted it, to have been the author
of the famous witticism 'he must be praised, honoured, - and
got rid of' (*laudandum, ornandum, tollendum*, Cicero, *ad Familiares* 11.20.1). The senate also tried to whittle down the
rewards promised to Augustus' veterans and was (understandably)
reluctant to offer him the vacant consulate which he felt he was
entitled to. For the sequel, see 26 n. *Augustus' consulships*.

Nursinos: Nursia was a town on the borders of Umbria, Picenum, and Sabine territory. This episode probably belongs to the war of Perusia (Dio 48.13.2): the 'freedom' for which the men of Nursia died was much more clearly identifiable in 41-40 B.C. (see 13.3-14 n. - *cf.* Propertius 1.21; 1.22; and 4.1.126-130).

13-15 These chapters relate episodes concerning the wars of Philippi and Perusia (42-40 B.C.), which are, in themselves, scarcely explained. Suetonius lays stress on two things: first, the number of dangers and narrow escapes Augustus encountered, and second, his resolute cruelty. Thus he points to two qualities admired in a leader, good fortune and constancy. Although, for the moment, the latter is perverted, it is an important characteristic of Augustus and valuable when directed to good ends (*cf.* 42.2).

13.1-2 After extorting the consulship from the senate, Augustus entered into negotiations with Antony and Lepidus. These culminated in a meeting near Bononia in Nov., at which the three men agreed to form what amounted to a joint dictatorship for five years (see 27.1-4 n.) and set in train arrangements to take vengeance on the murderers of Caesar. These led eventually to the campaign of Philippi, in northern Greece, when the forces of the triumvirate led by Antony and Augustus defeated those of the self-styled 'liberators' Brutus and Cassius in two battles, one on Oct. 23rd., 42 B.C. and the other about three weeks later. Brutus sacked Augustus' camp on the first occasion, while Antony was winning on the other wing; Augustus was never a very good general, apart from being troubled by sickness, which became severe on his return to Italy in the winter.

The stories which follow are doubtless derived from pro-Antonian writings of the period 34-31 B.C. or later, and it is impossible to know how much truth there is in them. Suetonius' purpose in retailing them is discussed above (13-15). Dio (47.49) and Appian (*BC* 4.135) suggest that everyone except the actual murderers and extreme anti-Caesarians (like Favonius) were given a chance of making their peace with the victors. Antony is said to have given Brutus' body proper burial, and the head to have been lost at sea while on the way to Rome. Augustus wrote in his memoirs that he had never refused to give a man's body back to his relatives for burial (Ulpian, *Digest* 48.24.1).

13.3 By the division of responsibilities agreed between the triumvirs after Philippi, Antony undertook the task of pacifying and administering the eastern half of the empire, while Augustus was to return to Italy and supervise the settlement of the soldiers now discharged. This was an extremely unpopular operation, since it meant large-scale evictions of the existing ocupants of the land marked down for the veterans.

14   Feeling ran so high that Antony's brother Lucius, who held the consulship in 41 B.C., assisted by Antony's wife Fulvia, a great political lady, raised a rebellion in the autumn against the authority of Augustus. After various military operations, from which Augustus was lucky to escape without being trapped, Lucius found himself besieged in Perusia (modern Perugia). Antony himself was spending a winter of pleasure in Alexandria as the guest of its queen and seems to have received no news of these startling events until they were over. At any rate, the Antonian generals in Italy and Gallia Cisalpina (Pollio, Ventidius, and Plancus) received no instructions from him and although they were in a position at Fulginium (modern Foligno) from which their watch-fires could be seen across the plain by the beleaguered forces in Perusia, they made no move to attack the besiegers and Perusia fell in Jan. or Feb. 40 B.C.

quattuordecim ordinibus: the first fourteen rows of the theatre were reserved for *equites* and a common soldier had no right to sit there.

15   trecentos ... ad aram Divo Iulio ... mactatos: it is impossible to believe this story of human sacrifice, though it occurs in Dio too (48.14.4): a) human sacrifice, although it occurred in 216 and 114 B.C. after the discovery of unchastity among the Vestal Virgins (Livy 22.57.2-6, Plutarch, *Qu. Rom.* 83) was un-Roman and no god received it; b) Augustus can hardly have wanted to give the new god Julius, whose paternity he proudly proclaimed, such a barbaric and bloodthirsty character: the mortal Julius had been famed for his clemency; C) Lucius Antonius and other leaders were allowed to go free, which indicates a policy similar to that followed after Philippi (see Carter 1970 111); d) Suetonius himself clearly does not believe it. On Julius Caesar's divinity, see Weinstock 1971. He had been officially created a god at the beginning of 42 B.C.
facultate L. Antoni ducis praebita: even more fantastic than the tale of human sacrifice is the idea that the whole Perusine war was a put-up job between Augustus and the Antonii. Suetonius' introductory formula - 'there were those prepared to allege ...' makes it quite clear what he thinks; by reporting two such incredible stories in this way he manages to reflect doubt on other less extreme but better documented examples of Augustus' severity.

16.1 THE SICILIAN WAR AGAINST SEXTUS POMPEIUS

After the murder of Caesar, the government had entered into negotiations with Pompey's younger son Sextus, who was still at large with a fleet in the western Mediterranean, and early in 43 B.C., in the context of the struggle with Antony, the senate officially recognised him as 'commander of the fleet and coasts' - a title which appears on his coins of 42-40 B.C. (Crawford 1974 no. 511). When the triumvirate was formed he was duly proscribed, and sailed to Sicily where he treacherously killed the

governor Pompeius Bithynicus and seized the island. He defied
attempts to eject him by Augustus and Salvidienus Rufus early
in 42 B.C. and was joined by survivors of Philippi and the proscriptions as well as less respectable fugitives from justice
like runaway slaves and criminals. His fleet bacame strong
enough to harry the Italian coasts and interfere with the corn
supply to Rome, so that in 39 B.C. the triumvirs were forced
to negotiate with him (at Misenum) and buy him off with a promise
of restitution of his property and the control of Sicily,
Sardinia, Corsica, and Achaea (Greece south of Macedonia). Not
receiving Achaea, he began hostilities again, thus provoking
the war of 38-36 B.C.

The two fleets of Augustus' whose loss Suetonius records were
destroyed within a few days in 38 B.C., though the first
disaster had nothing to do with the weather (Appian, *BC* 5.81-90)
and in both cases poor seamanship was largely responsible. But
Augustus would not make peace, even though Antony had never
agreed to the war. He devoted 37 B.C. to winning support for
his war from a reluctant populace and his colleagues, and to
the huge naval building and training programme (directed by
Agrippa) which Suetonius describes. Agrippa created *portus
Iulius* by joining the deep crater-lake of Avernus by a canal
to the shallow intermediate lagoon of the Lucrine lake, and
connecting the latter to the sea by breaching the dyke which
carried the coast road from Puteoli to Baiae and Misenum (Dio
48.50-51; Paget 1968). He thus obtained a naval base secure
from attack by Sextus' squadrons, and a suitably protected
expanse of water for training crews. His techniques proved
effective and enabled Augustus in 36 B.C. to transport his land
forces across to Sicily and join up with those which Lepidus
had landed from Africa, while he himself, as admiral, defeated
the fleet of Sextus first near Mylae, on the north coast, and
then decisively a few weeks later at Naulochus, a little east
of Mylae, on Sept. 3rd. 36 B.C. Neither Sextus nor Augustus
were on board, but awaited the outcome with their armies on
shore (Appian, *BC* 5.12; Dio 49.8.5-6).

16.1 XX servorum milibus manumissis: the freeing of such a large
number of slaves is proof that the fleets of the late Republic and early
empire did not use slaves as oarsmen. Most rowers appear to have been
free men, but not Roman citizens, from the eastern parts of the Mediterranean. To use freed slaves in this way in the armed forces was a sure
sign of crisis, cf. 25.2.

16.2 M. Agrippa: this is the first mention in the *Life* of Augustus'
great friend and helper M. Vipsanius Agrippa. Of obscure origins, he
was the same age as Augustus and was serving as a (presumably equestrian)
officer in Caesar's army at Apollonia in March 44 B.C. He very soon
established himself as Augustus' most determined and able supporter and
as the best of Augustus' generals (Salvidienus excepted, see 66.1).
Without his military abilities and total loyalty, it is improbable that
Augustus, whose own talents for generalship were not remarkable, would
have survived the civil wars. Agrippa played an important part in the

war of Perusia in 41-40 B.C., campaigned in Gaul and made a crossing of
the Rhine into Germany in 39 and 38 B.C., and was recalled to Italy to
assume the consulship in 37 B.C. and take charge of the naval offensive
against Sextus. For his success he was awarded not only the blue standard
mentioned in 25.3, but also the unique honour of a golden crown adorned
with ships' rams. He undertook a notable aedileship in 33 B.C. (see
29.5 n.), was admiral of Augustus' fleet at Actium, and was Augustus'
colleague in the two consulships of 28 and 27 B.C. which marked the re-
introduction of constitutional government. Thereafter he was in practice
vice-emperor. In the crisis of 23 B.C. (see 19.1 n.; 28.1-2 n.) he was
marked out as Augustus' personal, though not constitutional, successor.
In 21 B.C. he married Julia (see 63), in 18 B.C. he became associated with
Augustus in the tribunician power (see 27.5 n.), and from 16 to 13 B.C.
he held a general command over the eastern provinces (probably with
imperium maius, for which see Introduction §24). He died in 12 B.C. from
an illness contracted while campaigning in Pannonia the previous winter.
He never accepted a triumph, but his three consulships, his naval honours,
his tribunician power, and his marriage to Augustus' only child, together
with his record of civil and military achievement indicated plainly
enough his position in the state. We know nothing of him as a person;
but there is a magnificent portrait in the Louvre, and one quirk tells us
that for all his steely competence and complete devotion to Augustus he
was sensitive to his relatively humble origins - he did all he could to
drop his family name and become known, like any aristocrat, simply as
M. Agrippa (*cf.* 4.1 n.).

etiam invito Neptuno: Augustus' insults to Neptune must be understood
in the light of the fact that Sextus called himself 'Son of Neptune' after
the great storm which destroyed Augustus' fleet in 38 B.C. He thus
claimed equality with Augustus 'Son of the God Julius' and Antony 'the
New Dionysus' (see 7.2 n.). For the circus procession, see 43.5 n.

16.3 nec temere: 'scarcely', a favourite Suetonian idiom (*cf.* 53.2,
66.1, 73 and 77).

traiecto in Siciliam exercitu: Augustus was attacked unexpectedly
while bringing the first detachment of his army across the Straits of
Messina to Tauromenium, thinking that Agrippa had pinned Sextus and his
admirals Demochares and Apollophanes on the north coast near Mylae. Both
the other episodes here mentioned by Suetonius seem to belong to the
immediate aftermath of Augustus' escape from this attack, when he had some
difficulty in making his way from the remote spot where he landed and
establishing contact with his forces on the Italian side of the strait
(Appian, *BC* 5.110-112).

Aemili Paulli comitis: Paullus Aemilius Lepidus (consul 34 B.C.) was
a son of L. Aemilius Paullus (consul 50 B.C.), who had been proscribed
by his own brother the triumvir Lepidus. The slave doubtless regarded
Augustus as partly responsible, since the lists of victims were jointly
agreed. The elder Paullus escaped to fight at Philippi and stayed in
voluntary exile at Miletus afterwards (Appian, *BC* 4.37).

M. Lepidum: Lepidus owed his membership of the triumvirate to the
strong military force under his command and to his union with Antony in
43 B.C. He had neither Antony's personality and military expertise, nor
Augustus' Caesarian inheritance, and soon became the least important of
the three, in spite of the ancient glories of the Aemilii. His loyalty

was not above suspicion and after Philippi his portion of the Roman empire, which originally comprised both Narbonese Gaul and the two Spanish
provinces, was restricted to Africa. in 36 B.C. he brought twelve (weak)
legions across to Sicily as part of the attack on Sextus. In the sequel
to Agrippa's victory at Naulochus, when their leader had fled east,
Sextus' troops in Messina surrendered to Lepidus, who thus found himself
in command of 22 legions. He challenged Augustus' authority, but the
soldiers would not support him and he had to throw himself on Augustus'
mercy. Stripped of his triumviral powers, but remaining Pontifex
Maximus, he was allowed to live quietly, until he died in 12 B.C., in
the seaside town of Circeii south of Rome.

17-18 INCIDENTS FROM THE WAR WITH ANTONY

Suetonius avoids overlapping categories and the complexity of
historical explanation, and compresses the whole story of the
relations between Augustus and Antony from 41-33 B.C. into half
a sentence. All the details of 17 belong to the years 32-30
B.C. The qualities illustrated here are Augustus' determination, taken to the point of ruthlessness when necessary (e.g.
the opening of Antony's will and the killing of Antony's
eldest son), but also his capacity for respecting the motives
and circumstances of those who found themselves opposing him
(e.g. the people of Bononia and the younger children of
Antony). Chapter 18 rounds off the civil war period, emphas-
ising Augustus' standards of value and proper use of his
victory.

17.1-2 RELATIONS WITH ANTONY 41-32 B.C.

News of the Perusine war (see 14) brought Antony back to Italy,
allied now with the remains of the Republican fleet under Cn.
Domitius Ahenobarbus. Antony was ready for war and laid siege
to Brundisium, but once again the soldiers on both sides refused to fight their old comrades and the diplomacy of Cocceius
Nerva, Maecenas, and Pollio led to an accommodation (the so-
called 'Treaty' of Brundisium, autumn 40 B.C.). Peace and
friendship were proclaimed, both men entered Rome to an ovation,
and Antony, whose wife Fulvia had died in the summer, married
Augustus' recently widowed sister Octavia (see 4.1 n.). In the
following year agreement was reached with Sextus Pompeius at
the conference of Misenum (see 16.1 n.) and Antony returned
to the east with Octavia while Augustus gave his attention to
Gaul. The next year the war with Sextus broke out again; in
order to secure Antony's approval for it, Augustus asked him
for a meeting at Brundisium but did not keep the appointment
himself. Antony was angry, disapproving of the war, but since
he could in fact do nothing to stop his colleague, returned to
the east. In the winter of 38-37 B.C. Augustus, whose fortunes
were at a low ebb after the mauling of his fleet in 38, sent
Maecenas to mollify him and ask him for ships. Antony came to

Tarentum in the spring with 300 ships, and once again Augustus
did not meet him. He no longer needed the ships, thanks to
Agrippa's energy, while on the other hand Antony was anxious
to recruit in Italy for his forthcoming attack on Parthia. So
Antony waited, none too pleased, and eventually Octavia pre-
vailed upon her brother to negotiate with her husband. The
result, the 'Treaty' of Tarentum, gave approval to the war
against Sextus, arranged for Antony to lend 120 ships to
Augustus in exchange for four or five legions, and renewed the
triumvirate retrospectively for five years from Jan. 1st 37
B.C. Antony then left Italy, intent upon his scheme to conquer
Parthia, while Octavia and her two daughters by Antony stayed
behind - though there was nothing unusual about this under the
circustances. There followed Antony's resuscitation of his
affair with Cleopatra (whom he had not set eyes on since early
in 40 B.C., although she had subsequently borne him twins),
and his disastrous expedition in 36 B.C. through Armenia against
the Medes and Parthians, which had to stand comparison in Rome
with Augustus' complete success against Sextus in the same
year. Antony never returned to Italy. The east provided him
with all he needed: opportunities for military conquest, revenues from the richest provinces of the empire, and a regal
consort who bore his children and equipped and victualled his
armies - all, that is, except one thing, good fighting men
from Italy. Augustus never sent him the promised legions, and
at the same time embarked on a campaign in Illyria, from 35-33
B.C., whose chief purpose was to battle-harden his own recruits.
From then on the final breach and war was inevitable: the
young Caesar was too ambitious and ruthless to rest content with
a *de facto* partition of the Roman world. He mounted a campaign
of propaganda and diplomacy against his rival, designed to show
that his behaviour in the east was betraying the true interests
of Rome, while Antony, in spite of adding Armenia to the Roman
empire in 34 B.C., played into Augustus' hands by behaving like a
Hellenistic monarch with Alexandria as his capital.

At the end of 33 B.C. the triumvirate came to an end. In Feb.
32 B.C. Augustus staged a coup d'état by which he forced the
consuls C. Sosius and Cn. Domitius Ahenobarbus and some three
hundred other senatorial supporters of Antony to leave the
country. He then devoted all his efforts to manufacturing a
casus belli sufficiently convincing to justify leading an army
against his erstwhile colleague and the consuls of the Roman
people. Suetonius says Antony was proclaimed an enemy of the
state, but according to Dio (50.4.3) war was declared only
against Cleopatra - and that not until the end of the year. In
the meantime, in order to give his position as party leader
some kind of bogus legality, Augustus arranged that all the
inhabitants of Italy and the western provinces should swear an
oath of loyalty to himself. He himself claims (*RG* 25.2) that
the oath was spontaneous; but in that case it is not clear why
he needed to excuse the people of Bononia from swearing it,
and there were other places beside Bononia which supported

Antony, though they might not have had the traditionally res-
pected tie of clientship to justify them (Dio 51.4.6). The
opening of Antony's will occurred about July 32 B.C., as a
result of the defection from his camp of L. Munatius Plancus
(see 7.2 n.) and Plancus' nephew M. Titius. These two high-ranking
persons told Augustus that the will was in the keeping of the
Vestal Virgins. Augustus, sensing that its contents might give
him the proof he still lacked that Antony had ceased to be a
true Roman, illegally seized and opened it. The senate and
people learnt from Augustus' own lips that Cleopatra's eldest
son, Ptolemy Caesar, was indeed Julius Caesar's child; that
her children by Antony were to receive great legacies; and
that Antony wished his body, should he die in Rome, to be sent
to Cleopatra for burial. This was confirmation enough that the
wicked queen, who lusted to overthrow Rome and dine on the
Capitol, had corrupted and enslaved a once fine man to her
foul purposes. The way was open for the official declaration
of war.

17.2 Actium: this decisive naval battle took place off the mouth of the
Gulf of Arta on the west coast of Greece on Sept. 2nd. 31 B.C. Antony
had been blockaded for most of the summer, and disease and desertion were
rapidly weakening his forces. It was essential for him to break out, but
by making for Egypt with Cleopatra instead of trying to rejoin his army
elsewhere in Greece, he abandoned any chance of recovering the military
initiative. The break-out was comparatively successful under the circumstances, but Antony lost the majority of his ships and his army did not
manage to retreat very far before surrendering, so that the battle was
correctly represented as a victory by Augustus' side. Although Augustus
was at sea participating in the fight, Agrippa held the command. (See
Carter 1970 200-227.)

17.3 Samum: Augustus was in no hurry to follow up the victory of Actium,
as there were enemy forces still left in Egypt and the country was difficult to attack. The lapse of a winter gave him time to attend to the
diplomatic consequences of Antony's defeat amongst the kingdoms of Asia
Minor and the Syrian region, and to make proper preparations for the
assault. Samos was a convenient base for both purposes.
seditione praemia et missionem postulantium: after Actium, Augustus
found himself with an army of over 50 legions, far more than he needed,
composed of men to many of whom he had made a variety of expensive pro-
mises over the years. The end of the Sicilian war had taught him the
danger of such a situation, and he sent some of them back to Italy at
once to await formal discharge and the payment of their promised bounties.
They became mutinous, Agrippa was sent to keep them in order but failed,
and things became so serious that Augustus had to make the hurried winter
voyage here described; he was only able to pacify the veterans by agree-
ing to provide land for them by dispossessing (since he had no money)
communities which had supported Antony and risking the same ill-feeling
which had led to the Perusine war.
montes Ceraunios: also known as Acroceraunia, and notorious for sudden
storms, these mountains lay on the coast of Epirus near Apollonia.
Alexandria ... potitus est: C. Cornelius Gallus advanced with one

army along the coast of Cyrenaica, Augustus with another by way of Asia
Minor, Syria, and Judaea. Antony offered some resistance, but the decisive battle, of Aug. 1st. 30 B.C., was something of a fiasco: Antony's
fleet surrendered without a fight, his cavalry deserted, and his infantry
were defeated.

17.4 Antonium ... ad mortem adegit: while it may be true that
Antony tried last-minute negotiations, Suetonius is certainly wrong to
say that Augustus made him commit suicide. The lost battle and (false)
report of Cleopatra's death were responsible.
viditque mortuum: it was regarded as cruel to look upon the dead body of
your enemy (Caesar would not look at Pompey's head - Appian, *BC* 2.90).
Cleopatrae ... Psyllos admovit: Augustus had managed to seize
Cleopatra in her mausoleum before she could carry out her design of cre-
mating her treasure in it along with herself; but it seems likely that
once the treasure was safe he was not unwilling for her to commit suicide.
Otherwise, after she had walked in his triumph, he would either have had
to execute her (as tradition prescribed) or exile her (as clemency and
respect for a great house of kings counselled), and neither course was
attractive: one was barbaric, the other risky. The Psylli were a tribe
of Libya said to possess the art of curing snake bites (Pliny, *NH* 7.14).
The asp was supposed to deify those who died by its bite, and there is
thus good reason to believe that Cleopatra, a goddess in the eyes of her
subjects, would have chosen it as the instrument of her suicide.

17.5 Antonium iuvenem: M. Antonius junior, known as Antyllus, was
probably born not later than 45 B.C. He had assumed the *toga virilis*
after Actium and had been sent by his father on an embassy to negotiate
with Augustus in 30 B.C. (Dio 51.8.4). His brother Iullus Antonius,
born in 43 or 42 B.C., was brought up by Octavia along with her own
children by Antony and attained the consulship in 10 B.C. only to be executed for his involvement in the activities of the elder Julia in 2 B.C.
(see 65.1-3). Fulvia had been married to two outstanding political
figures before Antony, namely P. Clodius (died 52 B.C.) and C. Scribonius
Curio (died 49 B.C.).
Caesarionem: Ptolemy Caesarion, perhaps born in 47 B.C., was almost
certainly Caesar's son, in spite of C. Oppius' pamphlet purporting to
disprove the fact (*DJ* 52; Heinen 1969). Augustus, Caesar's 'son', could
not afford to let a real son live, even if he would not have been recognised in Roman law.
reliquos Antoni ... liberos: these other children were the twins
Alexander Helios and Cleopatra Selene (born 40 B.C.) and Ptolemy
Philadelphus (born 36 B.C.). The two boys disappear from history;
Cleopatra was married to Juba II of Mauretania (see 48 final n.).

18.1 Magni Alexandri: Alexander the Great died in Babylon. He
apparently wished to be buried at the shrine of Zeus Ammon in the Egyptian
desert, where he had been assured of his divinity by the god. There are
various versions of how the body came to be in Alexandria (Diodorus 18.
26-28; Pausanias 1.6.3 and 1.7.1; Strabo 17.1.8). As an all-conquering
superhuman ruler, Alexander was a potent inspiration to the generals of
Republican Rome (see Michel 1967). Dio (51.16.5) tells the same story

as Suetonius, adding that Augustus was said to have broken a piece off
the nose of the mummy.

Ptolemaeum: this was the burial place and shrine of the Ptolemies, who
had been the ruling dynasty of Egypt since the first Ptolemy had estab-
lished himself as king after the death of Alexander in 323 B.C.   The
Macedonian stock had been diluted somewhat by marriages with other
Hellenistic royal houses, but there was no Egyptian blood in the family.
Cleopatra herself was ethnically largely Greek and culturally entirely
Greek.

18.2 Aegyptum in provinciae formam redactam: the conversion of
conquered territory into a Roman province was normally done by a law
which sanctioned legal and administrative arrangements made by the
victor and/or a senatorial commission, but in this case all Augustus'
acts (since 32 B.C.), not only the annexation of Egypt, were ratified
by an oath of the senate on Jan. 1st., 29 B.C.   The government of Egypt
remained quite distinct from that of the other provinces: i)   it was
governed by an equestrian Prefect and no senator was allowed in the
country without express permission.   This was because Augustus, as ruler
of Egypt, became divine in the eyes of the people, and his deputy, the
Prefect, was scarcely less awesome.   ('He who is sent has the rank of
King', Strabo 17.1.12).   Egypt was also strategically strong, had a garrison
(at first) of three legions, and was very important as a source of grain
for Rome.   Such a heady combination had to be kept away from any ambitious man who had the prestige and connections to challenge Augustus -
and such a man could only be a senator.   ii)   There was only one city
of Greek type in the country, Alexandria, and even that was too turbulent
to be granted the usual local autonomy.   Otherwise Egypt consisted of
villages grouped into nomes (districts) within three great epistrategiai
('commands').   The whole was adminstered by an elaborate bureaucracy
answerable directly to the Prefect.   This system had been set up by the
Ptolemies but was in a bad way by 30 B.C.   Augustus simply made it work
properly again (the clearing of the irrigation ditches is symptomatic)
and substituted himself, represented by his Prefect, for the king.

COMMEMORATION OF ACTIUM

Augustus returned from Samos (where he had spent the winter of
30-29 B.C.) in the summer of 29, and put in at Actium to see to
three commemorative projects:

i)   He created a new city, Nicopolis ('victory-town'), on the
low neck of the northern peninsula, below the site of his camp,
by transferring the population from a number of places further
inland.

ii)   He enlarged the old temple of Apollo which stood on the
tip of the southern promontory, where Antony's camp had been,
and associated with it his new quinquennial games, the Actiaca
(cf. 44.4 n. and on super templa 59).   See Gagé 1936.

iii)   On the hill where his camp had been he erected a monument

incorporating prows of the various sizes of ship he had captured from Antony, and dedicated it to Neptune and Mars. Since
the restoration of the inscription given in $E-J^3$ no. 12 has
been superseded, the new text is given here: *Nep]tuno [et Ma]rt[i*
Imp. Caesa]r div[i Iuli] f. vict[oriam ma]rit[imam consecutus
bell]o quod pro [re pu]blic[a] ges[si]t in hac region[e c]astra
[ex] quibu[s ad hostem in]seq[uendum egr]essu[s est spoli]is
[ornat]a [dedicavit cons]ul [quinctum i]mperat[or se]ptimum pace
parta terra [marique. (See Oliver 1969, revised by Carter 1977.)

19   PLOTS AGAINST AUGUSTUS

Suetonius now inserts a chapter on plots and civil disturbances
whose material tends to overlap with that of chapter 66. In a
sense the theme of civil war continues, but the chapter is only
tenuously connected with its general military context. We
have here little but a catalogue, and Suetonius evidently
expects his readers to know all about the first six names on
his list.

i)   'Young Lepidus', son of the triumvir and nephew of M. Brutus,
formed a plot to kill Augustus on his return to Italy in 29 B.C.,
but was found out and put to death by C. Maecenas (see 66.3 n.)
who had been left in charge of Italy (Velleius 2.88).

ii) and iii) *Varro Murena* and *Fannius Caepio* were condemned
and killed as leaders of a conspiracy formed after Murena, as
counsel for M. Primus, the proconsul of Macedonia, who was
accused of making war outside the borders of his province without proper authority, had challenged Augustus' standing in the
case (Dio 54.3.2-8). The date of the conspiracy -- 23 or 22
B.C.? - and the identity of Murena - A. Terentius Varro Murena
(consul 23 B.C.) or his brother Lucius (no recorded office)? -
are much disputed (see Stockton 1965; Swan 1966; Jameson 1969;
Sumner 1978). Murena was Maecenas' brother-in-law, and the
conspiracy (if it really existed) represented a reaction against
the autocracy of Augustus' new republic; on this general topic,
see Sattler 1960 and Schmitthenner 1962.

iv) *M. Egnatius Rufus,* as aedile, probably in 22 B.C., won
enormous popularity by organising an efficient fire brigade
(cf. 30 n.) and was able to secure his election to the praetorship, unconstitutionally, in the next year or in 20 B.C. He
then tried to become, equally illegally, consul in 19 B.C.,
but the already elected consul Sentius Saturninus refused to
accept his candidacy and faction fighting broke out. Egnatius
and his followers were imprisoned and executed. (Dio 53.24.4,
misdated; Velleius 2.91-92; Dio 54.10.1; Sattler 1960 87 f.;
Millar 1964a 87-88).

v) *Plautius Rufus* is much more obscure but is generally
identified with the Publius Rufus of Dio 55.27.2, one of the

instigators of a poster campaign and seditious talk during the famine and military crisis of A.D. 6.

vi) *L. Aemilius Paullus* (consul A.D. 1), son of Paullus Aemilius Lepidus (consul 34 B.C. cf. 16.3) was married to Augustus' granddaughter Julia. The date and nature of his plot are not otherwise known; but Suetonius' arrangement of words makes it virtually certain that he is to be coupled with Plautius Rufus, both being introduced by *exin* in the same way that Varro Murena and Fannius Caepio, whom we know belong together, are introduced by *deinde*. All other single conspirators, except for the first named, have an adverb or adverbial phrase to themselves (*mox; praeter has; item; ad extremum*). Levick 1976 58 f., suggests that the activities of Rufus and Paullus were the last open political agitation of the reign and that when they were suppressed Julia and her brother Agrippa Postumus continued the struggle against their aging and tyrannical grandfather by more secret and sinister means, leading to their own exile, on the islands of Trimerus (off the Apulian coast) and Planasia (modern Pianosa, near Elba) respectively (see 65.1 n.). Paullus' fate is unknown; since Julia was accused of *adultery* he should have been alive in A.D. 8 (see 34.1 n.; note also *Claud*. 26.1 and *ILS* 5026, with elder Pliny, *NH* 18.6).

vii), viii) and ix) Of *L. Audasius, Asinius Epicadus,* and the remembrancer *Telephus* we know only what Suetonius tells us here. Augustus' daughter Julia was banished to the island of Pandateria (modern Ventotene, off the Campanian coast) from 2 B.C. to A.D. 4 after a supposed adultery scandal (see 65.1-3). For her son Agrippa, see vi above. It is possible that Suetonius has confused the two Julias; the younger seems a more likely principal in such a plot than her mother (see above) but since Suetonius neither gives dates nor makes it clear whether the activities of Audasius and Epicadus were connected, the matter remains in doubt.

20-23 Suetonius goes on to list Augustus' external wars. Augustus is now entirely 'good': he only makes war because he has to, he is successful, a paragon of good faith and moderation, an arbitrator of thrones, and a bringer of peace. In the face of disaster he acts decisively, makes the appropriate vows to the gods, and shows by his grief a proper sense of the responsibility vested in him.

20   (bellum) Delmaticum adulescens adhuc: the Dalmatian war took place in 35-33 B.C., so Augustus was *not* 'in his teens' (*GG*) but 'quite young'. This war was fought largely to harden new recruits who had replaced the seasoned troops Augustus had been forced to discharge at the end of the Sicilian war in 36 B.C., and to provide a counterpoise to any military success Antony might win in the east. Augustus' personal involvement in the fighting may have been intended to efface the memory of

his somewhat inglorious part in the Sicilian war (see Appian, *Illyr.* 16-28; Dio 49.35-38; Schmitthenner 1958).

(**bellum**) **Cantabricum:** the Cantabrian war belongs to 26-25 B.C. Even after nearly 200 years of Roman rule in Spain, the peninsula was far from completely subdued. Though probably not imposing a war, the raids of the Cantabri in northern Spain were a convenient excuse for Augustus to operate in the western half of the empire against a traditional and clearly non-Roman foe. Nor did he need a fleet, so he could stake a claim to the military abilities a military monarch ought to possess without having his victories won for him by Agrippa. He was not con-spicuously successful and retired in ill-health to Tarraco, leaving his legates C. Antistius and T. Carisius to finish the campaign, which they did well enough to enable Augustus to claim that universal peace had been established in the empire and close the shrine of Janus (see 22) for a second time (see Syme 1934; Schmitthenner 1962). In fact, Agrippa needed to complete the subjugation of Spain in 19 B.C.

reliqua per legatos administravit: there was one province, Africa, where wars were fought by proconsuls who were not legates of Augustus (see 47 n.); but these were not technically 'his' wars. Otherwise, since the commanders of armies in the imperial provinces derived their authority from him, he was nominally always the commander-in-chief. There was almost continuous warfare somewhere in the area of Illyricum, the Alps, and the Rhine, from 15 B.C. to the end of the reign.

21.1 partim ductu partim auspiciis: this formula is equivalent to that of *RG* 4.2 'by me or by my legates acting under my auspices' - *a me aut per legatos meos auspiciis meis.* Only the possessor of *imperium* conferred directly by the people had the right (and duty) of taking the auspices, and hence being able to claim the responsibility for victory and the honour of a triumph (see 38.1 n.)

Cantabria: see 20 n.

Aquitania: (south-western France), subdued by M. Valerius Messalla Corvinus in 28 B.C.; Agrippa had also operated there in 39 or 38 B.C.

Pannonia: (northern Yugoslavia and Danube valley), initially conquered by Tiberius in 12-9 B.C., following operations by M. Vinicius and Agrippa in 14 and 13 B.C., but rebelled in A.D. 6 and was not finally subdued by Tiberius until A.D. 9 (cf. *RG* 30.1; more fully, Dio 55.29f.; Velleius 2.110f.).

Dalmatia: (with Illyricum), shared in the revolt of Pannonia in A.D. 6, having been previously won by a process started by Augustus himself in 35-33 B.C. (see 20 n.) and continued by P. Silius in 17 and 16 B.C. *Illyricum* is an elastic region: it may include Pannonia, but Suetonius seems to use it here to mean the coastal belt (Dalmatia) together with the inland areas too far south to be included in Pannonia. It is ex-tremely unlikely that we possess the full record of campaigns in this area under Augustus, as it was chronically turbulent.

Raetia, Vindelici, Salassi: Raetia corresponds to parts of modern Switzerland, Austria, and Bavaria; the chief town of the Vindelici after the conquest was Augusta Vindelicum (modern Augsburg) lying some 20 miles south of the Danube. This area was conquered by Tiberius and his brother Drusus in 15 B.C., a campaign celebrated by Horace, *Odes* 4.4 and 14. The Salassi lived on the Italian side of the St. Bernard Pass, where the

colony of Augusta Praetoria (modern Aosta) was founded after their final
conquest in 25 B.C. by A. Terentius Varro; they had previously been defeated by C. Antistius Vetus in 35-34 B.C. and by Messalla Corvinus in
(?)27 B.C. The conquest of the Alpine regions was designed to pave the
way for the annexation of Germany (see Wells 1972 35-89).

Dacorum incursiones: 'Dacians' is used as a convenient label both by
Suetonius and by Augustus (RG 30.2), who speaks of his armies defeating
Dacians on each side of the Danube. The peoples meant are those who
lived on the north bank of the river, opposite the province of Moesia,
approximately in the area of modern Rumania. It is vain to try and
identify the episode(s) Suetonius alludes to: but probably the success
of M. Crassus, proconsul of Macedonia 30-28 B.C., is not one of them,
since he was awarded a triumph and must therefore have been fighting
under his own auspices (Dio 51.26.5). A more probable date is between
6 B.C. and A.D. 4, when senior army commanders were fighting in the
area and the province of Moesia was being formed (Syme 1939 400). The
Dacians also crossed the frozen river into Pannonia in the winter of 10
B.C. (Dio 54.36.2).

Germanosque ultra Albim fluvium summovit: Suetonius does not
mean that Augustus depopulated the region between Rhine and Elbe, but
that there were no unsubdued Germans left in that area. The conquest
of this part of Germany took a long time, starting with the campaigns in
Pannonia and Raetia (see above) to give a secure southern base, and continuing with the activities of Drusus (13-9 B.C.), Tiberius (8-7 B.C.),
Cn. Ahenobarbus (ca. 1 B.C.), M. Vinicius (ca. A.D. 2), and Tiberius
again (A.D. 4-6), who according to Velleius (2.108.1) completed the task
except for the subjugation of the Marcomanni in the south. But the new
province was lost in A.D. 9 when the German leader Arminius lured the
governor P. Quinctilius Varus (consul 13 B.C.), who was treating the
Germans as pacified, into a trap and destroyed him and his three legions
(XVII, XVIII, and XIX), causing near-panic at Rome (see 23; Velleius 2.
117-119; Dio 56.18-21; Tacitus, Ann. 1.60-61). The Romans were able to
hold the line of the Rhine, but never thereafter controlled territory
beyond it, except a small area in the angle between the upper Rhine and
Danube. In general, see Wells 1972.

Suebos et Sigambros: the Sigambri (spelling variable) lived in the
Ruhr area, and had contributed to the defeat of Lollius in 16 B.C. (see
23.1); they were transferred by Tiberius in 8-7 B.C. (Tib. 9). There
were several tribes of Suebi further west and south, but which one was
moved, and when, is not known; Wells 1972 156 links their deportation
with that of the Sigambri.

21.2 sine iustis et necessariis causis: all Roman wars (like all
modern wars) were just and unavoidable, and an elaborate religious ritual
was carried out by the priests called fetiales, whose duty it was to claim
restitution for the wrong inflicted on the Roman people before solemnly
declaring war. Augustus says (RG 26.3) that he pacified the Alps without waging an unjust war on any people, though the reader of the list of
Alpine tribes inscribed on the monument of La Turbie (E-J[3] no. 40) might
legitimately wonder what they had all done to rouse the ire of Rome, and
perhaps significantly Augustus himself does not make the same claim in
respect of the expeditions against Ethiopia and Arabia. Imperial expansion
was a desirable, even a necessary aim of a Roman leader, but to meet with

the blessing of the gods it required a steady supply of menacing enemies. The ideology of conquest and the requirements of piety lay uneasily together.

21.3 Indos ac Scythos: Indians and Scythians appear in the same guise, as peoples from the uttermost fringes of the civilised world, in *RG* 31 and Horace, *Carmen Saeculare* 55. Embassies from India are known in 25 and 20 B.C., and see Strabo 15.1.4 (Wheeler 1954). For Suetonius to say that these peoples were 'known by report alone' is a little strong, since Romans were trading regularly with South India early in the reign of Augustus (Schmitthenner 1979 103), but he seems to be paraphrasing Augustus' words 'not previously seen'.

Parthi quoque et Armeniam: public opinion expected Augustus to take action against the Parthians, who had captured legionary standards from Crassus at Carrhae in 53 B.C., from Decidius Saxa in 40 B.C., and from Antony in 36 B.C. (cf. *RG* 29.2); they had also overrun Armenia (newly annexed by Antony in 34) in 32/31 B.C. and installed a pro-Parthian king, Artaxes, on the throne. Diplomatic pressure failed and Augustus threatened military action in 21/20 B.C.; this was enough to make the Parthian king Phraates hand over the standards and any Roman prisoners who wished to return home. These events encouraged the pro-Roman party in Armenia to murder Artaxes, and Tiberius was able to enter the country unopposed and crown as king Artaxes' brother Tigranes II, who had been living first in Alexandria and then in Rome since his capture by Antony in 34 B.C. Augustus judged that Armenia was more valuable to Rome as a client-kingdom than as a province (see 48 n.; *RG* 27.2). For the hostages and struggles for the Parthian throne, see 43.4 n. The Armenian throne was also disputed: after the death of Tigranes II (not later than 6 B.C.) his son Tigranes III was placed on the throne by the anti-Roman faction, only to be ejected on Augustus' orders and replaced by Tigranes II's Romanised younger brother Artavasdes, who was in turn thrown out with Parthian help before 1 B.C. Then the new Parthian king Phraataces came to an understanding in A.D. 1 with Gaius, by which his half-brothers the hostages continued to stay in Rome, he refrained from interfering in Armenia, and Ariobarzanes (king of Media since 20 B.C.) became in addition king of Armenia - Tigranes III having opportunely been killed in a border disturbance. The importance of Armenia to Rome lay in its position on the flanks of Parthia and North Syria: a king friendly to Rome served as a check on Parthia and a shield to Syria, a king friendly to Parthia left the eastern frontier very exposed.

22 Ianum Quirinum: this was a small rectangular shrine with doors at both ends and the statue of the god facing both ways within (see Nash 1961 1.502). It stood in the Forum near the senate house, at the entrance to the Argiletum. It was also known as *Ianus Geminus* and *Ianus Bifrons*. The doors stood open in time of war, and the antiquarians of the late Republic held that they had been closed only twice in Roman history before Augustus' time, once in the reign of Numa and once in 235 B.C. (Varro, *LL* 5.165). They were closed again in 29 and 25 B.C. (Dio 51.20.4; 53.26.5) after the ending of the Alexandrian and Spanish wars respectively. The third occasion is unidentified but guaranteed by Augustus himself (*RG* 13); Orosius (6.22.1) puts it in 2 B.C. but activity at that time on the Rhine and Danube frontiers makes this implausible. 18 B.C., 13 B.C., or

sometime before 8 and 1 B.C. (Syme 1978 26) seem better guesses.
terra marique pace parta: variations of this formula occur in the
same connection on coins of Nero (*BMC Aug* Index *s.v.* PACE P.R. TERRA
MARIQ. PARTA), in Livy 1.19.3 and in *RG* 13. It was also used on the
Actium inscription of 29 B.C. (see 18.2 n.) and on the base of the
rostral column erected in the Forum after the defeat of Sextus Pompeius
(Appian *BC* 5.130). Links can be traced back to the Hellenistic regal
title 'ruler over Land and Sea', but the connection of universal rule
with universal peace seems to be an Augustan invention (Momigliano
1942 63).
bis ovans: Augustus' two ovations (a sort of inferior triumph, see
Gellius, *NA* 5.6.20f., 27) were in 40 B.C., after the reconciliation with
Antony at Tarentum, and 36 B.C., after the defeat of Sextus Pompeius
(*E-J*[3] pp.33-4; Dio 48.31.3 and 49.15.1; *RG* 4.1). Suetonius' words 'after
the war of Philippi' are, at the least, misleading.
curules triumphos: 29 B.C., August 13th, 14th, and 15th. See 38.1 n.,
Dio 51.21.7. Suetonius follows Augustus' own words at *RG* 4.1 very
closely.

23.1 clades ... Lollianam et Varianam: M. Lollius (consul 21 B.C.)
commanding forces in the Rhine area in 17-16 B.C. suffered an incursion
by the Sigambri, Usipetes, and Tencteri, was taken by surprise, and
defeated after his cavalry had been routed. Recovery was swift, and the
disgrace was caused chiefly by losing the eagle of the fifth legion
(Velleius 2.97.1; Dio 54.20.5). Lollius lost little credit: Augustus
appointed him chief adviser to Gaius on his important military and
diplomatic mission in the east (2 B.C. onwards). However, intrigue,
scandal, or guilt undid him and he died by his own hand in A.D. 2. The
notorious pearls of his granddaughter Lollia Paulina were said to be his
plunder of the provinces. (elder Pliny, *NH* 9.117). His minor reverse
of 17 or 16 B.C. was turned into a 'disaster' by writers favourable to
Tiberius, whose enemy he was. On Varus' defeat, see n. on *Germanosque*
21.1.
excubias: ιt is interesting that a disaster in Germany should have made
Augustus take steps to ensure order in Rome. Perhaps he felt unsure of
his own position after the disturbances of A.D. 6 and the banishment of
his own grandchildren in A.D. 8 (see 19.1 n. v and vi).

23.2 magnos ludos: 'Great Games': the term *Ludi Magni* was applied
to the *Ludi Romani,* the greatest of the regular annual festivals (Livy
1.35.9). Not exclusively, however; the sources exhibit confusion between
Ludi Magni, Ludi Maximi, and *Ludi Votivi,* the last of which were without
doubt specially put on in honour of a vow. The games Augustus vowed on
this occasion were clearly votive - as is proved by the reference to the
Cimbric (105-101 B.C.) and Marsic or Social (90-88 B.C.) wars, in both
of which Rome had armies annihilated. We do not know whether Augustus
carried out his vow before his death, unless 43.5 refers.
barba capilloque summisso: to go without shaving or having one's
hair cut was a sign of mourning; cf. *DJ* 67.2; Lintott 1968 16f.
diem cladis: the date is not known, but it was probably in late Sept.
(*RE* 24.955-6).

24-25 These two chapters bring to an end the 'military' part of

the work: they illustrate Augustus' attitudes to military discipline and rewards, and conclude with a few pithy sayings of
the emperor which both stress his policy of caution and make a
vivid ending to this section. Augustus is here pictured as
severe, but able to temper justice with mercy, and willing to
reward people, but strictly according to their deserts. His
concern for the preservation of status barriers is also evident.

24.1 in re militari et commutavit multa et instituit: in speaking
of military reforms, as is clear from what follows, Suetonius does not
refer to such strategic matters as the disposition and command of legions
and general terms of pay and discharge, for which see **49**, but to conditions
of service for the individual, divided under the two heads of discipline
(down to 25.2) and rewards (25.3). A major change, nowhere mentioned by
Suetonius and not specifically attributed to Augustus by any ancient
source, was the ban on soldiers' marriages which seems most likely to
have been introduced in 13 B.C. (Campbell 1978 154; cf. Ovid *Ars Am.*
1.131-2). On the other hand Augustus allowed soldiers to treat as their
own property, immune from the rules of *patria potestas,* their earnings
while they were in the army (known as *peculium castrense;* see Crook 1967
110-111). In general, see Watson 1969.
equitem Romanum: this story of the *eques* who cut off his sons' thumbs
to disqualify them from military service (*sacramentum* being the oath taken
on enlistment) is clear evidence for the survival of the compulsory levy
in Augustan times, in spite of the general tendency from the time of Marius
for the army to become a professional volunteer force. Compulsion was
applied on several occasions in the first century B.C. Since this episode
is undated, it may well belong before 31 B.C.; but men were dodging the
levy in 23 B.C. (*Tib.* 8) and the crises of A.D. 6 and 9 entailed even the
conscription of slaves, freed for the purpose (see **25.2**). Velleius
(2.130.2) writes of the levy as a thing of terror before Tiberius' time,
and it is likely that Augustus resorted to compulsory levies several
times in his reign. For full discussion, see Brunt 1971 408ff.
publicanos: it is not clear why Augustus was so disturbed at the prospect
of public contractors buying the unfortunate *eques.* Perhaps he suspected
that they were going to exploit the man's former rank in some undignified
way; certainly his action in making him over to an imperial freedman
suggests that he repented of an over-harsh decision.

24.2 decimam legionem: Syme 1933 15 conjectured that this was Caesar's
old tenth legion, which could have been amongst the mutinous troops at
Brundisium (see **17.3**) in the winter of 31/30 B.C.; but an (unspecified)
legion was disbanded for mutiny in 35 B.C. (Dio 49.34.4). Neither of the
two tenth Legions known after 27 B.C., Fretensis and Gemina (see **49** n.),
can be the one referred to here.
alias exauctoravit: *exauctoratio* is the technical military term for
'discharge', and is in itself neither honourable nor dishonourable; under
the empire it may imply 'early discharge' and can be contrasted with
missio 'full-term, pensionable, discharge' (e.g. Tacitus *Ann.* 1.36.4).
Suetonius refers to the trouble Augustus had with dissatisfied troops
after his defeat of Sextus Pompeius (Appian *BC* 5.129), as well as to the
unrest at Brundisium (see previous n.). On the latter occasion he plac-
ated some of the veterans by giving them money with the promise of land

later, and it is possible that they were never in fact given the land.
Suetonius' phrase *citra commoda emeritorum praemiorum* 'without all the
benefits of the rewards they had earned' is vague and need not mean that
the men in question received nothing at all. *commoda* is the technical
term under the empire for any allowance, including discharge bounty.
decimatas hordeo pavit: decimation was the clubbing to death of every
tenth man (chosen by lot) by his fellow-soldiers. The principle that
breaches of individual military discipline were punished by a man's equals
(Polybius 6.37.1ff.) is extended to become a kind of mass self-purification
and expiation on the part of the whole unit (see Lintott 1968 42, who
compares Germanicus' treatment of the Rhine army mutineers, Tacitus,
Ann. 1.44.2-5). Augustus is known to have used the punishment once, in
34 B.C. (Dio 49.38.4); in the civil war period Caesar, Domitius Calvinus,
and Antony also employed it (Dio 41.35.5; 48.42.2; 49.27.1), in some
cases, as here, joined with the ancient military punishment of distributing
rations of barley instead of wheat (barley being the diet of slaves and
animals).
cum decempedis vel etiam caespitem portantes: the point of this
is that surveying-poles and clods of earth were normally carried only by
common soldiers in the course of performing tasks which no centurion
ever had to demean himself by doing.

25.1 commilitones: the revolutionary implications of the term 'fellow-
soldiers' are patent. Augustus here reversed a practice of Caesar's, to
the evident approval of Suetonius (cf. *DJ* 67.2). His power depended on
his soldiers, but like every other part of society, they had to be in
their place.

25.2 libertino milite: freedmen were regularly enrolled for the corps
of *vigiles* (night-watchmen, firemen, and police); see 30 n. The two
military crises are those of A.D. 6 (the Illyrian revolt - see n. on
Pannonia 21.1 and Velleius 2.111.1, who confirms Suetonius' detail that
the rich were forced to manumit) and A.D. 9 (the disaster of Varus - see
n. on *Germanosque* 21.1). Macrobius (*Saturnalia* 1.11.32) says that Augustus
called these separate formations of freedmen *voluntariae cohortes*
('volunteer cohorts'); free men subjected to the levy had no choice (see
n. on *equitem Romanum* 24.1).

25.3 dona militaria: the military decorations here mentioned by
Suetonius were all in use under the Republic. *phalerae* were discs or
bosses worn on the chest, *torques* collars of twisted gold links (for illus-
trations, see Webster 1969 pl.VI and VII). Of the crowns, the *vallaris*
(called *castrensis* by Gellius) was given to the man who first climbed
the rampart into an enemy camp, the *muralis* to the man who first scaled
a city wall. Gellius, in his discussion of these and other crowns (*NA*
5.6), says they were usually of gold, but Suetonius (perhaps unintentionally) seems to imply the reverse.
M. Agrippam: for Agrippa and the Sicilian war, see 16.2 n. According
to Dio (51.21.3), the blue flag was awarded after Actium. A *vexillum*,
a small silver-mounted standard, was a usual military decoration for
senior officers.
solos triumphales: I take it that *triumphales* includes men who had
been granted the *ornamenta triumphalia* as well as those who had actually
celebrated a triumph (see 38.1 n.). By refusing to award decorations to

such men, Augustus attempted to maintain a little of the fiction that he
was only *primus inter pares*.
σπεῦδε βραδέως: 'more haste less speed' - *'festina lente'*. Gellius
(*NA* 10.11.6) confirms that Augustus used the Greek words.
ἀσφαλὴς γάρ ...: 'a safe general is better than a bold one' (Euripides,
Phoenissae 602).

26   The opening sentence of this chapter signals the third main
section of the book, 26-60. 'Magistracies and offices' are dealt
with in three chapters, but the subsequent transition to Augustus'
civil achievements is logical and fleshes out the catalogue of
office-holding. When at 57 Suetonius comes back full circle to
honores in the sense of 'honours' rather than 'offices', those
honours are now fully intelligible because we know what Augustus
had done to deserve them.

The structure of 26-28 follows, with digressions, the three
heads of magistracies 'held early', 'of a new sort', and 'perpetual'. The treatment is very uneven and anecdotal, gives
least space to what interests modern historians most, and omits
altogether the constitutional bedrock of Augustus' position after
23 B.C., his consular and proconsular *imperium* (see Introduction
§25).

AUGUSTUS' CONSULSHIPS

Apart from the introductory sentence, 26 is devoted entirely to
his consulships. The words *ante tempus* ('early') refer to tenure
of an office before the minimum normal age for holding it; the
minimum ages laid down by the *lex Villia annalis* of 180 B.C., re-
affirmed by Sulla, and observed, with occasional exceptions
allowed by the senate, down to 49 B.C. were: quaestor - age 30,
praetor - age 39, consul - age 42. Augustus held no qualifying
magistracies and entered his first consulship in August 43 B.C.,
a month before his twentieth birthday, filling with his cousin
Q. Pedius the vacancies created by the deaths of Hirtius and
Pansa at Mutina (see 11 n.). The story about the centurion is
found also in Dio 46.43.4. The threat was not enough, and
Augustus had to follow up the unsuccessful embassy by marching
with his army on Rome. The senate could not of course grant the
consulship: what Augustus needed from it was a dispensation from
the provisions of the lex Villia. The actual election by the
people was constitutionally anomalous (see Dio 46.45.3-5) but
preserved a veneer of respectability. Augustus abdicated when
the triumvirate was formed three months later.

His second consulship was in 33 (i.e. nine years intervening),
and his third in 31 B.C.; both these appear from the legends of
coins issued in 37 B.C. to have been agreed before his meeting
with Antony at Tarentum in that year (perhaps at Misenum in 39
when they came to some kind of arrangement with Sextus Pompeius
- though the details reported by Appian, *BC* 5.73, fit not 38-35

but 34-31 B.C. - or perhaps earlier in 39, as Dio 48.35 states).
He may have gone through the farce of the second consulship
in order to keep the tally of his consulships equal with
Antony's; for though the Fasti almost suppress the fact, the
coins show that Antony held *his* second consulship in 34 B.C.,
and such things were important for a leader's prestige. The
full record may be set out as follows, combining the information
of Suetonius with that of the Fasti (*Inscr It* 13.1.502ff.;
EJ[3]32ff. and no.323):-

Consulship	Year B.C.	Place of assumption	Date of abdication	Months held
I	43	Rome	Nov. 27	3
	(Aug. 19)			
II	33	Rome	Jan. 1	0
III	31	Rome	Apr. 30	4
IV	30	Asia (Ephesos?)	Jun. 30	6
V	29	Samos	Sep. 30	9
VI	28	Rome	-	12
VII	27	Rome	-	12
VIII	26	Tarraco	-	12
IX	25	Tarraco	-	12
X	24	Rome	-	12
XI	23	Rome	June	6
XII	5	Rome	Mar. 31 or Apr. 30	3 or 4
XIII	2	Rome	Mar. 31 or Apr. 30	3 or 4

Augustus' reasons for abdication can be inferred, where they are
not known. In the late Republic the consulship had become in
practice a civil magistracy and it could be administratively
inconvenient for a consul to be inaccessible on campaign.
Thus Augustus abdicated in 31 B.C. in time for the campaign of
Actium and in 30 B.C. for the final attack on Alexandria. In
29 B.C. he appears to have retained office until after his
triumphs of 12-15 Aug. (see 22), for which he would in any
case have had to be given a special grant of *imperium*. From
28 until the middle of 23 B.C. the consulship was the office
on which his power legally rested. His abdication in June 23 B.C.
marked a radical transformation of the principate (see 27.5 n. and
28.1-2 n.). Henceforth he refused to be considered a consular
candidate, and there was trouble and even rioting in Rome in
connection with the elections for the consulships of 21 and
19 B.C.; the people at that time insisted on keeping open for
him one of the two places, in his absence and against his will,
although other men were eventually appointed. By the time he
consented to hold the consulship again, to introduce first
Gaius, then Lucius, formally into public life, it had become
normal for the elected consuls (*consules ordinarii*) to resign
half-way through the year so that two more men (*consules suffecti*) could have the honour of reaching the highest magistracy
of state every year. By resigning after three (or four)
months, Augustus in effect allowed a man, whom he had by his
exceptional candidature kept out, to realise his ambitions after

all: in both 5 and 2 B.C. we find three *suffecti*, of whom the
first almost certainly held office for the unexpired portion
of the six months Augustus would by now have been expected
to remain consul.

Suetonius' final comment, on the places where Augustus entered
on his consulships, arises from the fact that a consul had
constitutionally to enter office at Rome.   There is no exception
before Julius Caesar in 46 B.C., unless one believes the
tradition hostile to C. Flaminius (consul 217 B.C.) found in
Livy 21.63; but Cicero nowhere mentions it in several contexts
where it would have suited him to have done so (*de Divinatione*
1.77-78; 2.21, 2.67 and 2.71; *de Natura Deorum* 2.8) and there is
good reason to doubt it. All Augustus' irregular assumptions
of consular office fall in his period of continuous tenure,
and were demanded, like Caesar's, by the necessities of warfare.
However, unlike Caesar (cf. *DJ* 76.2-3) Augustus tried not to
devalue the consulship or the other magistracies, at least once
the Civil War was over.

27.1-4   THE TRIUMVIRATE

The office created by Antony, Lepidus, and Augustus for themselves by the lex Pedia of 27th Nov. 43 B.C. was unique. Boards
of three were common for special purposes (e.g. the Gracchan
land commissioners), but had not adminstered the state since
the days of 'military tribunes with consular power' in the
fifth century. The formula *rei publicae constituendae* ('to
reconstitute the state'), with its clear implication that the
state had broken down, had been used by Sulla to define and
justify his new sort of dictatorship. It was ideally suited to
cloak autocratic power. Theoretically the three men possessed
no more than consular power (the dictatorship, and therefore
its powers, had been abolished in 44 B.C.), but they commanded
armies and were in fact a military junta. It is quite unclear
to what extent the normal institutions, such as elections and
the law courts, continued to function. The triumvirs certainly
overrode the people by appointing consuls for years ahead and
creating other magistrates wholesale; on the other hand we hear
of some contested elections and it is inconceivable that the
whole machinery of state suddenly required the exercise of
triumviral power in order to keep it functioning. (See Millar
1973.)

The lex Pedia conferred power until 31st Dec., 38 B.C. (*Fasti
Colotani* - E-J^3 p.32). This date passed without the triumvirs
having either laid down their office or taken any steps to
renew it, but no one was in a position to challenge them and
Antony and Augustus, meeting at Tarentum in the summer of
37 B.C., agreed to a retrospective renewal for another five
years from 1st Jan., 37, which it is hard to believe was not
ratified by the people, despite Appian's assertion (*BC* 5.95) to

the contrary. Thus the triumvirate expired on 31st Dec., 33 B.C..
Augustus laid down his title (RG 7.1), and after forcing the
Antonian members of the senate, including the two consuls, to
leave Italy, gave his position as leader of one party in a civil
war a bogus legality by organising the oath of personal loyalty
(see 17.2). Antony, more honest, continued to use the title as
well as the powers, as is proved by coins dated to his third
consulship of 31 B.C.; while Lepidus had already been stripped
of his office in 36 B.C. (see 16.3).

The proscriptions of late 43 B.C. were the most notorious act
of the triumvirs, and are described at length by Appian (BC
4.17ff.) and Dio (47.3ff.). They recalled the proscriptions
of Sulla, and arose from the same causes: the wish to stamp out
opposition and pay off old scores, and the need to obtain money
to pay the soldiery. Suetonius clearly draws on anti-Augustan
writings at this point, though he names no source apart from
the otherwise unknown Iulius Saturninus. The picture is dark;
but notice how Suetonius uses it to point up Augustus' later
magnanimity, in the case of Vinius Philopoemen, and even under-
cuts his own presentation by the frankly incredible detail of
Augustus putting out Q. Gallius' eyes with his own hands.

27.1 C. Toranium: Toranius is confirmed as C. Octavius' colleague in
   their aedileship (?64 B.C.) by Octavius' elogium (see 3 n.). Fatherless
   Roman children were required to have a male legal guardian (tutor) until
   they were 14 years old, and it was normal for a man to name his children's
   guardians in his will (cf. DJ 83.2). The reasons for Toranius' fall from
   grace are unknown, except that they existed already before 45 B.C., when he
   was apparently in exile on Corcyra (Cicero, ad Familiares 6.20 and 21).

27.2 Iulius Saturninus: not otherwise known.
T. Vinium Philopoemen ...:   the details are given by Dio 47.7.4-5.
   For an ex-slave to attain equestrian status was an exceptional honour (for
   Augustus' later atttitude cf. 44.1). When legal regulations were later
   laid down, in A.D. 23, no man was allowed to claim equestrian rank unless
   his father and grandfather had been freeborn (elder Pliny, NH 33.32).
   Philopoemen had incurred the death penalty by concealing his former master.
   Yet it was important for the fabric of Roman society that a freedman
   should be loyal to his patron, and the law treated him in some respects
   as though he were a son.

27.3 Pinarium ... Tedium Afrum: both otherwise unknown.

27.4 Q. Gallium: the episode belongs to late 43 or early 42 B.C. His
   brother M. Gallius, who served with Antony at Mutina (see 10-12), was
   also an opponent of Augustus; he died ca. 40-39 B.C., before Livia's
   marriage to Augustus, leaving the infant Tiberius as his heir and adoptive
   son! (Cicero, Philippics 13.26; Appian, BC 3.95; Tib. 6.3). Appian's
   version of Q. Gallius' fate agrees with that of Augustus given here by
   Suetonius, and conforms with Augustus' general policy in dealing with
   opponents of high social rank. Torture of free men (not to mention

putting out their eyes) was not permitted under Republican law and it seems
highly unlikely that Augustus, who needed all the popularity he could get
during these years, would have risked alienating the uncommitted by such
an act of illegal barbarism.

27.5 TRIBUNICIAN POWER

Augustus accepted tribunician power when he abdicated from the
consulship of 23 B.C. (*Fasti Capitol* E-J[3] p.36), and counted
his tribunician years from this date. Appian (*BC* 5.132) and
Orosius (6.18 and 34) say that he received the power in 36 B.C.,
Dio (49.15.6) that he was granted the inviolability (*sacrosanc-
titas*) of a tribune in 36 and the power (*potestas*) in 30 and
again in 23 B.C. (55.32.5). Various explanations have been
advanced of these contradictory data, but three things are quite
clear. First, so long as Augustus was triumvir or consul, i.e.
until 23 B.C. (excepting only the year 32, see 17.2), tribunician
powers afforded him no practical constitutional advantage; second,
he himself did not rate them important until he laid down the
consulship in 23 B.C.; and third, he himself distinguishes
(*RG* 10.1) between his sacrosanctity and his tribunician power,
although his language leaves it obscure whether they were conferred on him at the same time. The powers were:-

i)   *auxilium:* the right to intervene on behalf of citizens who
    were being unfairly treated by other magistrates.

ii)   *intercessio:* the right to veto the acts of other magistrates.

iii)   *coercitio:* the right to compel citizens to obey his orders,
    and impose sanctions if necessary.

iv)   legislative powers (*ius agendi cum populo* and *ius consulendi
    senatum*): the right to summon the people, address them,
    and put legislation to them, and the right to summon the
    senate and put motions to it.

A tribune could not exercise any of these powers outside the
city of Rome, though imperial holders of *tribunicia potestas* may
have done so (*Tib.* 11.3) and during his year of office he was
supposed to be available at all times to those whose interests
he guarded, the common people of Rome, and the doors of his house
were always open. The tribunate was a magistracy of the city of
Rome, and Rome alone. Its origins lay deep in the class struggles
of the fifth century B.C., and it symbolised above all the
successful defiance of an oppressive aristocracy by the ordinary
people of Rome. The opening sentence of *RG* informs us that
Augustus 'set free the state when it was labouring under the
tyranny of a faction'. The parallel is obvious, even if tendentious. As perpetual holder of tribunician power, Augustus
was perpetual watchdog of the interests of his clients, the
plebs of Rome. Watchdog against whom? In reality, no one,
except perhaps his own agents; but in the early days of the

principate, when there was a token measure of Republican freedom,
it may have seemed that there were potential enemies of the new
order and of the benefits it brought to Romulus' descendants.
It is clear that it was chiefly for symbolic reasons that
Augustus held the powers of a tribune, though there is a little
more to it than that. The Roman people did not like Augustus'
decision to cease holding an annual consulship (see 26 n.), and
it is possible that he though it politic to accept (or re-accept)
a grant of the powers of a tribune, never hitherto dissociated
from the office itself, in order to convince them that he would
still be able to represent their interests properly. Probably
the least important reason is that commonly advanced by con-
stitutionalists, that he needed the powers to compensate for
those that he lost by resigning the consulship. Formally, this
may be true (but note the hypothesis of Brunt 1962, 70ff. -
retracted Brunt and Moore 1967, 14 - that he may have held
imperium without the insignia from 23-19 B.C.). But in practice,
his personal authority, powers of patronage, and continued provincial commands were so powerful, even after 23 B.C. and before
he was formally invested with consular *imperium* (without the
office) in 19 B.C., that he did not stand in any need of the
personal right to convoke senate, put legislation to the people,
and so on. These were things he could do just as effectively
through others, and in fact did so throughout his reign (e.g.
the lex Papia Poppaea of A.D. 9, modifying his own earlier
marriage laws and undoubtedly representing his own wishes, but
brought in by the consuls of the year). For extended discussion,
see Last 1951.

Augustus had a colleague five times in tribunician power (*RG* 6):

Agrippa	18-14 B.C.	(Dio 54.12.4)
	13-(9) B.C.	(Dio 54.28.1)
Tiberius	6-1 B.C.	(Dio 55.9.4; *Tib.* 9.3)
A.D.	4-13	(Dio 55.13.1)
A.D.	13-23	(Dio 56.28.1)

Suetonius is thus in error in stating that all the grants were
for periods of a *lustrum* (five years), though they were certainly
for multiples of that period. (Amend *GG* to read 'for five-year
periods'.) For Augustus' use of the title tribune, see Lacey
1979.

PERPETUAL CENSORSHIP

By the words *morum legumque regimen perpetuum* Suetonius seems to
mean a kind of enhanced censorial power, extending beyond the
field of *mores* to that of *leges,* which had certainly never been
subject to normal censorial scrutiny. Although Dio (54.10.5)
gives Suetonius some support, Augustus himself says (*RG* 6) that,
when in 19, 18 and 11 B.C. the senate and people wished to
appoint him *curator legum et morum* (supervisor of laws and

morals), he 'would not accept any office inconsistent with Roman
tradition', and did what was needful at the time in virtue of
his tribunician power. Suetonius is consequently confused about
the legal basis of Augustus' three censuses, though he is correct
to state that Augustus did not hold the actual office of censor.
From RG 8 we learn that the first in 28 B.C. was carried out
with Agrippa as colleague, when they were actually consuls; and
that the second in 8 B.C., without a colleague, and the third in
A.D. 14, with Tiberius, were carried out by consular power.
Augustus received this power for life in 19 B.C. (Dio 54.10.5;
Jones 1960 ch.I); so in all three cases he could have acted in
virtue of an authority he already possessed. On the other hand
the Fasti of Venusia (E-J³ no.323) record that Augustus and
Agrippa held censorial power in 28 B.C., and Dio (54.10.5 and
54.30.1) says that he took it in 19 B.C., and again in 12 (or
11) B.C., for a five-year period.

We know that he was embarrassed about exercising the functions
of the censor in respect of his social equals (see 35), and he
may have felt that to take the office itself was inconsistent
with his political stance as first citizen and protector of the
people. As for the powers of the office, the censorship had
originally been created to assist the consuls; so it might be
said that consular power was not distinguishable from censorial
power. The chief duties of the censors (normally, under the
Republic, elected every five years, to hold office for 18 months)
were to compile up-to-date citizen rolls, let the state contracts
for taxation, supplies, and public works, and revise the membership of the two elite groups, the equestrian and senatorial
orders. This last duty involved not only promoting the worthy,
but demoting (or merely censuring) the unworthy, and to this end
they would take account of all aspects of a man's life, public
and private, moral and practical. A severe censorship, conducted
according to the moral criteria of a Cato, was theoretically
excellent, and accorded well with the view the Romans had of
the qualities which had made them a great nation; but it could
produce resentment, especially among a group as exclusive and
interrelated as the Roman aristocracy, and it is easy to see why
Augustus disliked this side of the censorship and did his best to
avoid it. A further point was that a censorship of high moral
tone could only plausibly be conducted by a man who himself
measured up to the standards he demanded of others, and Augustus
was notoriously open to attack on this ground (see 69-71). On
the other hand, a pair of censors derived credit from being able
to register a higher number of Roman citizens than previously
enumerated, and it is this aspect of censorial activity which
Augustus makes much of in RG, recording figures more than four
times higher than the last Republican count. It is noteworthy
that both Suetonius and Augustus himself clearly dissociate the
enumeration of the citizens from the revision of the roll of the
senate. See Jones 1960 ch.II; Astin 1963; and Brunt 1971, esp.
113ff.

28.1-2 CONTROL OF THE STATE

These sections sum up Suetonius' view of the nature of Augustus'
power: autocratic but benevolent. From a distance of 150 years
it seemed obvious that Augustus had always controlled the state,
and never yielded it up (cf. Dio 52.1). It is tempting to
identify the first of the two occasions on which Suetonius says
he thought of doing so with the constitutional normalisation
of 28-27 B.C., when Augustus claimed to have 'transferred the
republic from my power to the discretion of the senate and people
of Rome' (*RG* 34.1; cf. Dio 52.42 and 53.2; Velleius 2.89.3-4;
and, for a contrary view, Millar 1973). But that process culminated in the senate meetings of 13th and 16th Jan., 27 B.C.,
as a result of which Augustus received ten-year proconsular
commands over Egypt, Cyprus, and the three great military
provinces of Spain, Gaul, and Syria (see Lacey 1974). He also
retained the consulship (which is to say he did not wish to
stop the people electing him consul). This is the so-called
'first settlement', and since it remained the legal basis for
his power down to 23 B.C. it is very difficult to see how
Suetonius can have been thinking of this; for although Augustus
may stress the constitutional propriety of the way in which
his power was held after 27 B.C., Suetonius is interested not
in the propriety but in the reality of that power. Furthermore,
the phrase 'immediately after the death of Antony' more naturally
refers to 30-29 B.C. than to any later date. We know neither
the occasion, nor whether Suetonius is right.

As to the second occasion, Suetonius must be referring to
Augustus' critical illness of 23 B.C., when, according to Dio
53.30.1-2, he gave his fellow-consul Piso a statement of the
military forces and revenues of the empire (*rationarium imperii*)
and handed over his signet-ring to Agrippa (see 50 n.). In this
case it seems it was the imminence of death and the need to
attempt some kind of continuity in the management of the state
which forced this course upon him. As soon as he recovered, he
took steps to alter his constitutional position by resigning his
consulship (see 26), accepting perpetual tribunician power (27.5),
and having conferred upon himself a species of *imperium* (known
to later writers as *imperium proconsulare maius*, see Introduction
§24-25) which was formally superior to that of all other holders
in the provinces. He continued to hold the proconsular commands
which he had acquired in 27 B.C. (with adjustments as time went
on, see 47 n.), though he did for the most part administer them
through legates. Thus he was in a position to give direct orders
to all army commanders and provincial governors, whether or not
they had been appointed by himself; and he had also disembarrassed
himself of an annual consulship which, though prestigious, had
become somewhat anomalous because of his long absence from Rome
in 27-25 B.C., and had incidentally halved the number of consulships available to others whose support he needed and who like
their ancestors regarded that office as the crown of their
legitimate ambitions. This is the so-called 'second settlement'.

By it, Augustus freed himself from holding any of the actual
magistracies of the state, and strengthened the powers he possessed. He was granted consular power and insignia in 19 B.C.
(Dio 54.10.5), so that after this date he held *imperium* equal
to the consuls' in Rome and greater than anyone else's outside
the city. This grant was not essential to his position, which
was perfectly well safeguarded by his other powers and his
immense personal prestige and authority, but it conveniently
allowed him to exercise *imperium* in his own right in the city
and it gave him the formal prominence which the Roman people
evidently desired him to have. It also had the effect that
his edicts acquired the same consular authority as they had had
before 23 B.C. (on Augustus' *imperium*, see Last 1947, Chilver
1950, Jones 1960 ch.I, Grenade 1961, Brunt and Moore 1967).

It seems in fact unlikely that Augustus ever thought of becoming
a private citizen. The reasons Suetonius gives for his decision
can hardly be derived from anything said or written by Augustus,
but are a piece of historical analysis presented without the
qualifying 'doubtless' which would mark them in a modern writer.
The conclusion of the paragraph, with its impressive quotation,
leaves the reader in no doubt about the magnitude of Augustus'
achievement or its success.

The date of the edict from which Suetonius quotes is unknown,
but its tone and content would fit well in the years 17-16 B.C.,
when the *Ludi Saeculares* (see 31.4 n.) had inaugurated a new
age, and the coinage mentions public prayers and offerings made
to Jupiter Optimus Maximus for the health and safety of Augustus
quod per eum res publica in ampliore et tranquilliore statu est -
'because through him the state is in a better and more peaceful
condition' (*BMC Aug* pp.16-19). A magistrate's edict was the
formal communication to the Roman people of his views on a
matter of public importance. By a natural development imperial
edicts gradually came to have the force of law: cf. Augustus'
edict on the aqueduct of Venafrum, E-J[3] no.282, or the edict
on the torture of slaves of A.D. 8 (*Digest* 48.18.8).

28.3-31 SACRED AND PUBLIC BUILDINGS AND INSTITUTIONS IN ROME

28.3 For flood and fire, see 30. Augustus' boast that he found
Rome brick and left it marble is taken metaphorically by Dio
(56.30.4). Suetonius' literal interpretation is as good, provided that by 'brick' we understand not the familiar brick-faced
architecture of the empire, as yet undeveloped in Augustus' day,
but the unbaked brick which was the basic wall material of
ordinary buildings. There can be no doubt that the Augustan
period saw a transformation of the centre of Rome, both by the
creation of new monumental complexes like Augustus' own forum,
and by the rebuilding in more splendid materials of damaged
or dilapidated structures. Augustus mentions (*RG* 20.4) that
he restored 82 temples in 28 B.C. 'neglecting none that needed

restoration at the time' - doubtless using the spoils of his
victory over Cleopatra for the purpose.

29.1 Suetonius chooses to mention only three striking examples
of Augustus' building activity. For what Augustus himself
thought worth a mention, see *RG* 19-21, and for modern discussion,
Boethius and Ward-Perkins 1970, 183f. and Gros 1976. The best
guide to the individual remains is Coarelli 1974; for pictures,
Nash 1961; and for topography, Platner and Ashby 1929 and Lugli
Fontes.

The Forum of Augustus, lying to the east of its predecessors,
the Republican and Caesarian Fora, is named by the elder Pliny
(*NH* 36.102) as one of the three most beautiful buildings in
the world (the others being the Basilica Aemilia and Vespasian's
Temple of Peace). The materials, workmanship, and architecture
were all of the very highest quality, and the immediate model
was clearly the adjacent Forum of Caesar, completed by Augustus
after being left unfinished at the dictator's death. Vowed in
42 B.C., the temple itself was not completed and dedicated
until 2 B.C.; it stood at the end of the Forum (backing against
a massive stone wall which separated it from the crowded region
of the Subura just behind it) on a high podium, approached by
steps in front. It was flanked by porticoed hemicycles which
gave a cross axis and widened out the slightly restricted space
(cf. 56.2). The porticoes continued along the sides and across
the opposite end, and contained niches in which were set, with
appropriate inscriptions, two series of statues: one of members
of his own family, which traced its descent back to Aeneas, son
of Venus, and the other of those not so connected. According
to Suetonius, all were represented in triumphal garb (see 31.5),
and they were men who 'had raised the power of Rome from insig-
nificance to greatness', but we know of at least one, Ap. Claudius
Caecus, whose inscription has survived and makes no mention of
a triumph. While apparently subscribing to traditional Republican values of pride in family and respect for achievement,
particularly military, the whole complex underlined the extraordinary status of Augustus. See Rowell 1940; Dudley 1967,
123f.; Zanker 1968.

sortitiones iudicum: the jury for any particular trial was drawn by lot
    from a much larger panel constituted by the praetor from the *decuriae
    iudicum* (see 32.3 n.).

29.2 The Temple of Mars Ultor, the Avenger (i.e. of Caesar),
whose dedication might have served as an uncomfortable reminder
of the Civil Wars, was skilfully given another emphasis. By
placing in the temple the standards he had recovered from the
Parthians in 20 B.C., and enacting that henceforth similar
trophies were to be put here and not on the Capitol, Augustus
bought to the fore the idea of Mars as Avenger of the Roman people
on its enemies. And by the time the temple was eventually
dedicated, on 1st Aug., 2 B.C., the anniversary of the day on

which Augustus had entered Alexandria and thus in the words of
the official calendars 'freed the state from the most terrible
danger', memories of the original reason for its building would
have faded still further. The other functions or ceremonies
transferred here were clearly appropriate to Mars. The senate
had formerly met to consider a request for a triumph in the
temple of Bellona, which was (unlike Mars Ultor) outside the
pomoerium, so that the commander in question could attend the
meeting without having to lay down the *imperium* he required to
command his troops (Livy 28.9.5 and 28.38.2). It seems that
in the late Republic a special grant of *imperium* for the day
of the triumph could be made (e.g. Pompey's Pontic triumph was
held long after he had returned to Rome) and the need for the
senate to meet outside the ritual boundary of the city disap-
peared.

29.3 **The Temple of Apollo on the Palatine** has now been positively
identified with the foundations immediately adjacent to the
north-west corner of the palace of Domitian at the top of the
slope down to the Circus Maximus (Carettoni 1967). It was
begun on land which Augustus had acquired for an extension to
his own house in 36 B.C. (Velleius 2.81.3), and dedicated on
9th Oct., 28 B.C. The porticoed courtyard with the Greek and
Latin libraries lay to the south, at a lower level than the
platform on which the temple stood, and was balanced on the
north by the courtyard of Augustus' own house (see 72). The
meetings of the senate mentioned by Suetonius are attested in
two documents of the time (*Tabula Hebana* E-J[3] no. 94a, line 1;
Papyrus Oxyrhinchus 2435 = E-J[3] no. 379, line 32). The temple
contained statues of Apollo, Diana, and Latona by the great
fourth-century sculptors Scopas, Timotheus, and Cephesodotus
(elder Pliny, *NH* 36.5.24 - 25 and 32); the ivory panels of the
doors were worked with scenes of the god's wrath; and the
portico was embellished with statues of the Danaids and one of
Apollo himself singing to the lyre (Propertius 2.31.1-16). The
whole effect must have been magnificently impressive, with the
great platform thrusting forward and on top of it the temple
itself in gleaming Luna marble standing high above the other
buildings. Aside from the fact that the god had himself chosen
the site by striking it with lightning, sanctity was given to
the new temple by transferring to it the Sibylline books (31.1).
(The literary sources are numerous, see Lugli *Fontes* xix; and on
Augustus' 'special relationship' with Apollo, see Liebeschuetz
1979, 82f. and Gagé 1955, 523ff.)

haruspices: an order of priests concerned with the 'Etruscan discipline',
  in particular the interpretation of the signs afforded by the livers of
  sacrificial victims and by lightning. They might also be called upon by
  the senate to interpret prodigies.
decurias iudicum: the judicial panels, see 32.3 n.

The Temple of *Jupiter Tonans* (the Thunderer) has entirely dis-
appeared, but its importance is clear. It figures on the coinage

(*BMC Aug* nos. 362ff.) and was according to the elder Pliny (*NH*
36.50) one of the few buildings in Rome to be built of solid
marble, not just faced. If it is correctly placed by Gros
1976, 97-100, it stood on the west edge of the *area Capitolina*
near the head of the steps which led up from the Forum Holitorium.
The coins show it as hexastyle but given the conventions of Roman
numismatic representations this is no proof that it was so. It
was not as big as the Palatine Temple of Apollo (*ca*. 19.5 x
35.5m. to *ca*. 22 x 40m.) and both were smaller than the great
octastyle temple of Mars Ultor (*ca*. 35.5 x 43m., excluding that
portion of the podium which lay in front of the porch columns).
It was dedicated on 1st Sept., 22 B.C. and was thus completed
fairly quickly; Augustus' narrow escape from lightning must have
occurred in either 26 or 25 B.C.

The *Porticus Gai et Luci* seems to have been a kind of loggia
connecting the *Basilica Aemilia* (itself restored in 14 B.C.)
with the temple of Divus Julius, and forming a dignified entrance
to that corner of the Republican forum (see Gros 1976, pl.IX-X).

The *Basilica Gai et Luci* was the name Augustus intended for his
rebuilding of the *Basilica Julia* after it had been destroyed
by fire. It was still incomplete when he last revised the text
of *RG* 20.3 and Dio (56.27.5) may be wrong in ascribing its dedication to A.D. 12. But these are the only three passages which
associate it with the names of Augustus' grandsons, and to the
Romans it remained the *Basilica Julia*.

The *Porticus Liviae* was built on the Esquiline, on a site once
owned by Vedius Pollio, a man whose cruelty and extravagance
were so notorious that when he died in 15 B.C. and left his
property to Augustus, the emperor pulled down the house and
constructed a fine colonnaded square (Dio 54.23.6; Ovid, *Fasti*
6.639-648). Its plan is preserved on a fragment of the Severan
marble plan of Rome. It was dedicated in 7 B.C. (Dio 55.8.2;
cf. Strabo 5.236).

The *Porticus Octaviae,* here associated by Suetonius with
Augustus' sister, is to be identified with the portico so
labelled on the Severan marble plan, which ran around the temples
of Jupiter Stator and Juno Regina next to the *Circus Flaminius*.
It was a replacement or reworking, some time after 27 B.C., of
a portico of Metellus which existed from 146 B.C. in the same
area (Velleius 1.11). It is easily confused (e.g. by Dio
49.43.8) with the nearby Portico of Octavius (*Porticus Octavia*
or *Octavi*) mentioned by Augustus (*RG* 19.1), which was erected
in 167 and reconstructed by Augustus in 33 B.C.

The *Theatrum Marcelli,* lying between the Capitol and the river
opposite the island in the Tiber, was both a memorial of
Augustus' nephew Marcellus, who died in 23 B.C. (see 65 and
66), and a realisation of a project of Julius Caesar's. It was
vell advanced by 17 B.C. and was dedicated probably in 13 B.C.

(Dio 54.26.1) rather than 11 B.C. (elder Pliny, *NH* 8.65). A
large part of the semi-circular, arcaded, facade of the cavea
still exists, with modern apartments built around and on top of
it. Dramatic spectacles (more spectacle than drama, if Horace
is to be believed) were an important part of life in the capital,
but in the Republic permanent theatres had been banned. This
was why the first stone theatre, that of Pompey erected in 55-
52 B.C., took the form of a semi-circular flight of steps leading
up to a temple which stood high at the back. The theatres of
Marcellus and Balbus (see 29.5 n.) were a notable addition to
the amenities of the capital, and needed to pretend to no such
religious connection.

29.5 The structures Suetonius mentions in this section were
certainly erected from the spoils of victory (*ex manibiis,* cf.
E-J[3] no.187 = *ILS* 886). Their donors were all men who had
triumphed, and although there was no legal compulsion on a
general to use his spoils for the public benefit, political considerations had made this desirable and customary (see Shatzman
1972). The buildings may be tabulated as follows:-

Building	Location	Date of Dedication	Builder and date of consulship	Date of Triumph
Temple of Hercules Musarum (reconstructed)	North of Circus Flaminius	?	L. Marcius Philippus (38 B.C.)	33 B.C.
Temple of Diana (reconstructed)	Aventine	?	L. Cornificius (35 B.C.)	33 B.C.
Atrium Libertatis (census offices reconstructed, with added library)	Near Forum of Caesar	Before 28 B.C.	C. Asinius Pollio (40 B.C.)	39 or 38 B.C.
Temple of Saturn (reconstructed)	Republican Forum	?	L. Munatius Plancus (42 B.C.)	43 B.C.
Theatre of Balbus	North of Theatre of Marcellus	13 B.C.	L. Cornelius Balbus (40 B.C.)	19 B.C.
Amphitheatre of Taurus	Near Theatre of Balbus	29 B.C.	T. Statilius Taurus (37, 26 B.C.)	34 B.C.

With the exception of Balbus' theatre, and possibly Pollio's
Atrium Libertatis and Plancus' Temple of Saturn, the buildings

form part of the massive programme of urban renewal inaugurated
by Agrippa's aedileship of 33 B.C., which reached a climax in
Augustus' own restorations (together with the completion of the
Palatine Temple of Apollo) of 28 B.C. Only the Temple of Saturn
can still be seen, though the Temple of Hercules and the Theatre
of Balbus appear on fragments of the marble plan.

M. Agrippa never accepted a triumph; but his position as Augustus'
lieutenant is accurately reflected by the number of public works
for which he was responsible. His assumption of the relatively
lowly office of aedile in 33 B.C. was a striking way of demonstrating to the people of Rome that the Augustan party cared
for their physical well-being. As aedile he constructed a new
aqueduct (the Julia), added to and mended others, repaired
public buildings and streets, cleaned out the sewers, and installed ornamental fountains - in effect carrying out a huge
programme of public sanitation. Between 33 and his death in
12 B.C. he was responsible, amongst other things, for his
Pantheon (totally obliterated by the present Hadrianic rotunda),
the completion of the *Saepta Julia* (the voting enclosures), a
portico, baths, an ornamental lake, and another aqueduct (the
Virgo, still supplying the Trevi fountain). All these were on
the Campus Martius. He also built a bridge over the Tiber and
a set of granaries between the Palatine and the Vicus Tuscus.
When he died he bequeathed to the Roman people his baths and
gardens, lying between the river and the public part of the
Campus Martius which he had done so much to adorn, together with
an endowment to maintain them free of charge.

(On sections 29.4-5, see esp. Shipley 1931.)

30   THE ADMINISTRATION OF THE CITY

The elder Pliny (*NH* 3.66) tells us there were 14 regions and
265 *vici* (wards). These were instituted by 7 B.C. at the latest,
and the administration here described by Suetonius replaced the
former oversight of the city by the aediles. The urban areas
had increased enormously during the last years of the Republic
(see Quilici 1974, who places the extension of the city out
along the main highways at 5-7 km. from the centre) and maps
which show the Augustan regions bounded by the Aurelian walls
of *ca*. 273 A.D. are misleading. The praetors, aediles, and
tribunes (a total of 24 for most of the period) were those who
drew lots for the regions (Dio 55.8.7). The *vicomagistri*, four
per *vicus*, were predominantly freedmen, and they had control of
the public slaves who had earlier been at the disposal of the
aediles for fire-fighting purposes, until the institution in
A.D. 6 of the regular system of *vigiles* (nightwatchmen and
police) in seven cohorts of freedmen, under the command of the
urban prefect (see 37, Dio 55.26.4-5; Baillie Reynolds 1926).
After A.D. 6 the chief function of the *vicomagistri* was to give
individual *vici* a sense of identity, and to supervise the cult

of the Lares Compitales and the Genius of the emperor (see 31.4).
The office also allowed freedmen a niche in public life, from
most aspects of which they were debarred by statute. (See
Niebling 1956.)

30.1 alveum Tiberis: for the Tiber commissioners, see 37 n. A (iv).
Flaminia via: the inscription on the arch of Augustus at Rimini of 27 B.C.
  commemorates Augustus' restoration of this road, along with that of others
  not named, 'at his prompting and expense' E-J[3] no.286 = ILS 84).
triumphalibus viris: two of these were C. Calvisius Sabinus (consul
  39, triumphed 28 B.C.) and M. Valerius Messalla Corvinus (consul 31,
  triumphed 27 B.C.), who each refurbished part of the Via Latina (CIL
  10.6895; Tib. 1.7.57). On manubiali pecunia (money derived from booty),
  see 29.5 n. and Shatzman 1972.
aedes sacras: on the temples, see 28.3 n.; the remarkable single deposit
  of gold, jewels, and pearls in the temple of Capitoline Jupiter was surely
  made after Augustus' Egyptian triumph of 29 B.C. (cf. Dio 51.22.3), though
  Suetonius seems to have exaggerated the sum: 16,000 lbs. of gold = 67
  million HS, which with the 50 million HS of the gems and pearls exceeds
  on its own the 100 million HS which Augustus says (RG 21.2) was the total
  of his gifts to several temples, including this one.

31   This chapter contains a number of items related to the
themes of the preceding two, without being organically connected
to them: religious institutions, the calendar, and honours for
great men of the past. The quotation from an edict of Augustus',
at the end of the chapter, serves like the similar quotation at
28.2 to round off this sub-section.

31.1 Pontificatum Maximum: Lepidus had managed, as the price for his
  support of Antony in the confusion after the murder of Caesar, to have
  himself made Pontifex Maximus - the most prestigious priestly office in
  the state. After his downfall in 36 B.C. (see 16.4) he retained the office,
  probably because there was neither any real power attached to it, nor any
  mechanism whereby Augustus could decently strip him of it. Augustus took
  credit (RG 10.2) for this forbearance, and was duly offered the post by
  the people when Lepidus died in 12 B.C. Dio relates (44.5.3) that one of
  the honours conferred on Caesar in 44 B.C. was that any son of his should
  become Pontifex Maximus.
fatidicorum librorum ... Sibyllinos: the Sibylline books proper had
  been burnt in the fire which destroyed the Capitoline temple in 83 B.C.,
  and replaced by another collection of oracles gathered by a special
  commission. It is evident that a large number of 'prophecies' circulated
  under this and other names, many capable of bearing a political interpretation. It was important for Augustus to control them, because the
  people seem to have taken them seriously and the state religion provided
  for consultation of the Sibylline books under certain cirumstances.
  Augustus had the Sibylline books recopied on the grounds that they were
  becoming illegible, which afforded a good opportunity for the editorial
  work here described (cf. Dio 54.17.2). They were in the charge of the
  priestly college of quindecimviri sacris faciundis, who were bound to keep
  their contents secret.

31.2 annum a divo Iulio ordinatum ...: the Julian calendar, introduced in 45 B.C., had fallen into error through the insertion of a leap
year every three instead of every four years (Macrobius, *Saturnalia* 1.14.13-
15), and was corrected in 8 B.C. Macrobius also preserves (1.12.35 = E-J³
no. 37) the text of the decree of that year which changed the name of the
month Sextilis to Augustus: it is more accurate than Suetonius in placing
only one victory in the month, that of Alexandria (1st Aug.); Actium and
Naulochus fell on 2nd Sept. and 3rd Sept.

31.3 THE PRIESTHOODS

A priesthood was held for life and was amongst the highest
honours of state. Augustus himself not only belonged to the
four major priestly colleges (*pontifices, augures, quindecimviri sacris faciundis*, and *septemviri epulonum*) but was also
a *sodalis Titius*, a *frater Arvalis*, and a *fetialis* (*RG* 7.3 and
see Brunt and Moore, *ad loc.*). He seems to have been responsible
for the revival of the defunct Arval brethren some time before
21 B.C.; as *fetialis* he participated in the declaration of war
against Cleopatra; and as *quindecimvir* he took a leading part
in the celebration of his *Ludi Saeculares* in 17 B.C. (*ILS* 5050 =
LR II 57-61). This encouragement of the priestly colleges was
part of his programme to revive the state religion. He was permitted by a senatorial decree of 29 B.C. (Dio 51.20.3) to choose
supernumerary priests; it is the view of Lewis 1955 that the
first three colleges (nominal strength 15) normally had about
25 members, and the *septem viri* about 10. Thus Augustus widened
the circle of honour without significantly devaluing it.

As to the Vestal Virgins, it appears that ritual virginity and
honoured seclusion for their daughters were not as attractive
to the aristocracy as they had once been. When one of the
Vestals died, a girl of between six and ten was chosen to take
her place, normally from amongst the best families in Rome.
In A.D. 5 even daughters of freedmen were declared eligible,
though none were actually chosen (Dio 55.22.5). Augustus
increased the Vestals' material comforts (*commoda*) by resigning
to them the official residence of the Pontifex Maximus and by
giving them estates at Lanuvium (*Liber Coloniarum* I p.235 Blume).

31.4 augurium salutis: the 'Augury for Safety' was a ceremony to
  determine whether it was propitious for the consuls to offer a prayer
  for the safety of the state. It could only be performed in time of peace.
  We know of no instances of it between 63 and 29 B.C., and since Tacitus
  says (*Ann.* 12.23.3) that Claudius' performance of it in A.D. 47 was the
  first for 75 years, 28 B.C. must have been the last Augustan occasion.
Diale Flaminium: the *Flamen Dialis* was the priest of Jupiter and a
  member of the college of pontifices, but was subject to so many taboos
  (e.g. he could not sleep out of his own bed for more than three con-
  secutive nights, and could not look on a dead body) that the office had
  been vacant since the death of L. Cornelius Merula in 87 B.C. It is
  likely that Ser. Cornelius Lentulus Maluginensis (consul A.D. 10) was the

holder of the office from its restoration in 11 B.C. (Dio 54.36.1; Lewis
1955, 30.)

sacrum Lupercale: the *Lupercalia*, a festival (15th Feb.) centring on
the Palatine cave of Lupercus (an old Italian fertility god), and its
priests the *Luperci* were flourishing at the end of the Republic. The
celebration of 44 B.C. is notorious for the attempt of Antony, clad only
in the ritual goatskin in which the *Luperci* ran around the Palatine, to
crown Caesar; it was probably as a result of this that the senate withdrew
funds from the *Luperci* with which Caesar had favoured them (Cicero,
Philippics 13.31). Augustus' action is then to be seen as a re-enactment
of Caesarian policy.

Ludos Saeculares: Augustus' *Ludi Saeculares* were intended to inaugurate
a new age in which proper standards of religious and moral behaviour would
be restored and the gods would once again look upon Rome with favour after
the long years of civil war and neglect of ancient values (see Liebeschuetz
1979, 90f.). The celebrations took place on 1st-3rd June, 17 B.C., with
prayers and sacrifices by night to the Fates, Eilithyia (Hekate), and
Terra Mater, and by day to Jupiter, Juno, and Apollo and Diana (*ILS* 5050
= *LR* II 57-61). Horace wrote his *Carmen Saeculare* to accompany the last.
The sole resemblance between these ceremonies and their only two certainly
historical precursors, those of 249 and 146 B.C., is in the night-time
sacrifice to chthonic deities. This took place beside the Tiber at the
spot known as the Tarentum, because it was from that city that the wholly
Greek rite of a special sacrifice to Dis and Proserpina came - as a result
of consultation of the Sibylline books in a dark moment of the First Punic
War. The alleged celebrations of 348 and 509 B.C. are certainly a fiction
of the annalistic historians of the first century B.C., as is the whole
idea of inaugurating a new *saeculum* (100 or 110 years); there is no suggestion in any of our very full sources for 49-46 B.C. that *Ludi Saeculares*
were due then. In short, it seems that Augustus invented a large part of
the ceremonies for his celebration, and grafted them on to a notion of
the *saeculum* only recently developed (perhaps by the learned antiquary
Varro), to produce a splendid piece of bogus archaism - celebrated with
great solemnity, commemorated on the coinage of the state, and designed
to stress the continuing greatness of Rome as the new age dawned. (See
Weiss 1973.)

Compitalicios ... Compitales Lares: the *Compitalia* was an ancient
festival celebrated at *compita* (road junctions). With the urbanisation of
Rome the festival, which became fixed at 3rd and 4th Jan., fell under the
charge of local associations presided over by *vicomagistri* (see 30.1 n.).
These associations (*collegia*) were closed down by Caesar on account of
their political activities, but revived by Augustus in 7 B.C. as a means
of giving the reorganised *vici* a cult focus. The *Compitalia,* at which
the youths of the street participated in games under the direction of the
vicomagistri, had always been particularly celebrated by slaves and freedmen, and this continued to be true. The Augustan *vicomagistri* were almost
always freedmen, so this important social group, legally debarred from
almost all office and honour, gained a means of acquiring local status
and participating in the cult life of the state. By associating his *Genius*
(see 52 n.) with the *Lares Compitales* (so that the Lares came to be known
as the *Lares Augusti*) Augustus in effect transformed the cult into a disguised expression of emperor-worship on the part of the least privileged
sections of the urban population. The crowning of the Lares with flowers

was probably on 1st May and 1st Aug. (Ovid, *Fasti* 5.129 and 147; E-J[3] no.139 = *ILS* 3612); consequently there was some celebration of the cult, and thus of the emperor's divinity, approximately every four months (see further Ryberg 1955, 53f.; Kunckel 1974, 22f.; Liebeschuetz 1979, 70f.).

31.5 opera ... manentibus titulis: Suetonius means temples and other public buildings. Augustus himself cites one instance, that of the *Porticus Octavia* (*RG* 19.1).

statuas: see 29.1 n.

principes: 'leaders' in the plural is a pleasing echo of the vocabulary of Republican politics. The leading men might *be* emperors, but that was not what Augustus wished to stress here: the message of his edict is that the leaders of Rome should continue to increase the power and dominion of Rome. Its spirit is that of the prayer which Valerius Maximus (4.1.10) says the censors made down to 142 B.C., that the gods should 'expand and prosper the affairs of the Roman people' (*populi Romani res meliores amplioresque facerent*).

curia in qua C. Caesar fuerat occisus: Caesar was murdered in a hall whose foundations can still be seen on the west side of the Largo Argentina. It opened off the portico behind Pompey's theatre. Why Augustus moved the statue is unknown. Perhaps he closed or altered the hall in an attempt to break its associations with the murder.

32-34 These chapters are concerned with Augustus' achievements in the field of law and order, and follow on naturally after the ethical note struck in 31.5. The main theme of Suetonius' presentation is that Augustus was both fair and strict, and that his measures were motivated by a proper concern for an orderly and decent society.

32.1 SUPPRESSION OF CRIME

We first hear of detachments (*stationes*) of soldiers stationed about Italy in 36 B.C., when Augustus, after his defeat of Sex. Pompeius, was able to make Italy safe from the highwaymen (*grassatores*) who had flourished in the civil wars. Appian (*BC* 5.132) makes these troops the precursors of the *vigiles* (or urban cohorts?), so perhaps it was from these units that the regular detachments were later drawn. In spite of these measures, the menace of highway robbery was a continuing one. Tiberius had to increase the number of military pickets in his principate (*Tib.* 37.1).

ergastula: barracks in which the agricultural salves of large land-owners (*possessores*) were confined when they were not working in the fields. In his quaestorship or immediately after it Tiberius was charged by Augustus with the task of investigating these establishments (23 or 22 B.C. - *Tib.* 8) to see if free men or other men's slaves were illegally detained in them.

collegia: associations, generally formed for the purposes of trade, burial, or worship, were a notable feature of Roman life (see 34.4 n. on *Compital-*

icios; and esp. McMullen 1974, 73f.). They had elected officers, respectable aims, limited membership, and legal status. But in the late Republic
they came to be used as a covert means of mobilising a political force,
and this provoked attempts to control them, notably a *lex Iulia* of Caesar's;
Suetonius' words here suggest that the process had gone further and that
the *collegia* had actually become vehicles for organised crime. Dio (54.2.3)
places in 22 B.C. Augustus' regulation of the *collegia*. Apparently he
enforced Caesar's law banning all except long-standing *collegia*, but
relaxed its provisions to allow *bona fide* new associations to come into
being subject to senatorial approval (*ILS* 4966; de Robertis 1938, 171f.;
Treggiari 1969, 169f.).

32.2 tabulas ... debitorum: in 28 B.C. Augustus cancelled all debts
to the treasury incurred before Actium, except those concerned with buildings (Dio 53.2.3). Because there was no public prosecutor at Rome it
was open to any individual to prosecute those in breach of the law - a
process which was encouraged by the provision of statutory rewards for
successful prosecution. Thus even if the treasury officials did not take
any magisterial action to recover monies owed, the debtor was still liable
to be prosecuted (cf. Tacitus, *Ann.* 13.23.3-4).
diutinorum reorum ... sordibus: it was the custom for an accused man
to put on dirty clothes and remain unshaved and unkempt (to excite pity
and support) as soon as a charge was formally laid, regardless of how long
ahead the trial might be. The vindictive practice of accusing someone, so
that he became *reus,* and then delaying bringing the action was not stamped
out by Augustus, as a speech of Claudius to the senate reveals (Smallwood
1967, no.367 = *FIRA* 1.44).
maleficium negotiumve impunitate vel mora: take *maleficium* with
impunitate and *negotium* with *mora* - 'lest a crime should slip away unpunished
or a business suit collapse from delay'. Honorific holidays had been added
to the calendar at a prodigal rate in the late Republican and triumviral
periods.

32.3 THE JUDICIAL PANELS (*DECURIAE*)

The *lex Aurelia* of 70 B.C. had set up three panels of jurors for
the standing courts. Juries were made up of jurors drawn equally
from the three panels, one of senators, one of *equites,* and one
of *tribuni aerarii.* The last, which appears in practice to have
comprised an inferior sort of *equites,* was abolished by Caesar.
Antony reconstituted it (Cicero, *Philippics* 1.19 and 5.12) but
the details are unclear and it is generally presumed that the
three panels to which Suetonius here refers consisted of one of
senators and two of *equites* (cf. elder Pliny, *NH* 33.29-30 with
Frontinus, *de Aquis* 101 = E-J[3] no.278 A21). The minimum property
qualification of an *eques* was 400,000 HS, and of a senator 1
million HS (see 41.1 n.). The reduction in the age qualification
for jurors from 30 to 25 matches a similar reduction for the
quaestorship and hence for the start of a senatorial career. It
is not apparent how the system of years of duty mentioned by
Suetonius worked in practice: perhaps he has made a mistake,
and what actually happened was that a quarter of each panel was

excused every year.

iudices a vicesimo quinto aetatis anno: since we know 30 to have been the minimum age for jury service in the Republic (*lex repetundarum = FIRA* I no.7, line 13, translated in *HRFC* I p.123) the correct figure here must be 25. The corruption XXV to XXX would be very easy. (Amend *GG* to read 'from 30 to 25 years'.)

33   THE IMPERIAL JURISDICTION

The imperial jurisdiction grew up because Augustus was the most powerful man in the state and it was inevitable that appeal would be made to him by those who were dissatisfied with their treatment at the hands of other organs of the law.   None the less, one can construct a theoretical framework to accommodate his jurisdiction:

i)   Any *legatus* of his who governed a province, and so administered the law, was his deputy; appeal therefore lay from deputy to principal.   Such appeals must have been numerous, or he would not have had to delegate them to senior men, as Suetonius tells us at the end of the chapter.   On appeal under the empire, see Garnsey 1966.

ii)   From 27-23 B.C., and after 19 B.C., Augustus held *consulare imperium.*   This allowed him to exercise the normally dormant judicial powers of the consul and intervene on appeal in cases which did not come from the inappellable standing courts (*quaestiones*).   We also find under Augustus the beginnings of the jurisdiction of the senate (Kunkel 1969).   Since the consuls presided Augustus too could preside or sit with them (cf. Dio 55.34.1); see further 33.3 n.

iii)   After 23 B.C. Augustus also possessed *imperium proconsulare maius,* valid all over the empire (see 47 n.), and cases came to him from non-imperial provinces which ought in strict theory to have been taken by the *quaestiones* or dealt with by local law (e.g. the murder case from Cnidos, which was an independent city, E-J[3] no. 312; see Sherk 1969, 343f.)

iv)   He also had a complete military jurisdiction, based on his authority over all army commanders (created by his *imperium maius*) and on the fact that all soldiers swore an annual oath of loyalty to him.

v)   Like all Roman *patresfamiliae* (heads of families), he had power of life and death over those who were legally in his *potestas* - very roughly, his children, freedmen, and slaves (see Crook 1967, ch.4).   It appears to be in virtue of this power that he relegated his daughter and granddaughter to islands (see 65).

vi) The main problem is by what right Augustus heard cases for which inappellable standing courts existed. The present chapter is the chief evidence for this, *maiestas* cases excepted. Kelly 1957 argues that *ius dixit* here means no more than that Augustus was an ordinary member of the jury or at most presiding in place of the praetor (cf. Dio 55.34.1); but this contradicts not only the natural meaning of the Latin but the impression given by the whole chapter that Suetonius is describing trials by the free inquisitorial procedure known as *cognitio extra ordinem* which was the regular form for trials before the emperor. Note especially Augustus' readiness to alter normal procedure, and the phrase *simul cognoscentibus* which hardly suggests the jury of a regular court. (One would expect to read *simul iudicantibus*) Another possible escape route from the conclusion that Augustus encroached upon the jurisdiction of the standing courts is to place these two episodes in the provinces during the princeps' lengthy absences from Rome (cf. 51.2 n.). As to *maiestas*, it is generally accepted, in the light of such passages as Tacitus, *Ann.* 1.72.4 (Augustus was the first to take cases of libel under the law of *maiestas*) and Cyrene Edict II (E-J[3] no.311) line 45 (the ground for sending the offenders to Rome was that they were alleged to have knowledge concerning the emperor's safety and the state) that Augustus did exercise a primary jurisdiction in this politically sensitive matter. However, it is disputed whether the *lex Iulia Maiestatis* was a law of Augustus' or Caesar's (see Allison and Cloud 1962). If the former, it may have provided for trial by imperial *cognitio;* if the latter, it cannot have, and we are faced with a clear instance of encroachment on the *quaestio.* How this may have taken place is extremely obscure: some posit a specific law (or mandate), some derive the competence from Augustus' tribunician power and privileges, and some deny that any formal legal basis for it existed at all. All one can safely say is that by the end of Augustus' reign the emperor, whether *de facto* or *de iure*, had acquired the right to try in his own court (i.e. by *cognitio*) cases which could previously only have gone to the standing courts. We do not know the criteria for selection of these cases, nor whether they were restricted to *maiestas,* nor how exceptional they were. But the development was inevitable, given Augustus' position, and had immense consequences. See Jones 1960, ch.V; Bauman 1967; Bleicken 1962.

vii) It seems clear that Augustus was also prepared to exercise a primary jurisdiction in civil cases, when litigants approached him directly and were able to persuade him that they had a case (97.3 below; *Digest* 8.3.35; Valerius Maximus 7.7.3 and 4). The origin of this jurisdiction is as mysterious as that of (vi) above, but must, like it, derive from the fact that Augustus was the most powerful man in the state and as a holder of *imperium* had the basic power to deliver and enforce judgments (see Introduction §20-25 and Millar 1977, 465ff. and 528ff.).

33.1 ne culleo insueretur: the apparently archaic penalty of being
sewn up in a sack and drowned had first been used to punish *parricidium*
(murder of close relatives) in 102 B.C. (Livy, *Periochae* 68), and was
still prescribed under the *lex Pompeia de parricidiis* (see Lintott 1968,
37f.)

33.3 appellationes ... urbanorum ... litigatorum praetori
delegabat urbano: these appeals from litigants at Rome ('Roman
citizens' in *GG* is misleading) may have been either from the court of the
urban prefect, who exercised a summary criminal jurisdiction in and around
Rome, or more probably from the ordinary civil processes administered by
the urban praetor. In either case Augustus' tribunician and/or consular
powers gave him the right to override the magistrate. By sending these
appeals to the urban praetor, Augustus was directing them, or at least
the civil cases among them, back to the magistrate against whom the appeal
was being made. If the text is right, what Augustus did was effectively
to order a re-trial; but Lipsius, followed in more recent times by Savigny,
proposed to read *praefecto* for *praetori*. This correction would provide a
neat basis for the later well-attested jurisdiction of the urban prefect,
and would mean that this class of appeal was referred, like those from
the provinces, to a consular. But there is no MS support for the correction, and there remains the problem of why the other class of appeal, from
the prefect himself, should have been directed back to him - for the urban
prefect did not have a vast legal machine at his disposal and could not
easily arrange, like the urban praetor, for a genuinely new trial to take
place. If the case had criminal aspects, the praetor could send it to
the appropriate *quaestio* presided over by one of his colleagues (cf.
younger Pliny, *Epp.* 5.1.7); if civil, he could revise his *formula* and
choose a different *iudex* (or, in the centumviral court, different jurors).
It seems best to retain the MS reading. On the urban prefect, see 37 n.C.
consularibus viris: the subjunctive *praeposuisset* indicates that
consulars were appointed as the need arose, not on a regular basis. These
appeals are 'from the provinces', i.e. from the decisions of the provincial
governor, not 'from foreigners' (*GG*). Many Roman citizens lived or did
business in the provinces and it was only they who had the right of appeal
to the emperor, if they could reach him: there survives the record of a
murder case (E-J[3] no.312; Sherk 1969, no.67; Lewis 1974, 10) involving
only citizens of the 'free' state of Cnidos, which was brought to Augustus
in Rome in 6 B.C. and was referred by him for investigation to Asinius
Gallus (consul 8 B.C.)

34   THE LEGISLATION OF AUGUSTUS

There were eleven laws under which *quaestiones* (standing courts)
operated in the later empire; at least six of them are known
to have been revising or consolidating statutes, while eight
bear the name *Iulia* (*Digest* 48.1.1). The partition of these
between Caesar and Augustus (Tiberius being generally discounted)
is disputed, especially as both men were responsible for consolidating legislation. For the *new* legislation of Augustus,
Suetonius' list may be complete: There is only one certainly
Augustan *lex Iulia* not mentioned here, his *lex iudiciaria*

(actually two laws, one dealing with private courts, the other
with public; cf. Gaius 4.30), and what we know of its provisions
suggests that it was an administrative statute regulating procedure, the legal calendar, and so on, so that Suetonius may
well not have regarded it an essentially new.

34.1 sumptuariam: the Romans had a long history of attempts to regulate
ostentatious hospitality: for the latest, see *DJ* 43.2. Augustus' law provided for a normal limit on expenditure of 200 HS per guest, rising to
300 HS on the Kalends, Nones, Ides and certain other days, and to 1,000 HS
for weddings and similar parties (Gellius, *NA* 2.24.14). Like all its predecessors, it became a dead letter and does not figure in the Digest (cf.
Tacitus, *Ann.* 3.54).

de adulteriis et de pudicitia: this apparent pair of laws must be
the statute elsewhere known simply as the *lex Iulia de adulteriis;* the
reason may be that *adulterium* was a crime which could only be committed
with a married woman, while the law created a new and separate offence
called *stuprum* (for which *pudicitia* could be a polite circumlocution) to
cover virtually all other sorts of irregular sexual connection. Perhaps
one should read *de adulteriis et* [*de*] *pudicitia* or treat the whole group
et de pudicitia as a gloss.

The law itself was an attempt to tighten up the very free moral standards of late Republican and early Augustan Rome, and was passed in 18 or
17 B.C. along with the *lex de maritandis ordinibus* (below) as part of the
general programme marking the introduction of the new *saeculum* (Horace,
Carmen Saeculare 16-20); n. on *Ludos Saeculares* 31.4). The main source
is *Digest* 48.5; the terms of the law were briefly as follows:-

(a)   It made adultery a public offence; on conviction both parties
were relegated to different islands for life. The man lost half of
his property (to the treasury), the woman a third of her property
(to the treasury) and half her dowry (to her husband).

(b)   It set up a procedure requiring divorce in set form before the
husband, or anyone else, could prosecute, and all but abolished the
archaic right of husband or wife's father to kill one or both of the
guilty parties if they were caught *in flagranti*.

(c)   A case had to be brought within six months in the new *quaestio
de adulteriis* set up for the purpose.

(d)   It created a new and equal crime of *stuprum* covering liasions
not qualifying as *adulterium*, i.e. between a man (married or unmarried)
and a free widow, unmarried woman, or boy - unless registered as a
prostitute or concubine

The penalties prescribed make it certain that the law was directed only
at the wealthy classes, but it represented a massive intrusion into
private life and offered a fertile field to professional informers. Its
effect may be seen in the virtual drying up after 17 B.C. of Roman elegiac
and amatory poetry - whose theme is always a relationship which the law
had now made criminal; but whether it made the gilded society of Rome more
moral, as opposed to more cautious, is doubtful. See further Brunt
1971, 558f.

de ambitu: *ambitus,* essentially, was any attempt to procure one's election
to office by irregular means of winning support (notably electoral bribery).
It was the target of a number of laws in the late Republic, the most recent
being the *lex Pompeia* of 52 B.C. (Asconius 31 and 34). Tacitus (*Ann.* 15.20)

speaks of *leges Iulias,* which may be ascribed to 18 and 8 B.C. (Dio 54.16.1 and 55.5.3). The former penalised offenders by barring them from office for five years, the second required a cash deposit from candidates before the elections, to be forfeited in case of infringements. The disturbances which preceded the earlier law, in 22-19 B.C., are evidence that political life was vigorous for at least ten years of Augustus' principate; by 8 B.C. it was the honour rather than the political importance of the office which was attractive.

de maritandis ordinibus: for date and context, see on *de adulteriis* above. That law operated negatively, this one positively, to encourage marriage and the begetting of children. At the census, a Roman affirmed that he had a wife (if he did) for the purpose of getting children, and the censors were traditionally concerned with increasing the number of citizens. Augustus perceived (rightly or wrongly) that among the upper classes there were more men than women (Dio 54.16.2), and it was at the wealthy that most of the inducements of the law were aimed. The original law (*lex Iulia*) was tempered in A.D. 9 by the *lex Papia Poppaea.* The two laws are treated as one by the jurists, which mades it difficult to separate their provisions with certainty. Suetonius' account points to a revision (perhaps only projected?) earlier than A.D. 9, but it has left no trace other than the fact of the strong protests made by the *equites* in that year (Dio 56.1.2 corroborates Suetonius: Germanicus had children aged 3 and 2 in A.D. 9). The chief provisions of the two laws were as follows:-

LEX JULIA

(a)   Unmarried men between 25 and 60, and unmarried women between 20 and 50, were forbidden to accept inheritances from outside their agnatic family (to the sixth degree). Childless couples may have been treated as unmarried, or they may have been allowed to accept some fraction smaller than a half (see *lex Papia Poppaea* (a) ii below).
  (1)   An heir thus barred was allowed a limited time (probably 100 days) to acquire spouse/child(?).
  (2)   Divorcées were given six months, widows twelve, to marry again.
  (3)   Betrothal to a girl under 12 counted as marriage for the purposes of the law.
  (4)   One surviving child was sufficient to exempt a man from the restrictions of the law (perhaps a woman needed three, Dio 55.2.5).
(b)   Marriages between freeborn (except senators and their descendants in the male line to the third generation) and freed slaves were expressly validated, unless the latter were *famosae* (prostitutes, actresses, adulteresses, or convicted persons).
(c)   (i) Celibacy could not be specified as a condition of inheritance by testators, nor a condition of manumission by patrons.
        (ii) Fathers could not obstruct their children's marriages by the exercise of *patria potestas.*

LEX PAPIA POPPAEA

(a)   Modified (a) above of the *lex Iulia:*
        (i)   Spouses, if childless, and within the age limits, could inherit one-tenth of each other's property. Each surviving child of a previous marriage and up to two deceased children of the existing marriage increased the proportion by a tenth. One common child

surviving till puberty, or two to three years old, or three to
nine days old, freed them from all restrictions of the law.
(ii)   The childless married could now take half of what they might
have had if they had had a child.
(iii)   Divorcées were now allowed 18 months, widows 2 years to
remarry.
(b)   (i)   Candidates for public office might anticipate the statutory
qualifying ages by as many years as they had children, up to three.
(ii)   A freeborn woman with two children (or a freedwoman with
three) gained the old Republican rights of a male patron over the
estate of her freedman (see (v) below).
(iii)   A freeborn woman with three children also
   (1)   probably escaped the provisions of the Lex Voconia which
      stopped a woman in the first property class being instituted
      heir or receiving as legatee more than the heir(s);
   (2)   escaped from guardianship (*tutela*), as did a freedwoman
      with four children.
(iv)   A freedman with two children was exempted from performing
compulsory service (*operae*) for his patron.
(v)   A freedman now needed three children (previously only one)
to prevent his patron participating equally with the other heirs
in his estate - provided this were worth over 100,000 HS.
(c)   Introduced a system of rewards for informers.

All these inducements to marry are either pecuniary or apply only to
candidates for public office, so it is scarcely surprising that it was
the moneyed class, the *equites*, whose protests were so loud. Note that
the practice of leaving substantial legacies to, or instituting as heirs,
non-relatives was common among the often childless Roman wealthy. The
attention paid to freedmen and -women is very striking, and bears out the
impression gained from other sources (literary and epigraphic) that this
class controlled considerable wealth. It is not clear whether the main
purpose of the provisions regarding freedmen was to ensure that more of
their property than hitherto came back to their patron's estate, or to
encourage them to have a large number of children who would of course be
freeborn Roman citizens. As to the 'legitimising' of marriage between
free non-senators and freedwomen, there is no indication that this had
ever been prohibited; but by affirming its complete propriety, Augustus
may have hoped to remove the social prejudice which evidently existed
against it. See further Brunt 1971, 558f.; Corbett 1930.
vacatione trienni data: this three years' grace is not the period
allowed an individual between death of spouse and remarriage (so *GG*), but
a moratorium granted before the provisions of the law came into force (cf.
Dio 56.7.2; Ulpian, *Tituli* 14). Since the only provisions of the *lex
Papia Poppaea* as set out above which appear possibly harsher than those
of the *lex Iulia* are those relating to inheritance by spouses from each
other, the three year period could have given couples with one child time
to have a second in order to free them from all restrictions. (There may
of course have been other clauses of which we are ignorant; see n. on
immaturitate sponsarum 34.2).

34.2 Germanici liberos ... iuvenis exemplum: in A.D. 9 Germanicus
was 24, and had two sons, Nero (born A.D. 6) and Drusus (born A.D. 7),

though he was still below the age set by the law for marriage. On imperial attendance at the games, see 53.1 n. immaturitate sponsarum et matrimoniorum crebra mutatione: since betrothal to an infant counted as matrimony, it was possible to have a whole string of 'fiancées' under 12 and never in fact get married. Augustus altered the rule so that the girl must be at least ten (Dio 54.16.7). Dio seems to ascribe this change to 18 B.C., which is impossible, while Suetonius speaks of it as though it were subsequent to A.D. 9. If it was in fact part of the *lex Papia Poppaea*, it would provide a satisfactory reason for the three-year period of grace (above). 'Frequent changes of marriage' must refer to divorcées who reaching the end of their six-month (later eighteen-month) period of permitted celibacy, contracted a marriage of convenience and immediately got divorced again. Men might also abuse the law by acquring a temporary wife within the permitted 100 days in order to accept a legacy. In either case *modum imposuit* surely means 'placed a numerical limit on', in spite of the fact that the jurists make no mention of such a rule.

35-40 These chapters describe measures concerning the senate and senatorial offices (35-38.2), the equestrian order (38.3-40.1), and the plebs (40.2-5). Augustus is shown as the great regulator of the institutions of the Roman state, sometimes innovating, sometimes reforming, sometimes reviving good customs of the past. He is always rational, moderate, and humane. Order in society implies clear definition and gradation of status (cf. Cicero *de Republica* 1.43: democracy is 'unfair (*iniqua*) since it has no grades of esteem'); the empire became progressively more status-bound, and it would never have occurred to Suetonius to question or analyse the assumptions according to which Augustus articulated the Roman society of his day, or do anything but approve of the measures here set out.

35.1-2 MEMBERSHIP OF THE SENATE

Caesar was attacked in his lifetime for admitting to the senate foreigners (*DJ* 80.2), soldiers (i.e. centurions), and freed-men (Dio 43.47), and is said to have increased its numbers from 600 to 900. The rule of the triumvirs severely reduced the importance and standing of the senate, and there can be little doubt that they too admitted their partisans on a generous scale. *Orcivus* (later *Orcinus*), from Orcus = Hades, was a term applied to slaves freed under a will, that is owing their status to a death.

Augustus himself says (*RG* 8.2) he put through three revisions of the senate's membership (*lectiones*). The first was in 29 B.C., as part of the censorial activities carried out with Agrippa in that year and 28 B.C., when he tactfully removed 190 senators, amongst them 50 who resigned voluntarily and were allowed to keep the privileges mentioned here by Suetonius (cf. Dio 52.42.2); this is Suetonius' 'second' *lectio,* and the precautions described

are appropriate to the uncertain political atmosphere in which
Augustus began the return to constitutional government. The
second *lectio* (Suetonius 'first') is that of 18 B.C., when
Augustus, wishing to reduce the senate to 600, tried to avoid
the opprobrium of himself expelling senators by setting up an
elaborate system of co-option (see Dio 54.13). It did not work
and he had to act himself. The third, not mentioned by Suetonius
must have been in either 13 or 11 B.C., probably the latter (Dio
54.26.3 and 54.31.1; Jones 1960, 21f.). There was another *lectio*
in A.D. 4, carried out by three senators (see 38 n.D).

35.2 Cordus Cremutius: the senator Cremutius Cordus (for the inversion
see 4.1 n.) wrote a history of the civil wars and the reign of Augustus,
which Augustus himself had read, apparently without taking any great
offence. But in A.D. 25 he offended Sejanus, was prosecuted for having
called Cassius the last of the Romans and shown insufficient respect for
Augustus, senate, and people, and committted suicide. His works were
ordered to be burnt. (Tacitus, *Ann.* 4.34-35; Dio 57.24; Younger Seneca,
ad Marciam 22.4.)
insigne vestis: the distinguishing marks of the senatorial dress were
the broad purple stripe on the toga and the special senatorial boots.
spectandi in orchestra: see 44.1 n.
epulandi publice: on feast days the senate dined publicly on the Capitol.

35.3-4 SENATORIAL PROCEDURE

The changes here described were consequent upon the establishment
of *de facto* monarchy. The offering by each senator as he took
his seat gave a solemn and ritual quality to meetings which
helped to conceal the fact that they were no longer important;
but it was this very fact which enabled Augustus to prescribe
regular meeting days (*legitimus* is confirmed as the technical
word by a fragment of a municipal calendar recently discovered
at Viterbo, *Notizie di Scavi* 1975, 39), to institute a quorum for
the vacation months of September and October, and to break with
the Republican custom of asking the most senior men for their
opinions first - a custom which had resulted in others seldom
doing more than indicate their agreement with one of the first
speakers. Had the senate still been a place for real political
debate and decision, none of this would have been necessary.

The *consilium semenstre* (six-monthly committee) is more fully
described by Dio (53.21.4-5); it consisted of the consul(s),
one praetor, one aedile, one tribune, and one quaestor, and
fifteen other senators chosen by lot. Thus every year thirty
non-magistrates would work closely with Augustus, and after a
period of years a majority of the senate would have served in
this way. Augustus thus had an opportunity to get to know new
senators (recruited at the rate of twenty a year through the
quaestorship) and to obtain opinions about plans and policies
which ordinary senators might have been unwilling to air in full
senate. This body had no executive power, but in practice it

formulated business for the senate and anticipated its decisions
(*Cyrene Edict* V = E-J[3] no.311, 87). It should not be confused
with the true council of state created in A.D. 13 when Augustus
was too infirm to attend the senate regularly; this was composed
of 20 annual counsellors, himself, Tiberius, the consuls, the
consuls-designate, Germanicus, Drusus, and any others he wished
according to the business involved, and its decrees had the
force of *senatus consulta* (Dio 56.28.2-3). Nor should it be
confused with the emperor's *consilium,* his inner circle of
advisers or 'cabinet', which had no formal constitutional
existence but immense importance; Suetonius makes no mention
of this, but see Crook 1955.

36   acta senatus: see 5 n.
magistratus statim in provincias: the normal republican practice
   after Sulla's reforms of 80 B.C., had been for a consul or praetor to
   proceed to his province as soon as his year of urban office was over.
   His *imperium,* conferred on him in virtue of his election to a magistracy,
   was simply extended by the senate. In 52 B.C. Pompey, in order to moderate
   the scamble for office, imposed a five-year interval between magistracy
   and governorship, but this law was either repealed or ignored in the
   period of the Civil Wars. According to Dio (53.14.2), Augustus prescribed
   the same five-year interval for both praetors and consuls, but only with
   regard to the senatorial provinces; he appointed as he pleased to his
   own provinces; see also 47 n.
cura aerari: the *aerarium* was the official state treasury and was located
   in the massive podium of the Temple of Saturn in the Forum. The two
   urban quaestors were the original financial officials of the republic,
   although they were never responsible for policy or judicial decisions, only
   for payments, receipts, and custody of the cash. In 29 B.C. Augustus replaced them by two *praefecti* of praetorian rank, and these again in
   23 B.C. by two praetors appointed by lot from amongst those elected, now
   increased to ten (Tacitus, *Ann.* 13.29; Dio 53.2.1). Perhaps Augustus saw
   administrative advantages in having a holder of *imperium* in charge of
   the treasury (cf. n. on *tabulas debitorum* 32.2). See Jones 1960, 99f.;
   Millar 1964b; Corbier 1974.
centumviralem hastam: the centumviral court dealt with civil cases
   involving inheritance (and therefore property and many related legal
   questions) which were sent to it by the praetor (Cicero, *de Oratore* 1.173).
   It seems likely to be of ancient origin, but we only know that in the late
   Republic its jurors numbered 105, three from each of the 35 tribes. (On
   the competence and constitution of the court, see Kelly 1976, ch.I). A
   panel of jurors would hear any particular case, under the presidency (after
   the change here described) of one of the *decem viri stlitibus iudicandis:*
   these ten were one of the four boards of junior magistrates which made
   up the vigintivirate, the others being *tres viri monetales* (moneyers),
   tres viri capitales (magistrates of summary jurisdiction), and *quattuor
   viri viis in urbe purgandis* (road maintenance board). Augustus made it
   compulsory for a man entering upon a senatorial career to perform a period
   of military service and to hold one of the offices of the vigintivirate
   before becoming qualified, at the age of 25, to stand for the quaestorship
   and thus secure entry into the senate (see Dio 54.26.5). On the Republican
   functions of the *decem viri,* see Kelly 1976, 66f.

37 nova officia excogitavit:

(A) The first four of these new posts reflect the increase in size,
complexity and facilities of the new capital city, which had by now completely outgrown the ability of the aediles to maintain it adequately.
Augustus' technique was to mount a massive restoration programme and
then or later create an appropriate body of curators.

(i) The aqueducts were refurbished and improved in 33 B.C. by Agrippa
(see 29.5 n.), who continued to take responsibility for them until his
death, and added the *Aqua Virgo* in 19 B.C. His large workforce of
skilled slaves passed to Augustus by his will, prompting the senatorial
decree of 11 B.C. which set up the board of *curatores aquarum* (E-J^3 no.
278 = *LR* II.69f. = *HRFC* II.207). An inscription of 5 B.C., commemorating
Augustus' repair of all the aqueducts, signifies the end of the long
process of major restoration carried out at his expense (*ILS* 98 =
E-J^3 no.281; cf. *RG* 20.2). The president was a consular and had two
assistants, one at least praetorian. He had *imperium* and two lictors.
The Augustan holders of the office were M. Valerius Messalla Corvinus
(consul 31) from 11 B.C. to A.D. 13, and C. Ateius Capito (consul
5 B.C.), from A.D. 13 to 23 (see Frontinus *de Aquis;* van Deman 1934;
Ashby 1935).

(ii) For the roads, see 30.1 and the coin of 16 B.C. showing a *cippus*
with the inscription 'Senate and People of Rome to Emperor Caesar because
the roads have been made up with the money which he contributed to the
treasury' (E-J^3 no.287 = *BMC Aug.* nos.79ff.). Augustus' curators replaced
the old Republican *duo viri viis extra urbem purgandis,* a junior magistracy
no longer equal to the task. They were of praetorian rank, and appear to
have been established by 20 B.C. (Dio 54.8.4; *ILS* 915 = E-J^3 no.197).

(iii) The full title of a curator of public buildings under Augustus
appears as *curator aedium sacrarum monumentorumque publicorum tuendorum*
(*ILS* 932 = E-J^3 no.205); by Suetonius' own time the formula generally
includes the words *operum publicorum,* with or without the reference to
sacred buildings. Under the Republic, the descendants of a man who had
erected a temple or other public building expected as a matter of family
pride to look after it; otherwise, the censors were supposed to see to
it. But families died out or became impoverished, and censors had been
infrequently appointed in the late Republic. Hence the tally of 82
temples mentioned at *RG* 20.4 as needing repair in 28 B.C. After 30 B.C.
the emperor's own benefactions, and those of this family and relations,
were on such a scale as to need more than his personal supervision. We
are not informed how the expenses of the necessary work were met.

(iv) There is no inscriptional evidence to corroborate Suetonius'
statement that Augustus set up the curatorship of the bed (and banks)
of the Tiber. In the Republic the censors were responsible for it.
Cippi restored by the board of five set up in A.D. 15 by Tiberius (Dio
57.14.8) reveal that the consuls of 8 B.C. defined and cleared the bed
(E-J^3 no.295 = *ILS* 5923d), a task which was finished by Augustus himself
(*ILS* 5924); see 30.1. The first known *curatores alvei Tiberis* are C. Ateius
Capito, who in A.D. 15 joined the office to his existing post of *curator
aquarum,* and L. Arruntius (Tacitus, *Ann.* 1.76.3).

(B) After the famine of 22 B.C., when he took over general responsibility
for the corn supply (*annona*), Augustus arranged that 2 annual prefects
(4 after 18 B.C.) appointed by the senate from ex-praetors should take

charge of distribution of grain to the people (Dio 54.1.4 and 54.17.1).
Their title, *praefecti frumenti dandi (ex senatus consulto)* marked their
difference from the Republican *curatores frumenti,* who were of a more
junior status and must presumably have assisted the aediles whose task
it had been, before 22 B.C., to arrange the distribution (*ILS* 887,907,
932 = E-J[3] no.205). In A.D. 6 another famine caused the additional
appointment of two ex-consuls to have general oversight of the whole
system of supply and distribution (Dio 55.26.2 and 54.31.4); but by the
end of his reign Augustus had assumed full personal responsibility and
created, to direct the entire operation, an equestrian prefecture with
no limit of tenure and answerable only to himself. Significantly, the
man chosen, C. Turranius (Tacitus, *Ann.* 1.7), had been previously prefect
of Egypt and would thus have been familiar with the main supply source,
quite apart from the prestige and experience he had gained from holding
this great office. The efficient provisioning of the city was of cardinal
importance in preserving popular support for Augustus' rule. See van
Berchem 1939 and 1974; Pavis d'Escurac 1976.

(C)   The urban prefecture of the principate, though having a superficial
connection with the Republican institution, was in fact a new creation.
In the Republic, if both consuls were out of Rome, a *praefectus urbi*
could be appointed to exercise consular power in their absence; he was
a representative, not a subordinate, and had full consular *imperium* and
fasces. Once the praetorship had been instituted (367 B.C.) the need
for the office vanished, and it survived only in the honorific appointment
of a *praefectus urbi* for the period of the Latin Festival (a custom which
endured to Tacitus' day). Under Augustus we know of both unofficial
and official prefectures: the unofficial ones were those held by Maecenas
in 36-33 B.C. and 31-29 B.C. and by Agrippa in 27-26 B.C.(?) and 21 B.C.,
when Augustus was away from Rome and wished to leave it in no doubt who
was to be the ultimate authority in his absence, although no special
grant of constitutional power was made. The official holders (Tacitus,
Ann. 6.11.4-6) were M. Valerius Messalla Corvinus (see 58.1 n.), who
resigned after a few days in 25 B.C. on the ground that he 'did not know
how to exercise his powers' (which probably means that he was forced to
resign because of opposition - see Sattler 1960, 58f.); T. Statilius
Taurus (consul II 26 B.C.), perhaps in office from 18 B.C. (Dio 54.17.2),
certainly from 16 to 13 B.C. (Dio 54.19.6), and possibly later since
Tacitus speaks of his advanced age; and L.Calpurnius Piso Frugi (consul
15 B.C.) who held the post from A.D. 12 -32 and whose tenure marks its
establishment as a permanent office of state. Messalla and Taurus were,
it seems, intended to stand in for Augustus in some way, but the matter
is very obscure as Augustus possessed, in theory, no powers which some
other magistrate did not already exercise. (Caesar, when in Spain in
46-45 B.C., had been represented by Lepidus and eight *praefecti*). As
for Piso, his post cannot be connected with Augustus' absence like the
other two. What is certain is that the urban prefect was a senior consular
whose job was to maintain public order in the capital. He exercised (in
virtue of his powers of *coercitio* and *iurisdictio*) a summary 'police-
court' jurisdiction in and immediately around Rome, and commanded the
urban cohorts and the *vigiles* (see 30 n. and 49 n.). He lost his powers
if he left the city. We do not know how he was appointed, though this
should have been by election since his powers were magisterial and urban;
he does not seem to have been a delegate of the *princeps*, but a magistrate

in his own right (see Cadoux 1959).

(D)   The two triumvirates for revising the senate and the squadrons of
equites were another device by which Augustus tried to avoid exercising
the functions of the censors (cf. 27.5 n.):

(i)   The senatorial lectio of A.D. 4 was performed (uniquely) by a
board of three senators selected by lot from ten nominated by Augustus
(Dio 55.15.3; cf. 35.1).

(ii)   The equestrian order was the second order in the state (see
Nicolet 1966; Wiseman 1970; Millar 1977, 279f.). It was composed of
men enrolled in the 18 centuries of equites equo publico ('cavalry
mounted at public expense'); these had originally been the cavalry,
i.e. the wealthiest members of the citizen army, but after the second
century B.C. they merely comprised voting units in the centuriate
assembly. Membership was a mark of social distinction: senators
excluded, this group represented the cream of Roman society. Property
worth 400,000 HS was a necessary, but not sufficient, condition for
membership, and sons and relatives of senators formed a significant
proportion of the order. It is likely that under Augustus military
service as an officer became a necessary qualification, although in
the early years membership could be claimed on hereditary grounds
(Ovid, Amores 3.15.5-6). Equestrian rank could also be granted as
an honour to men who would not otherwise be entitled to it, e.g. freedmen. Augustus desired to recall the military aspects of the order
and reintroduced the annual parade on horseback (travectio, see 38.3),
for which the centuries were grouped into six turmae (squadrons) of
three centuries, each commanded, for the purposes of the parade, by
a sevir - normally a young man of very high birth, who held office
for the day (see le Bohec 1975). Those members of the order who
attained the quaestorship and so became senators left it; but the
others remained equites so long as they were fit to appear at the
travectio. Suetonius gives the details at 38.3, from which it is
clear what the original purpose of the Republican travectio had been
and how Augustus modified it to enable older equites to retain the
rank which they would otherwise, on practical criteria, have had to
forfeit. We learn there that the emperor often carried out the
inspection (recognitio) himself, so that the triumvirate - whose title
was tresvir centuriarum equitum recognoscendarum censoria potestate
(ILS 9483 = E-J[3] no.209) - can hardly have been a regular office.
The parallel with other occasions when Augustus delegated censorial
functions suggests that the triumvirate may have been created to carry
out a serious examination and reconstitution of the order, the normal
recognitio being little more than formal. In the Republic, travectio
(annually on 15th July) and recognitio (by the censors) were separate,
but Augustus appears to have combined them (cf. Ovid, Tristia 2.89).

censores: the appointment of censors had become very irregular after 80
B.C., although in theory two ought to have been elected every five years
to hold office for 18 months. The last pre-Augustan pair had held office
in 42 B.C., but there were no more until L. Munatius Plancus and Paullus
Aemilius Lepidus were appointed in 22 B.C. They fell out with each other
and did not complete their duties, but had the distinction of being the
last non-imperial censors in the history of Rome (Dio 54.22.2). For the
duties of the office and Augustus' avoidance of it, see 27.5 n. Many of

the new offices mentioned in this chapter were concerned with some part
of the original censorial functions.

numerum praetorum: the number of praetors increased steadily during
the Republic until it reached eight under Sulla, the reason being the
roughly parallel increase in the number of provinces which required
governors (see 47 n.). Caesar raised the number to sixteen (Dio 43.51.4),
but eight was felt to be the norm when constitutional government returned
in 28-27 B.C. Augustus added two more in 23 B.C. when he placed praetors
in charge of the *aerarium* (see 36), and another two in A.D. 12 - apparently
because there were was such competition to attain the office that in the
previous year he had allowed all sixteen candidates to be elected (Dio
56.25.4). The praetorship was the 'career grade' for a senator; over
half of all entrants would reach it.

38.1 iustos triumphos et ... triumphalia ornamenta: a triumph
was the highest military honour which could be won by a Roman general.
The *triumphator* entered the city in solemn procession, riding in a splendid
chariot and wearing the dress of Jupiter Optimus Maximus, accompanied by
his soldiers, booty, captives, and tableaux or pictures of his exploits;
he made his offering at Jupiter's temple on the Capitol, and then feasted
the populace (see Versnel 1970). Triumphs were granted increasingly
frequently in the later Republican and triumviral periods but after the
first ten years of Augustus' reign they were practically eliminated: the
last private citizen (i.e. non-member of the imperial family) to triumph
was L. Cornelius Balbus in 19 B.C., and after that the only triumphs Rome
saw in Augustus' lifetime were those of Tiberius in 7 B.C. and A.D. 12.
The reasons were partly technical, in that to triumph a general had to
be fighting under his own auspices, that is holding a command directly
conferred on him by the people (Cicero, *de Divinatione* 2.76), and nearly
all major wars occurred in imperial provinces where the generals were
Augustus' subordinates; and partly political, in that Augustus, as founder
of a military monarchy, had a strong interest in denying to outsiders
access to the highest military honours. Thus the full (*iusti*) triumphs
were replaced by the triumphal decorations (*ornamenta triumphalia*) which
allowed a man to enjoy the status and privileges of one who had triumphed,
but robbed him of his day of glory. Counting from the establishment of
the triumvirate in 43 B.C., we know the names of 20 men who actually
triumphed, apart from Augustus and Tiberius, and 17 of them belong in or
before 27 B.C.; but we have no similar corroboration of Suetonius' statement about the number receiving the *ornamenta*.

38.2 liberis senatorum: the custom under the Republic (cf. Cicero,
pro Caelio 10-11) had been for the sons of senators and others who wished
to embark on a senatorial career to be introduced by their fathers or
important friends, when they had assumed the *toga virilis* (cf. 8.1), into
the social and intellectual world of the governing elite at the same time
as they pursued their studies in rhetoric and law. Augustus formalised
the process by allowing young men (and not only senators' sons - cf. Ovid
Tristia 4.10.29) who intended to become senators to assume the senatorial
toga with its wide purple stripe and to attend meetings of the senate.
This treatment reflects the creation of a senatorial class seen elsewhere

in the Augustan principate, e.g. in the marriage legislation which forbade a senator *or his descendants* to the third generation to marry a freedwoman.
militiamque auspicantibus: 'making a start' because later in their careers senators could expect to return to the legions for periods of service as senior officers and generals.
non tribunatum modo legionum sed et praefecturas alarum: the command of a squadron of auxiliary horse was later an equestrian post, but there is epigraphic confirmation of Suetonius' statement here (*ILS* 911 = E-J[3] no.195) - though not of the more remarkable information about joint prefectures of horse. The usual military post for a *laticlavius* (would-be senator) was a legionary tribunate. Each legion had six tribunes, normally five equestrian and one senatorial, who ranked below the commander and above the centurions. The 28 (or after A.D. 9, 25) legions should thus have been able to absorb each year's crop of 20+ young men who wished to qualify for the 20 quaestorships which would be available to them in due course. That they could not suggests either that Augustus expected more than a year's military service from senatorial tribunes, or else that at times there was considerable competition for entry to the senate and more men were qualifying than would be able to enter.

38.3 equitum turmas ...: see 37 n.(D)(ii).
reddendi equi gratiam fecit ... nollent: Mommsen emended *nollent* to *mallent,* to give the sense 'he allowed those who preferred, to retain their horses after reaching the age of 35'. This entails supposing an otherwise unknown regulation bringing equestrian service (and membership of the order?) to an end at that age. The transmitted text is perfectly satisfactory: 'he excused those over 35 from keeping their horses if they did not want to' (*sc.* while still remaining members of the order). The horse was called a 'public horse' because it was conferred by the censors (or whoever performed their function - cf. Ovid, *Tristia* 2.89-90), and its owner received an allowance from the state towards its upkeep. Originally this had been to ensure adequately mounted cavalry, but since the equestrian centuries were no longer a military force, Augustus was prepared to tolerate an unfit *eques* in the interests of preserving the dignity, and so commanding the gratitude, of the older men of the order.

39   decem adiutoribus: this commission of ten is not mentioned elsewhere and was probably unique (cf. the triumvirate of ch.37). It would fit in well with the 'normalisation' programme of 28 B.C., or it may be connected with the investigations referred to in a muddled fashion by Dio (54.26.8-9) as occuring in 13 B.C. (so Jones 1960, 22-23).

40.1 comitiis tribuniciis, si deessent candidati senatores: for the tribunate of the plebs, see 27.5 n. The office was a considerable tie, and unattractive once it had suffered political emasculation. Dio (54.30.2) bears out Suetonius precisely in his account of events in 13 B.C. (Cf. also E-J[3] no.371.)
e quattuordecim ... metu poenae theatralis: the first 14 rows of the theatre had been reserved for the *equites* by the *lex Roscia* (67 B.C.), which also provided a special place for those bankrupt through no fault of

153

their own (Cicero, *Philippics* 2.44). Augustus was evidently enlarging this category so as to preserve inherited status and avoid inflicting public humiliation on the undeserving.

40.2 populi recensum vicatim egit: this enumeration by *vici* (see 30 n.) was a separate count from that of the ordinary census; instituted by Julius Caesar, its prime purpose was to determine the number of those qualified for the corn dole - i.e. Roman citizens domiciled in Rome. On the *frumentatio* see 41.2 n.

THE ELECTIONS UNDER AUGUSTUS

Under Caesar and the triumvirs the elections had been largely taken out of the hands of the people, certainly in the case of the more important offices, and the minor offices had become devalued. Restoration of genuine elections and of proper limits on magisterial powers was one of the most important aspects of the return of constitutionality in 28 B.C. The reality of competition is shown by Augustus' law on electoral bribery (*ambitus*, see 34.1 n.) and by the disorders and irregularities attending the elections in 22-19 B.C. and again in A.D. 6 or 7 (Dio 55.34.2 and cf. 55.27.1-3). Suetonius, and all our literary sources, are quite silent about the *lex Valeria Cornelia* of A.D. 5, which set up a special assembly consisting of senators and *equites* aged over 25 to deliver an advance vote which served as a lead (*destinatio*) to the normal assembly in some way which is not clear (E-J[3] no.94a; Brunt 1961; Stavely 1972 218f.; Pani 1974); but by the end of the reign true popular election must have been dead, because Tiberius was able to transfer the elections to the senate (Tacitus, *Ann.* 1.15.1) without provoking any protests.

Fabianis et Scaptiensibus: Augustus belonged by adoption to the tribe Fabia, and by birth to the Scaptia. It was accepted that a man might distribute gifts or other favours, if he were a candidate, to his fellow-tribesmen. The point of Suetonius' remark is that Augustus was so certain of election that he had no need to do this, but none the less did so.

40.3-4 civitates Romanas parcissime dedit et manumittendi modum terminavit: On the whole subject of Roman citizenship, see Sherwin-White 1973. In the Augustan period it could be obtained (other than by birth) in the following ways:

    (i) By becoming a magistrate in a community which possessed the Latin citizenship (see 47 n.) or by belonging to an existing community which collectively had Roman citizenship conferred upon it (e.g. Carthage - Sherwin-White 1973, 227).

    (ii) Possibly, on discharge from service as an auxiliary soldier, though evidence is lacking between *ca.* 40 B.C. (E-J[3] no.302) and Claudius' regularisation of the practice.

    (iii) By a special grant for services rendered, as must be the case with the requests of Tiberius and Livia here. An attested example is

Seleucos of Rhosos in Syria, given the citizenship before 33 B.C. for service as an admiral under Augustus (E-J[3] no.301 = Sherk 1969, no.58 and Lewis 1974, 20). What Suetonius says about Augustus' attitude has been confirmed by the recent discovery at Aphrodisias of the text of his reply to a Samian request for freedom (Reynolds 1982, no.13; trans. only, Millar 1977, 431; ?38 B.C.). He refuses, on grounds very similar to those on which he refused the Gaul whom Livia supported (as she also did the Samians). In both cases he dismisses financial considerations as trivial. The Gaul cost the provincial treasury (*fiscus*) money, because had he become a Roman citizen he would still have paid tax - unless he had also been granted the *immunitas* which was all Augustus was prepared to offer him.

(iv) By manumission. A freed slave had a position in law analagous to that of a son, and though he himself was subject to certain statuory disabilities his children were fully free. Since nearly all slaves were non-Italian, and manumission was very common, the free population of Rome was steadily becoming more racially mixed. Augustus attempted to control the process by two statutes:

(a) The *lex Fufia Caninia* of 2 B.C. restricted the number of slaves a man could free by will: if he had one or two slaves, both could be freed; if 3-10, half of them; if 10-30, a third; if 30-100, a quarter; if 100-500, a fifth; and if over 500, 100 only. To free large numbers of slaves by will was an extravagant gesture which cost the testator nothing, but created new (and chiefly non-Italian) Roman citizens to draw the corn dole. The passing of the law shows that the practice was not uncommon, and slave establishments liable to be large.

(b) In A.D. 4 the *lex Aelia Sentia* tightened up the regulations for manumission while the master was alive:

(1) Manumissions designed to defraud patrons or creditors were forbidden.

(2) A master under 20 years old could not manumit at all without showing good cause to a tribunal.

(3) A master over 20 could formally manumit only a slave over 30; if the slave were under 30, manumission could only be informal (*inter amicos*) and the slave, though in practice a freedman, was in law still a slave. Such a slave (known later as a Junian Latin) could attain full legal freedom (*libertas iusta*) by marrying and having a child (or, after the *lex Visellia* of A.D. 24, by completing six years service in the *vigiles*).

(4) A criminal slave (*vinctus ... tortusve quis*), if manumitted, joined the category of *peregrini dediticii,* who were not Roman citizens, yet not citizens of any other state, and had to live over 100 miles from Rome (*pessima libertas eorum* Gaius 1.26).

(5) All legitimate births had to be registered within 30 days (in the interests of later proof of origin, status, and entitlement to privileges such as the corn dole).

Suetonius' comments on the barriers erected by Augustus between a slave and full freedom become intelligible in the light of these provisions, to which should be added that of the *lex Papia Poppaea* which required a freedman to have three children (formerly only one) before his patron lost all claim on his estate (see 34.1 n.). For discussion of why the Romans

freed slaves, see Hopkins 1978, 115f., and on manumission in general,
Buckland 1908, 533f.

40.5 pullatorum: *pullati* were those who wore the *pulla vestis,* the
dark grey (and probably dirty) everyday garment of the common people.
en, Romanos rerum dominos ...: Virgil, *Aeneid* 1.282. The Aeneid had
not been published when Virgil died in 19 B.C. That Augustus could quote
it like this shows its instant success as a national classic.

41-45 These chapters deal with Augustus' liberality to the people
as a whole. *liberalitas,* no more than a welcome attribute of
a Republican politician, rapidly became an essential quality
of the emperor, since he could no longer do his clients political
favours. Also relevant is the idea that the possessor of great
wealth had a duty to share it, and that offices of state (even
humble ones) carried with them the obligation to expend private
funds. The four cardinal virtues of the emperor may have been
iustitia, clementia, pietas, and *virtus* (*RG* 34.2), but *liberalitas* had a greater practical value than any of them. It could
be abused by a bad emperor: Suetonius is therefore careful to
contradict any impression that Augustus' notable largesse had
selfish motives by his famous verdict *salubrem magis quam
ambitiosum principem* ('an emperor who sought not his own popularity but his people's health'). Augustus is presented as a man
of generosity tempered by strictness and a strong sense of
moral values -- in fact as a good father to his people.

Two main categories of benefaction appear, as they do in
Augustus' own statements (*RG* 15 and 22-23): distribution of
money and grain (41-42) and giving of shows (43), to which is
appended other matter relevant to this important aspect of city
life (44-45). For a different viewpoint, one need only cite
Juvenal's bitter comment (10.77-81) on the Roman people:

> qui dabat olim
> *imperium, fasces, legiones, omnia, nunc se
> continet atque duas tantum res anxius optat
> panem et circenses.*

'they used to confer consulships, power, armies, everything - but
now they do nothing and long anxiously for just two things: bread
and the games'

See further Kloft 1970; Yavetz 1969, 88ff.

41.1 Alexandrino triumpho regia gaza: the Alexandrian triumph was
the third of Augustus' three triumphs, 15th Aug., 29 B.C. The treasure
of the Ptolemies, which had fallen into his hands with the capture of
Cleopatra (Dio 51.8.6 and 51.11.1-4), was the last major collection of
wealth left in the Mediterranean world not in the hands of Rome, and its
release into the economy made the rate of interest drop from its normal

figure of 12 per cent to 4 per cent (Dio 51.21.5).

quotiens ex damnatorum bonis pecunia superflueret: property of condemned men which fell to the state went into the *aerarium,* but why it should thus have been treated as a special category of money is not clear - unless it was very substantial, and we have no record of large-scale prosecutions under Augustus. It is possible that the estate of an occasional offender of very high rank (e.g. Cornelius Gallus, or Murena - see 19.1, 66.2) might be large enough to merit such treatment. But in general, the *aerarium* did not lend money and one should perhaps draw the conclusion that it was unusual for its liquid assets to be in long-term surplus. Augustus' purpose in making these interest-free loans, against generous security, can only be guessed at. The context suggests that he wished to encourage investment in Italian land and to compensate in part for the rise in its price.

senatorium censum: Suetonius' figure of 1,200,000 HS for the senatorial census is not supported by Dio (54.26.3) or Tacitus (*Ann.* 1.75.5 and 2.37.2), who say or imply that the figure was 1,000,000; nor is there any evidence elsewhere that it had ever been fixed at 800,000, though this could have been an intermediate step in the raising of the sum from the 400,000 HS which *equites* (and *a fortiori* senators) were required to possess. Nicolet 1976 has shown that there was no senatorial census as such in the Republic, and has argued that the senatorial *lectio* of 18 B.C. and the impending marriage legislation of that year or the next provide the context for its introduction, and the effective establishment of a senatorial class (cf. 38.2 n.).

41.2 congiaria ... frumentum: Augustus lists and dates his largesse to the civil population (*RG* 15), showing Suetonius to be less than strictly accurate: 400 HS three times (29, 24 and 11 B.C.), 300 HS once (by Caesar's will), and 240 (not 250) HS twice (5 and 2 B.C.). He made only one gift of free corn to the whole plebs, that of 23-22 B.C. when he distributed a whole year's rations at his own expense (see n. on dictatorship 52); from *RG* 18 we learn that from 18 B.C. on he made sundry distributions, both of grain and money, 'sometimes to 100,000 persons, sometimes to many more', but evidently not to all. For a full discussion of Augustus' expenditure, see Brunt and Moore 1967, 57f.

ab undecimo aetatis anno: the figure must be corrupt, as eleven was not a qualifying age for anything. Recently edited Oxrhynchus papyri make it almost certain that the correct figure should be fourteen, *quarto decimo* (Rea 1972), the textual corruption being either from *iiiidecimo* to *undecimo* or from xiv to xi.

tesserasque nummarias duplicavit: the context makes it difficult to believe that *tesserae nummariae* can have had any other purpose than to allow their recipients to buy grain. The later *tessera frumentaria* was a permanent possession of its owner and had stamped on it the day of the month and the counter number at which he was to draw his ration; but the Augustan system seems to have involved the surrender of a monthly *tessera* (not particular to its holder). Thus it functioned much more like money (*nummus*), and is therefore termed a *tessera nummaria* by Suetonius. Dio mentions (55.26.3) that Augustus doubled the corn ration in A.D. 6, evidently, if this interpretation of Suetonius is right, by issuing two *tesserae* to each recipient. See van Berchem 1939, 85f.

42.1 a genero suo Agrippa perductis ... aquis: for Agrippa's activities as builder and overseer of aqueducts, see 37 n.A(i). He became Augustus's son-in-law in 21 B.C. when he married Julia.

42.2 multos manumissos insertosque civium numero: a freed slave became a Roman citizen and so entitled to the corn dole, and to any other distribution made on the basis of the same list; see 40.3-4 n.(iv).

42.3 THE FAMINE OF A.D. 6 AND THE FRUMENTATIO

It is clear from Dio (55.26.1 - 2), who gives many of the same details, that Suetonius refers to the famine of A.D. 6. Even doubling the corn dole was not enough, and the mob clamoured for more. Hence Augustus' reappraisal of the institution. To abandon the dole was not simply a political but also a social and economic impossibility; but what Augustus meant was that the existence of the dole tempted men to abandon farming and come to the city - i.e. to forsake the mode of life which had made Rome great (cf. Horace, *Odes* 3.6.33 - 44). He was making an ethical, not an economic comment. The land thus left (if it *was* left) would have been take back into cultivation by others; the archaeological record suggests that agriculture in Italy prospered in the Augustan period. We hear of no more grain distributions after A.D. 6; so perhaps Augustus' way of 'taking account of the interests of growers and merchants' was to allow the price of grain in the open market to find its natural level -- while still keeping the free issue in being at its standard amount of 5 *modii* a month (more than enough for a single man, not enough for a family). It is notable that Augustus does not make the complaint often voiced by Republican opponents of the grain distributions, that the treasury was being exhausted (e.g. Cicero, *pro Sestio* 103).

43 PUBLIC SHOWS

Providing entertainment for the city populace had long been a function of the ruling class, and became, in the political struggles of the late Republic, an important way of winning support and publicity. Augustus thus continued a well-established tradition, but on a colossal scale in keeping with his political dominance and financial resources. The large number of festivals and holidays must be set beside the lack of a regular Sunday or weekend in the Roman calendar. Augustus' own list of the shows he gave is at *RG* 22-23.

'Games' (*ludi*) had originally had a religious significance, and all the regular *ludi* were associated with the festival of a god. They comprised dramatic performances and chariot races; gladiatorial shows being reckoned separately, like the wild beast hunts. See in general Piganiol 1923 and Harris 1972.

43.1 fecisse se ludos ... ter et vicies: Suetonius gives an almost

verbatim quotation from *RG* 22, with a gloss of his own inserted. The
four games Augustus gave in his own name were probably the following,
of which the third and fourth are guaranteed by his own words:-
- (i)   The games following his triumphs and the dedication of the temple
of Divius Iulius in 29 B.C. (Dio 51.22.4-9)
- (ii)   The *Ludi Apollinis* at the dedication of the Palatine temple of
Apollo in 28 B.C. (see 29.3; Dio 53.1.4)
- (iii) The *Ludi Saeculares* (see 31.4 n.; *RG* 22.2)
- (iv) The *Ludi Martis* of May 12th., 2 B.C., preceding the dedication of
the temple of Mars Ultor on Aug. 1st. (see 29.2; *RC* 22.2).

The occasions when he stood in for others are too numerous to identify,
though some are mentioned by Dio; the most noteworthy are the *Ludi
Victoriae Caesaris* of 44 B.C. (see 10.1).

⟨circensibus ... venationes⟩ non in foro modo: the context and
comparison with *RG* 22 show that a reference to gladiatorial games (which
traditionally, before the Augustan period, took place in the forum) and
to wild-beast hunts (*venationes*) is required to fill the evident lacuna
after *histriones*. I print Roth's supplement ('he very often gave games
in the circus and gladiatorial shows, diversifying them quite frequently
with hunts of African wild beasts'). Augustus himself does not mention
the Saepta as a location, although Dio does (55.10.7).

navale proelium: cf. *RG* 23: a lake 1800 x 1200 feet was excavated,
capable of holding thirty heavy warships and many smaller ones, fed by
a special aqueduct (*Alsietina* or *Augusta*) of low-grade water. The year
was 2 B.C., the place just across the Tiber. Suetonius again quotes
Augustus, whose exact words are *in quo loco nunc nemus est Caesarum;* the
site was converted after the deaths of Gaius and Lucius into a memorial
grove.

43.2 Troiae lusum: the 'Troy' game is described by Virgil, *Aeneid*
5.553-602 and fully discussed in the edition of R.D. Williams (Oxford 1960)
ad loc. The word *Troia* appears to be etymologically distinct from the
name of the city and originally to have had nothing to do with it. The
game was a kind of cavalry tournament performed by the young sons of the
upper classes, involving mock battles and elaborate formation riding. The
two age divisions (*maiores* and *minores*) are referred to by Suetonius also
in connection with Caesar's staging of the game (*DJ* 39.2). Suetonius
himself wrote a lost work on boys' games, including this (Servius on
Virgil, *loc.cit*.).

Nonius Asprenas. it is not clear which Asprenas this was; but probably
a son of the consul of A.D. 6, as the father is never surnamed Torquatus.
We hear of a L. Nonius Calpurnius Torquatus Asprenas, consul in A.D. 93,
who must be a descendant. The Nonii Asprenates were very close to
Augustus; see 56.3 n.

Asinio Pollione oratore. this episode provides a *terminus ante quem*
for the stopping of the Troy game, since C. Asinius Pollio died in A.D. 4.
Suetonius labels him an orator, but he wrote history and tragedy as well,
had wide literary and critical interests, and had been at one time the
patron of Virgil. Nothing survives of his literary output, and he is
better known to us for his prominent part as an army commander and
sympathiser of Antony's in the events of 43-40 B.C. He held a consulship
in the latter year and triumphed in 38 B.C. after a campaign in the region
of modern Albania; but thereafter he declined to take sides in the quarrel

of Augustus and Antony, and offered himself as a prize to the victor (Velleius 2.86). In the reborn Republic of Augustus, this great man devoted himself to literature and preserved his integrity; aloof, independent, and severe, when Pollio spoke, even the emperor had to take note. None the less, the game was reintroduced: the young Nero took part in it *ca.* A.D. 47 (*Nero* 7.1).

43.3 et equitibus Romanis aliquando usus est: Roman *equites* appeared in the games on two occasions mentioned by Dio: in 23 B.C. (53.31.3) before the passing of a senatorial decree which, in deference to social prejudice, forbade the practice (54.2.5); and in A.D. 11 (56.25.7-8) when the rule was waived for some reason not at all clear from Dio's account. For senators as well as *equites* competing in this way, see *DJ* 39.1-2. Both acting and gladiatorial professions were traditionally the preserve of slaves and freedmen, and actors were, like prostitutes, discriminated against by the law.

43.4 Parthorum obsides: Phraates, king of Parthia, at some time between 20 and 8 B.C., because he was threatened by dissident nobles and wished his bastard son Phraataces to succed him, sent his four legitimate sons to Rome so that they could not be put on the throne (Strabo 16.1.28, dating the episode to Titius' governship of Syria, i.e. either 19 or 13-8 B.C.; see Syme 1939, 398 n.1 and cf. 21.3). Augustus' exceptional treatment of them is explained by their royal status. Of the four, Seraspadanes and Rhodaspes died in Rome (*ILS* 842 = E-J^3 no.183); Vonones was sent to be the Parthian king *ca.* A.D. 6, but was expelled and, after an abortive attempt to become king of Armenia, was put to death in A.D. 19; and Phraates, backed by Rome in a bid to secure the throne of Parthia in A.D. 35, died of illness.

rhinocerotem ... tigrim ... anguem: for Augustus' interest in natural curiosities of all sorts, cf. 43.3 (the Lycian midget) and 72.3 (his villa on Capri).

43.5 votivis circensibus ... tensas deduceret: *ludi votivi* were special games celebrated in fulfilment of a vow (cf. 23.2). The giver of games opened them by leading into the circus the *pompa circensis,* a procession of statues of the gods, each in its own special cart (*tensa*) whose reins were held by boys whose parents were both alive (*patrimi et matrimi*). He himself rode in a chariot and wore triumphal insignia (cf. Juvenal 10.36ff.).

theatrum Marcelli: on Marcellus' theatre, see 29.4 n.

44.1 spectandi ... morem correxit: in Rome, senators had from 194 B.C. enjoyed the privilege of sitting in the orchestra of the theatre. Elsewhere a senator was a personage of such importance and comparative rarity that he could expect to have a good seat cleared for him, and no law had been necessary. But at Puteoli on the bay of Naples where a large number of senators owned villas and other property (see D'Arms 1970), familiarity appears to have bred contempt, and led to this decree - presumably that of 26 B.C. referred to by Dio 53.25.1. No such regulation applied to the circus until A.D. 5 (Dio 55.22.4).

   The ban on other states' delegations sitting in the orchestra alongside

senators, their Roman equivalents, because there might be freedmen amongst
them, reveals once again (as do the sentences which follow) Augustus'
concern with defining and erecting status barriers in his new state; cf.
74.

44.2 maritis e plebe: granting special places to the married was
part of Augustus' campaign to improve the legitimate birth rate.
Comparison with e.g. early Victorian London suggests that regular marriage
was infrequent amongst the poor. (*plebs* means those who were neither
senatorial nor equestrian).
pullatorum: see 40.5 n.

44.3 praetoris tribunal: 'the praetor's platform' because the president
at the games was normally a praetor.

44.4 pontificalibus ludis: the games in honour of Actium, instituted
in 28 B.C., were celebrated every four years; each of the major priest-
hoods (see **31.3 n.**) took it in turn to celebrate them (Dio 53.1.5; cf.
54.19.8).

45.1 cenaculis: if these are really 'attics' or 'penthouses', according
to the literal meaning, the apartment blocks to which they belonged must
have been very close to the circus. It seems more probable that they
were private boxes of some sort, either high up, or constructed like
penthouses.
ex pulvinari ... cum coniuge: the *pulvinar*, built by Augustus, was
the platform where the statues of the gods were placed after the procession,
in full view at the front (cf. *RG* 19.1; *Claudius* 4). The comment about
Livia and the children is explained by what Suetonius has just said about
the separation of the sexes at the games (**44.2**).
petita venia: see 53.1 n; the people expected their leaders to take as
much interest in the games as they did themselves. To attend, but do
office work at the same time, was an insult.

45.2 corollaria ac praemia: these were prizes and sums of money, the
kind of thing described at 85 . By distributing these at games given by
others, the emperor was putting his position as unique patron of the plebs
beyond all challenge.
Graeco certamini: games on the Greek model included athletics and
musical contests, neither of which formed part of ordinary Roman games.
Cicero, *Ad Atticum* 16.5.1, speaks slightingly of *ludi Graeci,* which
involved the performance of Greek plays.

45.3 SPECIAL TREATMENT OF ENTERTAINERS

In the Hellenistic Greek world artists and entertainers formed
professional corporations (e.g. the Dionysiac Artists) and were
commonly granted special privileges, such as immunity from civic
duties, in recognition of their services to the community and
to the festivals of the gods. Of the three categories Suetonius
mentions, the athletes (presumably Greek, see 45.2 n.) are
likely to have been just such a corporation. Gladiators were

normally slaves; having attained their freedom by risking their
lives they were of course free to go on being gladiators (cf.
Horace, *Epistles* l.l.4). Actors had long been discriminated
against by the law (*infames*) even when they were not slaves or
of servile origin; *coercitio* here seems to mean flogging (cf.
Tacitus *Ann*. 1.77).

45.4 xysticorum: 'wrestlers', because they practised in *xysti*, a Greek
term indicating porticoes with special facilities for athletes to
exercise (Vitruvius 5.11.3-4).

severissime egit: reluctant combatants are spoken of by Seneca
(*Epistulae Morales* 7.5) as being urged on with whips and hot irons.

Stephanionem togatarium: Stephanio specialised in *fabulae togatae*,
plays with subjects taken from Roman history. His offence consisted in
the fact that his disguised lover was a married woman (*matrona*), and the
pair of them were flouting Augustus' adultery law (see 34 n.) in a
spectacular manner. The three theatres were those of Pompey, Marcellus,
and Balbus. *Togatarius* occurs nowhere else, and has been emended to
togatarum (gen. pl.); but there is no good reason to suspect the
formation, which is very common in words denoting occupation, e.g.
navicularius, sandaliarius, tignarius.

Hylan pantomimum: a *pantomimus* ('mime-all') was a solo performer of
dramatic scenes, using dance and gesture to accompany words from a
chorus. Augustus is said to have introduced this form of entertainment
to Rome. Hylas was a pupil of Pylades, who was allowed to return from
exile in 18 B.C. (Macrobius, *Saturnalia* 2.7.12f.; Dio 54.17.5).

querente praetore: the fact that the praetor, who was presiding when
Hylas transgressed, complained to Augustus shows either that summary
punishment was in fact rare, or else that Hylas' crime was very serious
- perhaps an insult to Augustus, as Suetonius does not report it.

46 This is the sole chapter of the work devoted specifically
to Italy, almost as though the peninsula was nothing more than
a huge appendix to Rome. On the other hand, Suetonius' subject
is Augustus and it is true that the emperor's direct inter-
ventions in Italy were limited to such acts as are summarised
here. The *effects* of the Augustan peace and of Augustus' social,
financial, and military policies - all topics alluded to elsewhere by Suetonius - were no concern of Suetonius', and he
never embarks on this kind of analysis.

duodetriginta coloniarum numero: the figure of 28 colonies is taken
from *RG* 28.2. Identification is difficult: Pliny (*NH* 3.46ff.) names 46
towns as colonies, practically confining the title to those founded by
Augustus, and it is possible on the basis of other evidence to compile
a list of between 34 and 42 colonies of the triumviral and Augustan
periods. Colonies normally bore their founder's name in their titulature,
e.g. Capua was called *Capua Concordia Iulia Felix Augusta*, but there are
two difficulties with this criterion: one is that the name *Iulia* was borne
by colonies of Caesar, of Antony acting in Caesar's memory, and of
Augustus; the other is that a second title, as in the case of Capua *may*
indicate only an additional settlement of colonists not substantial

enough to rank as a re-foundation (cf. Cicero, *Philippics* 2.102), or
denote nothing more than a favour conferred.

There was at this time no juridical difference between *coloniae* and
municipia, though forms of government differed slightly. But *municipia*
were civil communities, while *coloniae* had always been military in
character (apart from some in the second century B.C.) and enjoyed
greater prestige. It is safe to assume that all Augustus' colonies were
settlements consisting almost exclusively of veterans. The problem of
providing land for discharged soldiers was with Augustus all his life,
until the institution of the *aerarium militare* in A.D. 6 (see 49 n., last
paragraph). Some of the colonies (e.g. those of Regio XI - see below)
performed the original purpose of such settlements, to secure a quasi-
military grip on outlying territory. The rest had no overt military
purpose, though they served as important foci of loyalty to Augustus and
remained a potential source of armed support in a crisis.

We do not know on what basis Augustus restricted his total of colonies
founded to 28; the candidates appear to be, by region:

I	(Latium and Campania)	Capua, Calatia, Aquinum, Suessa, Venafrum*, Sora, Puteoli?, Nuceria?.
II	(Apulia and Calabria)	Luceria*, Venusia.
III	(Lucania and Bruttium)	none
IV	(Samnium)	none
V	(Picenum)	Asculum, Falerio*, Hadria.
VI	(Umbria)	Fanum Fortunae, Hispellum, Tuder.
VII	(Etruria)	Luca, Pisa, Lucus Feroniae, Rusellae, Saena, Sutrium, Perusia?, Florentia?.
VIII	(Cispadana)	Ariminum, Brixellum, Parma, Placentia, Mutina?.
IX	(Liguria)	Dertona.
X	(Venetia)	Concordia, Tergeste*, Pola*, Cremona, Brixia*, Ateste*.
XI	(Transpadana)	Augusta Taurinorum*, Augusta Praetoria*.

*   certainly Augustan
?   not very likely to be Augustan

(I have excluded from the above list the triumviral colonies of
Ancona, Bononia, Beneventum, and Pisaurum, which are known to
have been founded by Antony. See further Brunt 1971, 608f., and
Salmon 1969.)

operibus ac vectigalibus publicis: outstanding examples of such
endowments made by Augustus are the aqueducts of Puteoli and Venafrum and
the walls of Fanum (*RE* 22.5057; *ILS* 5743 = E-J[3] no.282; *ILS* 104), and the
revenues of land near Cnossos in Crete presented to Capua (Dio 49.14.5).

excogitato genere suffragiorum: this system of 'postal voting' is
not heard of in any of our other sources and must have lapsed very soon.
It became a worthless privilege after Tiberius transferred the elections
to the senate in A.D. 15 (see 40.2 n.). It is significant that Augustus
restricted it to the *decuriones*, the members of the local senate: his

object was not to ensure that votes taken in Rome were more representative, but to confer privilege (and thus status) on the local notables. Every other Roman citizen had to travel to Rome to cast his vote. Most of course never did so.

aut honestorum ... aut multitudinis: from the context, *honestis* must mean not just 'respectable', but actually 'equestrian': Suetonius is using the terminology of his own day, when *honesti* were well on the way to becoming a legal category quite separate from the bulk (*multitudo*) of Roman citizens (Garnsey 1970).

equestrem militiam petentes: see 37 n.D and 38.3 n. for the equestrian order. Permission to qualify for the order by taking a post as an officer (legionary tribune or prefect of a cavalry or auxiliary formation - see 38.2 n. and 49 n.A) was granted by the emperor. It has been suggested that the mysterious *tribuni militum a populo* of the Augustan period (E-J[3] no.224 = *ILS* 9007) are those who were recommended by their communities in the way Suetonius describes (Nicolet 1967, 29).

regiones: these must be the regions of Italy, for which see on *duodetriginta coloniarum numero* above. GG interpret as the regions of Rome, but this flies in the face of Suetonius' principles of arrangement. 1000 HS = 250 *denarii* = 10 *aurei*, slightly more than a year's pay for a common soldier. Such a large amount was presumably not only to encourage the production of children (and hence soldiers, who were largely recruited from the country districts) but also to compensate for not receiving the electoral largesse and *congiaria* of the city plebs (see 40.2 and 41.2).

47-50 These four chapters deal in a very summary way with the provinces, client kingdoms, military forces, and communications of the empire. The information given is for the most part so brief and generalised as to be useless to a historian; but Suetonius' purpose is different, namely to show Augustus as a man who administered the empire responsibly and with due regard for order, discipline, efficiency, and humanity.

47(A) 'IMPERIAL' AND 'SENATORIAL' PROVINCES

In the Late Republic, provinces were normally governed by proconsuls, who held office for a year; these men were ordinarily the consuls and praetors of the preceding year, who drew lots among themselves for provinces which had already been designated by the senate. The assembly of the people, being sovereign, could override this system and appoint anyone it chose, for as long as it liked, to govern a province. Hence Julius Caesar's ten-year tenure of Gaul, and the five-year commands of Crassus in Syria and Pompey in Spain. The latter is particularly relevant to Augustus' practice, because Pompey remained in Rome, and even contrived to become consul (in 52 B.C.), while governing his province through *legati*. As in other fields, Augustus was able to build a new system by skilfully combining elements which all had Republican precedents.

The 'First Settlement' of 27 B.C. (see 28 n.) established the division between those provinces which Augustus undertook to

administer, and those to which annual governors were appointed
under the Republican system outlined above (see also 36.1). The
former, conventionally termed 'imperial', comprised Spain
(except Baetica), all Transalpine Gaul, Syria (including
Cilicia), Cyprus, and Egypt; the latter, or 'senatorial'
provinces, were Africa (including Numidia), Illyricum, Macedonia,
Achaea, Asia, Bithynia with Pontus, Crete with Cyrene, Sicily,
Sardinia with Corsica, and Baetica (Dio 53.12.4 - 8: the modern
doctrine that Baetica was created at a later stage, perhaps
16-13 B.C., is flimsy). The list given by Strabo (840C) dates
from a period when Narbonese Gaul and Cyprus had been made
senatorial and when Illyricum had not yet been taken under
imperial control, that is apparently between 23 (or 22) and 12
B.C. (cf. Dio 54.4.1 and 54.34.4; Syme 1939, 394 n.2). Later,
Sardinia became imperial (in A.D. 6 - Dio 55.28.1) and the new
province of Moesia took over the legions hitherto stationed in
Macedonia (probably *ca.* A.D. 3). Other new provinces, all
imperial, created after 27 B.C. were Galatia (25 B.C.), Raetia,
Noricum (both 15 B.C.), and Judaea (A.D. 6).

The governor of a senatorial province was called *proconsul;* of
an imperial, *legatus Augusti pro praetore* - unless he was the
equestrian governor of Raetia, Noricum, Judaea, or Sardinia,
when his title was *praefectus* (or, from Claudius' time, *procurator*). These titles bear no reference to the previous
status of the holder. A *legatus Augusti pro praetore* is in
fact much more likely than a *proconsul* to have already held the
consulship. During Augustus' reign the convention became
established that Africa and Asia went to ex-consuls, and the
remainder of the senatorial provinces to ex-praetors. In the
emperor's provinces the situation was more fluid, but in general
the great military commands went to ex-consuls. The *imperium*
of Augustus' *legati* was 'propraetorian' because it derived from,
and was subordinate to, his 'proconsular' variety. Hence appeal
was possible to Augustus from the judicial (and other) decisions
of his *legati*.

Technically the senate controlled all the provinces in that it
decided (even if only through the drawing of lots) who was to
govern them, and before 23 B.C. Augustus was on a par with any
other duly appointed proconsul. But there were important
differences: first, he was governor of several provinces, not
all adjacent, at the same time; second, he was appointed for
a period of ten years; and third, he was permitted to govern *in
absentia* through *legati* chosen and appointed by himself alone.
The fact that the Roman people happened to elect him consul in
each of the first five years of the new system did not
essentially alter his constitutional position as a provincial
governor. His authority remained identical. He did not have
to be 'acting consul' (if one may. so render *proconsul*) since
he was in fact consul. After 23 B.C. the position was slightly
different: in that year Augustus resigned the consulship and
was granted *imperium maius,* by which his *imperium* was formally

declared to be greater than that of any other proconsul and he
acquired the legal power (in addition to the moral authority
he already possessed) to issue edicts and decisions in any
part of the empire. But the distinction between imperial and
senatorial provinces remained unaltered. See further Millar
1966.

The official propaganda of the regime maintained that the
purpose of the division was to leave Augustus with the troublesome and possibly dangerous border provinces to pacify (a task
which, according to Dio 53.13.1, he promised to complete within
his allotted ten years), while others could enjoy governing the
rich and peaceful provinces of the remainder of the empire.
This is explicit in Augustus' contemporary Strabo (840C); but
Suetonius' own words here, though apparently conveying the same
information, start to seem ambiguous once the reader ponders
whose ease and safety are in question: the emperor's, or the
Roman people's? And Dio, writing another hundred years later,
when it was quite plain that Augustus had in fact established
a monarchy, says:

> 'His professed reason was that the senate might enjoy without
> fear the best parts of the empire, while he himself had the
> trouble and the danger; but really he wanted an excuse for
> them to be unarmed and incapable of fighting, while he alone
> had arms and maintained soldiers' (53.12.3).

This explanation is over-simplified. Of the original senatorial
provinces, Africa, Illyricum, and Macedonia contained legions,
probably to a total of between six and nine, or a quarter to a
third of the army (see 49); but the loyalty of the whole army
to the victor of Actium and 'son of the Divine Julius' was such
that there was no possibility of armed revolt. What Augustus
had to fear was not insurrection, but competition for military
glory and prestige from members of his own class, the semi-
hereditary ruling aristocracy of Rome. The division of 27 B.C.
removed nearly all the significant military commands from the
arena. Certainly, men had to govern these provinces, but their
status as mere *legati* of Augustus, their direct dependence upon
imperial favour for their appointment, and their inability to
claim credit in their own right for any victories they might
win (see 21.1 n.) effectively prevented any challenge to
Augustus' position as supreme trustee of the greatness of
Rome's empire.

(B) STATUS AND TREATMENT OF PROVINCIAL COMMUNITIES

'Federated' cities (*urbes foederatae*), mostly Greek, had an
independent treaty of alliance (*foedus*) with Rome. The exact
terms of their 'freedom' varied, but normally meant freedom
from the authority of the Roman governor, from Roman taxes,
and from Roman law. The unreality of the status is well
illustrated by the unilateral cancellations of it here mentioned

by Suetonius, and by the terms of the extant treaty with
Mytilene (E-J³ no.307) whereby the Roman people solemnly promise
not to allow the enemies of the Mytilenaean people to pass
through Roman territory 'so as to make war on the people of the
Mytilenaeans or on their subjects or on the allies of the people
of the Mytilenaeans' and the Mytilenaeans promise the same
mutatis mutandis. Cities which we know to have been deprived
of their independence include Cyzicus, Tyre, and Sidon (Dio
54.7.6), all indeed displaying Suetonius' *licentia.*

Foreign communities which were not 'free' could be granted Latin
or full Roman citizenship. *latinitas* derived from the original
relationship of the cities of the Latin League with Rome in
the early days of the Republic. After the whole of Italy had
been granted Roman citizenship in 90-89 B.C. *latinitas,* now
outmoded in its original sense, flourished in the non-Greek
parts of the empire as a means of marking a half-way stage in
the transformation of foreign communities into Roman towns.
The chief features of Latin status were the ability to contract
under Roman law valid matrimonial and commercial relations with
Roman citizens, and the possibility of becoming a full Roman
citizen by holding a local magistracy. Since the children of
Roman citizens were themselves Romans, as time passed an
increasing proportion of the office-holding, that is the better-
off, class came to be Roman rather than Latin in status. Hence
Roman law, institutions, and culture were slowly diffused
through the southern, western, and northern regions of the
empire in the first two centuries A.D. - the process known as
'Romanisation'. When sufficiently confident of its Roman-ness
a Latin community could apply for the full citizenship just as
it had previously done for the Latin. The process is nowhere
fully recorded, but Suetonius' *adlegantes merita* ('claiming a
record of service to Rome') gives an idea of the grounds on
which a petition could be based. In Claudius' time Volubilis
in Mauretania obtained the full citizenship by sending a
deputation of leading men to the emperor (*AE* 1916, 42 and cf.
POxy 2435 = E-J³ no.379) and no doubt this was the usual method.
See further Abbott-Johnson 1926, Sherwin-White 1973, Millar
1977, 394ff., and (for the west) Clavel-Lévêque 1971.

aere alieno laborantes ... terrae motu subversas: debt, being
    often caused by failure of the harvest, was almost as much a natural
    disaster as earthquake. For Augustus, Dio (54.23.7) mentions Paphos
    specifically and adds that aid was given on so many occasions that he
    could not feasibly produce a list. A decree of Cos (*Olympia* V,53)
    speaks of Augustus as surpassing the founder Merops by restoring the
    city after a 'quake. See Robert 1978.
traicere ex Sicilia apparentem: cf. Dio 49.34.1; the episode
    belongs to the winter of 36-35 B.C.: Sardinia had been held by Sextus,
    Africa by Augustus' disgraced fellow-triumvir Lepidus (see 16). The
    emperor is alleged by Nicolaus of Damascus (*Vita* 11-12) to have
    visited Africa in the train of his great-uncle in 45 B.C.

48   RELATIONS WITH FOREIGN KINGS

The 'few' kingdoms which Augustus did not give back to native
dynasties included Egypt, a sizable portion of Spain, the
Alpine region, the provinces of Illyricum and Moesia, and
(until the disaster of Varus) Germany between the Rhine and
Elbe!

Suetonius' statement remains accurate for North Africa and
the eastern frontier between Egypt and the Black Sea. In the
latter area Roman policy had long operated with buffer states
or 'client-kingdoms', a system first given proper cohesion
by Pompey in 65-63 B.C. After Actium Augustus could be said
to have 'conquered' these kingdoms, but he wisely confirmed
on their thrones the more important kings: Amyntas of Galatia
(who had already deserted Antony at Actium), Polemo of Pontus,
Archelaus of Cappadocia, and Herod of Judaea. In Armenia, he
attempted no revenge on Artaxes, son of the king whom Antony
had defeated and deposed in 34 B.C., for the Romans he had
massacred in 32, but simply recognised him. When there was
trouble in the kingdom in 20 B.C. he intervened by sending
Tiberius to replace Artaxes by his brother Tigranes (RG 27.2).
Augustus knew that Armenia was too troublesome and difficult
to be worth annexing (though he made capital out of Tiberius'
success by issuing coins bearing the legend ARMENIA CAPTA),
but when Amyntas and Herod's successor Archelaus died (in
25 B.C. and A.D. 6 respectively) Galatia and Judaea became
imperial provinces. For a complete treatment, see Pani 1972.

In Africa, the only considerable independent kingdom was
Mauretania. Augustus had annexed it as a province in 33 B.C.
on the death of King Bocchus - no doubt to counterbalance
Antony's annexation of Armenia in the previous year. But,
with Antony defeated and Armenia under local rule again, he
found it convenient to let Mauretania revert to the status
of a client-kingdom and in 25 B.C. he installed as king
a native African, the Romanised and scholarly Juba II whose
father, the last king of Numidia, had been deposed by Julius
Caesar.

necessitudinibus mutuis iunxit...:   examples are the marriage of
   Polemo, king of Pontus, to Dynamis, queen of the Bosporan kingdom
   (Dio, 54.24.6) and of several connections of Herod's family (Josephus,
   Antiquitates Judaicae 18.135-140).
nec aliter universos...habuit: 'he treated them all as component
   parts of the empire'. These kings were not Romans; yet Augustus dealt
   with them in the manner prescribed by Roman law if they were minors
   or insane, by appointing a guardian.
plurimorum liberos...et instituit: examples are Agrippa the
   grandson of Herod, brought up at Rome with Tiberius' son Drusus
   (Josephus, Antiquitates Judaicae 18.143); Juba II, who was about ten
   years older than Augustus' stepsons Tiberius and Drusus and later
   married Cleopatra Selene, Antony's daughter by Cleopatra (Dio 51.15.6);

and probably Tigranes II of Armenia, captured by Antony in 34 B.C. and
then, after Antony's death, resident in Rome until he was placed on the
Armenian throne in 20 B.C.

49(A) DEPLOYMENT OF MILITARY FORCES

After Actium, Augustus reduced his swollen army of some 50
legions to 28, a number which was further diminished to 25
in A.D. 9 when Varus lost three in Germany (see 23). We
cannot discern any stable pattern of deployment before about
16 B.C., when most of the other fronts were quiescent and
the legions were positioned for the long and in the end
fruitless struggle to annex the whole of Germany. Even after
16 B.C., it would be wrong to think of the Augustan legions
as having any kind of 'normal' distribution of permanent bases
in spite of the fact that some of them may actually have been
stationed in the same places for years at a time. There was
fighting in the Danube regions, in Asia Minor, and on the
eastern frontiers, quite apart from the great Pannonian revolt
of A.D. 6-9, all of which entailed the movement of legions.
The following table, based on Tacitus, Ann.4.5 and the re-
searches of Parker (1928) and Syme (1933), is over-tidy and
cannot represent the likely complexity of troop transfers,
but may serve to give some idea of the military importance
of the various provinces:

Province	No. of legions before A.D. 6	No. and probable identification of legions A.D. 10-23
Spain	4 (5?)	3 (IV *Macedonica*, VI *Victrix*, X *Gemina*)
Germany (Rhine)	5	8 (I,V *Alaudae*, XX, XXI *Rapax*, II *Augusta*, XIII *Gemina*, XIV *Gemina*, XVI)
Raetia-Vindelicia	2	0
Illyricum	5	5 (VII, VIII *Augusta*, IX *Hispana*, XI, XV *Apollinaris*)
Moesia (Macedonia)	3	2 (IV *Scythica*, V *Macedonica*)
Syria	4	4 (III *Gallica*, VI *Ferrata*, X *Fretensis*, XII *Fulminata*)
Egypt	3	2 (III *Cyrenaica*, XXII *Deiotariana*)
Africa	2 (1?)	1 (III *Augusta*)
	28	25

The *auxilia* were non-citizen forces, often either lightly or
specially armed (e.g. slingers, bowmen, cavalry). From the
second century B.C. the Republican army had made use of such
units. Under Augustus we can see the beginnings of the pro-

fessionalisation of *auxilia*, but the situation is very fluid. There were two sorts of unit, the cavalry *ala* and the infantry *cohors* (some of whom might be mounted), and they were normally about 500 strong. In time, they came to be commanded by a Roman officer of equestrian rank, but this had not yet become the regular practice under Augustus, and both senatorial (see 38) and native commanders (e.g. *ILS* 847 - a chieftain of the Trumplini commanding his own men) are recorded. Although they operated *with* legions, it is not clear how firmly they were *attached* to the legions. It is difficult to estimate the proportion of auxiliary to legionary soldiers in the Augustan army. Velleius (2.113.1) records that Tiberius in A.D. 7 commanded an army of 10 legions, more than 70 (auxiliary) *cohortes* and 10 or 14 *alae* (the figure is corrupt in the text). If this is typical there were not many fewer auxiliaries than legionaries. Such a conclusion is in harmony with Tacitus' vague remark at *Ann.* 4.5 about the comparative equality of numbers of the two classes. (On the army in general, see Watson 1969 and Webster 1969; on the *auxilia*, Saddington 1975).

The navy was not dissimilar to the *auxilia*. The rowers were generally free non-citizens, the captains often freedmen (not slaves - see Kienast 1966 on E-J[3] nos. 274 and 276), and the admirals of the two great fleets equestrian. The bases at Misenum and Ravenna, and another at Forum Julii (Fréjus) east of Massilia, mentioned by Strabo (184C) and Tacitus (*Ann.* 4.5), were all constructed by Augustus. After the end of the civil wars the main function of the fleets must have been to keep down piracy and convoy important personages, since there was no rival power left in the Mediterranean. Perhaps the continued existence of these fleets was due to reluctance on the part of Augustus to destroy the arm which had won him the battle of Actium and, earlier, driven Sextus from Sicily. Tacitus says that the ships stationed at Forum Julii were those which Augustus had captured from Antony at Actium. See in general Starr 1960 and Kienast 1966.

The forces stationed in and around Rome were the nine cohorts of the praetorian guard and the three urban cohorts (for the *vigiles* see 30 n.). The former received more than three times the pay of ordinary legionaries (750 *denarii* a year as against 225), and existed from the start of the principate (Dio 53. 11.5). The latter received half the pay of the praetorians, were certainly in existence by the end of the reign, and were probably under the command of the urban prefect, although there is no necessary connection between the institution of the urban prefecture as a regular post (? A.D. 12, Tacitus, *Ann.* 6.11.3) and the establishment of the urban cohorts. These cohorts were numbered X, XI, and XII in sequence with the praetorian cohorts. They were a sort of security force, standing in the same kind of relationship to the praetorians as in London the Metropolitan Police do to the Guards - except that

in Rome both were military units and promotion could take
place from one to the other. There seems to be no reason
for believing that the number of three cohorts, which
Suetonius says was the maximum Augustus permitted in the
city, did not include the urban cohorts. In later reigns,
when the praetorians had their own barracks instead of
being billeted round about as they were under Augustus, only
one praetorian cohort was normally on duty at the palace.
Perhaps the Augustan practice was to have one praetorian and
two urban cohorts in the city. On the praetorians, see
Durry 1938; on the urban cohorts, Freis 1967.

We first hear of definite periods of service in 13 B.C.,
when fixed terms were introduced - 12 years for praetorians,
16 for others (Dio 54.25.5). In A.D. 5, evidently in response
to recruitment difficulties, these were raised to 16 for
praetorians and 20 for others. At the same time regular
money pensions were introduced - 20,000 HS for praetorians,
12,000 HS for others. These replaced the rather hand-to-
mouth Republican system which Augustus had so far followed
of settling retired soldiers either on individual parcels
of land ('viritane assignments') or in new colonies, which
after the early years of the reign had all to be overseas
since there was no more room in Italy. In the following
year the military treasury (*aerarium militare*) was set up,
funded by an initial 'float' from the emperor of 170 million
HS (*RG* 17.2), by a new tax of 5% on inheritance (*vicesima
hereditatum*) which was payable only by Roman citizens (Dio
55.25.5), and by the existing 1% tax on goods sold at auction
(*centesima rerum venalium* - Tacitus, *Ann*.1.78). Augustus had
clung so long to personal responsibility for settling veterans on discharge, because this was a potent factor in
ensuring the loyalty of an army to its commander, as the
last years of the Republic and the civil wars had so power-
fully demonstrated. But by A.D. 6 even the imperial coffers
could no longer stand the strain, and there can have been
only a handful of soldiers still serving who had ever known
any commander-in-chief other than Augustus. See Brunt and
Moore 1967, 41-43, and Brunt 1971, 332ff.

Miseni: the great base at Misenum was established c. 30-20 B.C.
  to replace *Portus Iulius* which Agrippa had created in 37 B.C. for
  the naval campaign against Sextus Pompeius (see 16.1).
Ravennae: the new port of *Classis* was connected to the city of
  Ravenna by a causeway, and to the mouth of the Po by a canal through
  the lagoons.
Calagurritanorum: from *Calagurris Nasica* (modern Calahorra), a
  Roman *municipium* in Hispania Tarraconensis.
Germanorum: perhaps the Batavian horsemen of Dio 55.24.7. The
  Germans were employed again by A.D. 14 (Tacitus, *Ann*. 1.24) and
  remained as a bodyguard until dismissed by Galba in A.D. 68. For
  the disaster of Varus, see 23.1.
aut aetate aut inopia: if *aetate* is to be taken according to the
  normal use of Latin, as a parallel alternative to *inopia*, with *post*

missionem construed closely with what follows so that the sense is 'they should not be able to be incited to revolution after discharge on account of either *aetas* or *inopia*', *aetas* can surely only mean 'youth' - i.e. what Augustus avoided was discharging relatively young men, with inadequate pensions, who might be potential revolutionaries. He had nothing to fear from old men *after* discharge; they were only to be feared if they were not discharged at the proper time (cf. the complaints of the mutineers of A.D. 14 - Tacitus, *Ann.* 1.17.3).

(B)   THE IMPERIAL POST

There was no regular postal system in the Republic, and even Augustus' system was supposed to be entirely for public business; private individuals had to obtain special permission to use the post for their own purposes. The great financial companies (*societates publicanorum*) kept a postal service of messengers, but otherwise communication depended on sending a slave or freedman of one's own, or making use of the journeys of one's friends or their agents.

Suetonius makes it clear that Augustus' original system passed a message through many hands, but that later the same messenger would use relays of vehicles. Once available, the vehicles could also be used as transport by public officials. They were provided by local communities along the roads, and were supposed to be paid for by the user; but inscriptions show quite plainly that not only did official users avoid payment, but others who had no right to use the service at all did so. (See in particular the interesting and detailed inscription from Pisidia - *JRS* (1976) 106ff., from which it appears that overnight accomodation had to be provided free of charge for the emperor's staff, agents, and soldiers).

vehicula: not 'chariots' (*GG*), but 'carts' (*carra* in the Pisidian inscription). Mules or donkeys were also provided.

50   SEALING OF LETTERS

In the late Republic and early Empire, a signet-ring was still simply the personal seal of its owner and was not what it later became, a badge of office or a means of symbolising the conferment or transference of power (cf. 66.3 n.). We are told that the sphinx ring existed in duplicate, in order that Maecenas and Agrippa could issue commands in Augustus' name when he was absent from Italy (see Dio 51.3.4 - 6; elder Pliny, *NH* 37.10). It was, therefore, in use before 29 B.C. and was inevitably associated with a rule which many Romans considered illegal or at least tyrannical. The Alexander-ring, on the other hand, had clear reference to world-rule (achieved or projected) and was particularly appropriate after the capture of Alexandria (cf. 18.1). Alexander was well understood

and used in the self-assertive world of late Republican
politics as the type of all-conquering, superhuman ruler
(Michel 1967). It is not known when Augustus gave up using
this ring in favour of one bearing his own portrait; the
engraver of this, Dioscurides, was the most famous exponent
of the art in Augustan times and half-a-dozen of his gems are
still extant. For full discussion, see Instinsky, 1962.

diplomatibus: originally any document folded or closed in on itself,
diploma came to mean a document authorising an official privilege like
the use of the imperial post, and later particularly a grant of Roman
citizenship made to an auxiliary soldier on discharge.

libellis: the term is used here in the technical sense of 'petitions'
to which the emperor generally replied by writing his answer at the
foot (*subscriptio*). The word can also mean 'notebooks' or, as in 55
'pamphlets'.

51-56 These six chapters form the last section of Suetonius'
treatment of Augustus as a public figure in the civil sphere,
which began at 26. The first two words, *clementiae civili-*
tatisque, function as a main heading for all that follows in
these chapters, which prepare us for the climax reached at
57-60.

51.1 clementia: this was one of the four cardinal virtues inscribed
on the golden shield voted by the senate to Augustus in 27 B.C. and set
up in the senate-house (*RG* 34.2). It was not a Republican virtue,
clemency, at least in the political field, being an autocrat's privilege.
civilitas describes the quality of decent relations between citizen-equals.

ne enumerem...Iunium Novatum et Cassium Severum: Suetonius'
reasoning is this: 'if Augustus could pardon even common people for
apparently serious offences, he of course pardoned men who were of more
exalted status or had committed lesser crimes'. The assumption is that
common people deserve - or at least get - harsher treatment, a proposition which became a fact in the legal framework of the Roman state not
long after Suetonius' time (Garnsey 1970).

It is possible that Junius, by uttering a forged document, laid
himself open to the penalties of the *lex Cornelia de falsis*. However,
what we know of the law suggests that it dealt with forgery for financial gain (especially forgery in wills), and since Tacitus, *Ann.* 1.72,
says 'Augustus was the first to deal with defamatory pamphlets under the
law of treason (*maiestas*)', it is likely then that this is a case in
point. The crime of Cassius (see 56.3) can hardly be brought under any
other head than that of *maiestas,* a vague but serious offence whose scope
became widened under Augustus and especially Tiberius to cover virtually
any form of opposition to or criticism of the regime. Seee Bauman 1974,
27f.; Allison and Cloud 1962.

Agrippae iuvenis: see 19.2 n.

51.2 quadam vero cognitione cum Aemilio Aeliano...: *cognitio*
extra ordinem was a judicial hearing before a Roman magistrate, conducted
at his discretion and in virtue of his *imperium,* and obeying no set rules

of procedure. It was the normal means by which Roman justice was
dispensed outside the city of Rome, though it could be employed there
too and appears to have been the usual way in which the (exceptional)
jurisdiction of consuls and emperors was exercised (Jones 1960, 85).
Corduba was in Baetica, the senatorial province of Spain, and its
inhabitants possessed the Roman citizenship. A constitutional problem
then arises: by what right did Augustus hear a case against a Roman
citizen from a senatorial province? Such a case ought either to have
been taken by the proconsul, or referred to the courts at Rome, from
which there lay no appeal. If Augustus heard the case in Rome, it
provides support for the thesis of Kelly (1957) that the emperor
possessed or at any rate exercised a primary criminal jurisdiction in
cases involving *maiestas*. But there is no need to suppose a hearing in
Rome. The most attractive and economical explanation is that the
incident occurred on one of Augustus' visits to Spain - probably that
of 15-13 B.C. when he was in formal possession of *imperium maius* (see
47 initial n.) and was clearly the highest judicial authority in the
province, rather than that of 27-24 B.C. when his *imperium* was in
theory no more than equal to that of the proconsul. The reply to
Tiberius with its reference to his youth will suit either of these
occasions but precludes any later date.

52(A) RULER-CULT

Suetonius is not interested in this phenomenon (perhaps because
it had become routine in his day) and appears to place temples
and honorific statues in the same category. In fact, ruler-
cult helped to hold the empire together. The inhabitants of
the eastern provinces had long been accustomed to worship their
monarchs; and just as Alexander and his successors were heirs
to the Achaemenids and the Pharaohs, so Augustus and before
him the proconsuls of the late Republic, were the heirs of
Alexander. The goddess Roma had first made her appearance in
the East for diplomatic reasons, early in the second century
B.C. (the first cult attested is that of Smyrna in 195 B.C.).
When the Romans rapidly became *de facto* and eventually *de jure*
rulers of these regions, Roma stayed on to receive the gratitude of those who were now kingless; but since she was
somewhat colourless, her temporal (and temporary) representatives, the proconsular governors of the eastern provinces,
quite frequently found themselves honoured with the trappings
of the cult - temples, sacrifices, and games (for a list of
known cases, see Bowersock 1965, 150).

Between 42 and 30 B.C. Antony had been worshipped as a god
in the East. His conqueror would have found it impossible
to avoid the same treatment, the more so as he advertised
that he was the 'son of a god' in his official nomenclature.
But the fate of his divine "father" and the barrage of anti-
monarchic and anti-oriental propaganda laid down by his own
side before the campaign of Actium made it impossible for
Augustus to assume *tout court* the role of king and god in

the East. Hence the compromise indicated here by Suetonius
(see further Dio 51.20.6-8). It is interesting that cult
honours are attested as late as 2/3 A.D. for a non-imperial
provincial governor, but clearly the cult of the emperor
(which spread to his family) was far more important. It was
regularised on a provincial basis by the appointment of a
high priest - the highest honour a native could attain within his province - and by the grafting of the cult, with its
annual gathering for prayer, sacrifice, and games, on to the
existing institution of the provincial *koinon*. Deputations
from all the cities of a province were accustomed to meet
regularly to discuss matters of common concern. The assembled
delegates constituted the *koinon* (council) of the province
and were able to give some political expression to its
feelings by (for example) passing decrees laudatory (or otherwise) of the governor or even deciding to prosecute him. In
the western provinces and Italy, where there was no previous
tradition of ruler-worship or provincial assemblies, the cult
of Augustus and Roma was deliberately promoted as an instrument of political cohesion - notably by the altar at Lyon
dedicated by Drusus in 10 B.C. as a gathering-place for the
representatives of the Gallic tribes - but was slower to take
root.

Below this 'official' provincial level things were different.
Tiberius, we know, tried to discourage divine honours (Tacitus,
Ann. 4.37 cf. his letter to Gytheion, E-J[3] no.102) and we can
be certain Augustus had done the same. But municipalities
and groups of private citizens were free to worship whom they
liked (subversion apart), and we find for example that the
Roman merchants at Thinissut (Africa) made an offering to
'God Augustus', and one L. Calpurnius of a leading commercial
family from Puteoli (near Naples) erected a temple to Augustus
(E-J[3] nos.106 and 111). It was partly in response to this
kind of pressure that after he became Pontifex Maximus in
12 B.C. Augustus instituted a public cult of his spirit (*genius*)
in association with the *Lares Compitales* (see 31.4 n.). This
acted as a veiled form of ruler worship and managed to avoid
giving that offence which Julius Caesar's striving towards
personal divinity had provoked. The *genius*, though an aspect
of the individual (or of the collective represented as an
individual, e.g. *Genius Populi Romani* as figured on coins and
sculpture) nevertheless signified the divine and life-giving
element in him. The *genius* of the *paterfamilias*, the head of
the family, who embodied the continuing existence of that family, was worshipped under the form of a bearded snake. Thus
the *Genius Augusti* was simultaneously unique to Augustus and
represented something far less transitory than the mortal
emperor himself. It also tended to be identified, especially
after Augustus had become *Pater Patriae* (see 58.1 n.), with
the *Genius* of the Roman People to whom Augustus was now *paterfamilias*.

Some modern scholars regard ruler-cult as a purely political phenomenon, devoid of any real religious content; but this view stems from a sharp distinction between mortal and divine which is not found in ancient thought. The Greeks rather conceived of many gradations between the fully human and the fully divine, exemplified by Naiads, heroes, demi-gods, and even founders of cities, and met no conceptual obstacle when wishing to recognise a degree of divinity in men like Alexander, or Augustus, who were plainly out of the ordinary.

See Taylor 1931; Weinstock 1971; Deininger 1965; Habicht 1973; Mellor 1975; Liebeschuetz 1979,65f.; Fishwick 1969.

argenteas statuas: silver statues were an oriental extravagance. Those of the Pontic kings Pharnaces and Mithridates were carried as spoil in Pompey's triumph of 61 B.C. (Elder Pliny *NH* 33.151). Dio (53.22.3) records that Augustus, by striking coin from silver statues set up 'by his friends and some communities', and disbursing it on public projects as his own money made it appear that his personal generosity was greater than it really was. (For the Temple of Palatine Apollo, see 29.1 n.). Augustus himself says he melted down about eighty silver statues to provide the gold offerings to Apollo (*RG* 24.2).

(B)   REFUSAL OF DICTATORSHIP

The occasion was the spring of 22 B.C., the first year since the restoration of regular government in 27 B.C. that Augustus had not been consul. Disease, floods, and scarcity of corn provoked the people to besiege the senate house and demand that Augustus be given special charge of the corn supply (*praefectura annonae*) and be made dictator (Dio 54.1; *RG* 5.1). The latter office was anathema to the Roman upper classes after the use made of it by Sulla and Julius Caesar, and had been constitutionally abolished by Antony in the reaction after Caesar's murder; the present demand shows how differently the lower classes felt, and to what lengths Augustus had to go to dissuade them. They clearly wished Augustus to possess open and unambiguous authority, if he would not hold the consul-ship. He did, however, accept charge of the corn supply, and to such effect that 'within a few days I delivered the whole city from apprehension and immediate danger at my own cost and by my own efforts' (*RG* 5.2). If this statement is true, it must raise the suspicion that Augustus had been stockpiling corn (and thus helping to create the shortage?) against just such an eventuality, in order to be able to play the part of larger-than-life benefactor to his stricken people; for how could a man, given the slow and cumbersome systems of communi-cation and transport available then, relieve a major shortage in a city of nearly a million inhabitants 'within a few days' without having massive stores ready to hand?

deprecatus est: 'begged them not to (force the dictatorship on him)' rather than 'implored their silence' (*GG*).

53 Augustus' avoidance of any title, pomp, or flattery which smacked of monarchy was a necessary part of his political stance. As 'leading citizen' (*princeps*) it was important for him to accept no more honour than a citizen should from his fellows, and to be accessible, good-humoured, and courteous.

domini appellationem: the title *dominus* (master) was associated with slavery, whether actual or metaphorical. Augustus' successors were less modest: Gaius (Caligula) had himself made a god, and Domitian was called *dominus et deus*.

spectante eo ludos: his position obliged the emperor to attend the games (which included dramatic performances). They afforded the populace a good chance to demonstrate their sympathies (see Millar 1977, 368f.). This episode appears to be dated later than 17 B.C. by the reference to Augustus' 'children' as it was in that year that Gaius and Lucius were adopted. Cf. Cicero's account of the discomfiture of Pompey and Caesar on a similar occasion in 59 B.C. (*ad Atticum* 2.19.3).

ne quem officii causa inquietaret: it was a well-established Roman custom for a procession to meet a returning magistrate or commander, or accompany him on his departure (cf. Cicero, *Philippics* 2.106). In 30 B.C. the Senate decreed that on Augustus' return from the East the Vestal Virgins, the Senate, and the whole people with their wives and children should turn out to meet him (Dio 51.19.2), and in 19 B.C. they sent the consul Q. Lucretius and a deputation of other magistrates and leading men as far as Campania to greet him - 'an honour that up to the present day has been decreed to none but myself' (*RG* 12.1). But special occasions apart, Augustus was doubtless as keen to spare himself the tedium of endless municipal welcomes and farewells as he was to relieve his hosts of time-consuming and unproductive formality. He was not long imitated. By the second century the imperial *Adventus* (arrival) and *Profectio* (departure) had become ceremonial occasions.

adaperta sella: 'an open sedan chair'. I adopt the conjecture of Beroaldus for the MSS' *adoperta* 'closed', which was a sign of pride, secrecy, or stand-offishness; cf. Cicero, *Philippics* 2.106; Gellius, *NA* 10.3.5.

promiscuis salutationibus: the *salutatio* was the early morning call paid by friends and clients on the great, an institution famous from the later strictures of Martial and Juvenal. Augustus refused to join those who followed the practice of C. Gracchus, whom Seneca alleges to have been the first Roman to have divided his callers into grades of precedence and had 'first friends, second friends, but no true friends' (*de Beneficiis* 6.34.2).

die senatus: to be taken closely with what precedes: the inference is that on other days senators would attend the *salutatio*, but that on a senate day Augustus wished to preserve the fiction that he was of the same status as his fellow-senators. (Cf. Dio 54.25.4 - 5 and 56.41.5). Julius Caesar had caused great offence by failing to treat the senate with respect (cf. *DJ* 78). To know the senators by name, without calling on the services of a remembrancer (*nomenclator*), and to greet them in their seats, indicated Augustus' tact and political sensitivity.

Gallum Cerrinium: the cognomen is placed first; see 4.1 n. This man is not otherwise known, though L. Cestius Gallus Cerrinius Iustus Lutatius Natalis, a senator of the later second century A.D., may be a descendant.

54-55 The theme of Augustus' respect for the senate leads to his tolerance (not always cheerful) of (verbal) opposition from it. The examples of free speech given by Suetonius, though innocuous by the standards of the departed Republic, will have seemed bold under the developed principate of Trajan and Hadrian.

54   si locum haberem ...:   'if I had the chance to speak'. Senators were normally called to speak in order of seniority, and many would not get the chance (but cf. 35.4).

Antistius Labeo: a famous jurist and antiquarian, of incorruptible independence, described by his great rival Ateius Capito, who was a friend of Augustus', thus: 'the man was driven by a spirit of freedom so excessive and intense that even when the late Augustus was *princeps* and master of the state, he considered nothing to be important or valid which had not be prescribed and hallowed according to his reading by the ancient usage of Rome' (Gellius, *NA* 13.12.2). His father had been one of the conspirators against Caesar and committed suicide after Philippi. Dio (54.15.7) relates the same episode, but makes Labeo reply 'What have I done wrong by keeping in the senate a man you still allow to be Pontifex Maximus?' The occasion was the *lectio* of 18 B.C. (see 35.1 n.); for Lepidus, see 16.4.

55   libellos aut carmina ad infamiam cuiuspiam ...:   *libelli* here are 'pamphlets', the origin of English 'libel', while *carmina* are not, as sometimes, 'magic incantations', but verse *libelli*. The prose pamphlets were a more modern form of the older verse attack already provided against in the XII Tables. Suetonius seems to be stressing two aspects of Augustus' action - that libel of anyone, not just himself, was wrong and that libel was just as reprehensible under a false name as a true one. Tacitus (*Ann.* 1.72.4) says Augustus was the first to proceed against libellous publications under the law of treason (*maiestas*) - see 33 n.; Bauman 1974, 27 f. The date is probably A.D. 6 (cf. Dio 55.27.1 - 3).

56   A final, miscellaneous chapter, giving more instances of Augustus' moderation and forming a general conclusion to the section introduced in 51 by the leading words *Clementiae civilitatisque eius.*

56.1 testamentorum licentia: 'freedom of speech in wills', often the only safe place to attack the powerful. Note Fulcinius Trio, who driven to suicide by informers 'wrote in his last testament many terrible charges against Macro and the principal freedmen of the emperor' (Tacitus, *Ann.* 6.44).

candidatis suis: those candidates to whom Augustus had promised his support were known as *candidati Caesaris*. They were, presumably, sure of election, but Augustus thought it proper to go through the motions of soliciting votes on their behalf. This process was called *suffragatio*. When as a result of age he found it difficult to go round in person, he resorted to *commendatio,* a public announcement in which he 'commended' certain candidates to the people as particularly worthy of their votes

(Dio 55.34.2). It is unlikely that he ever commended the same number of candidates as there were vacancies, and he never apparently commended to the consulship (except perhaps in the disturbances of 19 B.C. and A.D. 6 - Dio 54.10.2 (cf. 6.1-3 and 55.34.2).

56.2 forum angustius fecit: for his forum, see 29.1. The plan is slightly assymetrical at one end; but perhaps Suetonius means more than this, as the flanking colonnades do seem to crowd the temple a little. **praetextatis ... assurrectum ... et ... plausum:** the important word is the first one. What Augustus objected to was not the demonstration as such, but the fact that it was in honour of mere boys who had not yet officially emerged into public life. This episode (cf. Dio 55.9.1) is presumably to be placed in or not long before 6 B.C., when Tiberius retired from Rome and his stepsons, Augustus' 'sons', became so popular that Gaius, not yet fifteen, was elected to a consulship, in defiance of the constitution and Augustus' wishes. Dio (54.27.1) speaks of a similar incident, involving only Gaius, as early as 13 B.C.

56.3 Asprenas Nonius: a *cause celèbre;* Quintilian (10.1.22) recommends the student to read the speeches of Cassius, prosecuting, and Asinius Pollio, defending. Asprenas was alleged to have poisoned 130 guests (elder Pliny, *NH* 35.164), but Quintilian at any rate regarded the charge as malicious (11.1.57). This man was the father of the consuls of A.D. 6 and 8, and brother-in-law to the ill-fated P. Quinctilius Varus (see 23.1) and his sister Quinctilia who was married to Sex. Appuleius (consul 29 B.C.), Augustus' nephew (see 4.1 n.). **Cassius Severus:** 'this man, an able and vigorous orator of obscure origin, resembling a gladiator in appearance, was hated and feared for his bitter tongue and incorrigible love of independence' (Syme 1939, 486). When the dangerous historical writings of another notorious opponent of the regime, T. Labienus, were burnt towards the end of Augustus' life, Cassius remarked that it was no matter, as he knew them all by heart (elder Seneca, *Controversiae* 10. *praefatio* 8). He was himself prosecuted (?A.D. 12) and condemned under the law of *maiestas* (see 55 n.) to exile first in Crete and finally on the rocky islet of Seriphos (Tacitus, *Ann.* 1.72 and 4.21). **superesset:** the technical term for one who appeared in court to support another, especially by delivering an encomium (*laudatio*) of the accused. **Castricium, per quem de coniuratione Murenae cognoverat:** for the conspiracy of Murena, see 19.1 n. There exists an Augustan inscription (E-J[3] no.235) relating to one 'A. Castricius, son of Myriotalentus' which has given rise to the speculation that Myriotalentus ('Moneybags') may be Augustus' informer - who will not have gone unrewarded (Stockton 1965, 27).

57-60 Suetonius now passes, by an entirely natural transition, from Augustus' acts of kindness and moderation to their recognition by his grateful people. His arrangement is skilful. First come relatively ordinary celebrations and pecuniary gratitude; the tone rises as Augustus is named Pater Patriae; then we hear how important his very life was for Romans; and finally comes the astonishing information that even kings ceased to pretend they were kings when they were in his

presence. Augustus is truly King of Kings, though Suetonius
is careful to avoid the title. In musical terms, this movement
ends with a fortissimo climax.

57.1 senatus consulta: to Suetonius' contemporaries fulsome praise of
the *princeps* in decrees of the senate would have seemed routine; but even
in Augustus' own lifetime the currency of official praise had been devalued
by extravagant decrees in honour of Julius Caesar (*DJ* 70 and 78) and of
himself (Dio 51.19).

equites R. natalem eius ... biduo semper celebrarunt: Augustus'
birthday, September 23rd. (5.1) had been honoured by an official thanksgiving since 30 B.C. (Dio 51.19.2), and by praetorian games, which however
did not become part of the official calendar as the Augustalia until 11 B.C.
(Dio 54.34.2). It is not known why the equestrian order celebrated for two
days (23rd and 24th), but their lead was soon followed: decrees from Narbo
and Forum Clodii (Etruria) attest two days of celebrations and point to
some confusion as to which day actually was Augustus' birthday (*E-J*[3] nos.
100A and 101). The confusion may have arisen as a result of Julius Caesar's
calendar reform.

Lacum Curti: this was a well or pool in the Forum, with paving around it
by Augustan times. The Romans connected the name variously with a Sabine
leader who fought against Romulus, a consul of 445B.C., or a young man who
'devoted' himself to the gods, to save the community, by leaping into a
chasm on the spot in 362 B.C. (Livy 1.12-13 and 7.6; Varro, *de Lingua
Latina* 5.150; Dudley 1967, 95-97; Nash 1961, I.542-4). The custom of
casting coins or precious objects into water for good luck was practised
then as now: see Pausanias 1.34.4; *Tib.* 14.3.

strenam: 'we call that *strena* which is given for the sake of the omen on
a holy day' - Festus 410L. This practice became institutionalised (cf.
Tib. 34; *Gaius* 42) and gradually turned into a kind of tax. Augustus at
least used it for the ornamentation of the city; cf. **91.2.**

57.2 Palatinae domus: Augustus' house was burnt down about A.D. 3
(Dio 55.12.4-5). For the house, see **72.1.**

veterani: veterans had a civic identity as colonists, most of Augustus'
colonies being founded to settle them on discharge.

decuriae: Cicero, *pro Plancio* 45, which has been cited in support of the
theory that tribes had subdivisions known as *decuriae*, in fact proves the
reverse: the process of *decuriatio tribulium* there referred to is the
electoral malpractice by which political agents broke up the tribal lists
into quite unofficial sub-groups for the easier organisation of bribery
(cf. Cicero, *Philippics* 7.18 - *non decuriabit improbos?*). GG's 'guilds'
must be right. *CIL* 6. (1802ff.) yields many examples of *decuriae* of
scribes, lictors, heralds, etc. attendant upon magistrates. There were
also the grander *decuriae* of jurors (see **32.3** n.), and the word came to
be used of the various corps of freedmen and slaves within the emperor's
own household (cf. Petronius, *Satyricon* 47.11-13).

58.1 Patris Patriae: the senate bestowed the title *Pater Patriae* on
Augustus on February 5th 2 B.C. (Ovid, *Fasti* 2.127ff; Fasti Praenestini
- *E-J*[3] p.47). In *RG* Augustus places this honour last, after the great
roll of kings who acknowledged his superiority, and so makes it the
climax of his achievements. Suetonius reverses the emphasis.

The penetrating study of Alföldi (1952-4) has shown how *pater* (or *parens*) *patriae*, as used in the late Republic, always has connotations of 'saviour of the state', apart from the obvious elements of guardianship and authority; and this links the title not only with the world of the Hellenistic kings, who were often called 'Saviour', but with both the ideal Roman statesman, the *conservator* or *rector rei publicae* which Ciceronian political theory sought, and the actual achievement of Augustus commemorated by the oak wreath bestowed on him in 27 B.C. for 'saving the citizens' (*RG* 34.2; Dio 53.16.4). As applied by Livy to Romulus (1.16.6), Camillus (5.49.7), Manlius Capitolinus (6.14.5) and others, by Cato and Catulus to Cicero (Appian, *BC* 2.7; Cicero, *in Pisonem* 6), and by Cicero to Marius (*pro Rabirio perduellionis* 27), it had no formal existence as a title. This first occurred when the senate decreed that Julius Caesar should be called *Parens Patriae* (*DJ* 76.1 appears to be in error; cf. Alföldi 1953, 107) though this is not attested on coins or inscriptions until after his death (see *ILLRP* nos. 407-10; Crawford 1974, 494; *DJ* 85; Cicero, *ad Familiares* 12.3.1). Since the term was already clearly established in the vocabulary of political praise and had no unique reference to Caesar, it is scarcely surprising to find it applied to Augustus before 2 B.C. (e.g. Horace, *Odes* 1.2.50 - *hic ames dici pater atque princeps; ibid* 3.24.27 - *si quaeris PATER URBIUM subscribi statuis;* denarius of 18-17 B.C., *BMC Aug.* nos.397ff. - *SPQR PARENTI CONS(ervatori) SUO; ILS* 96 and 6755 - both *patri patriae*). There can be little doubt, in view of this, that the sequence of events related by Suetonius was carefully orchestrated. Note that it happens in the special year of 2 B.C., the year of Augustus' final consulship, of the entry of his younger 'son' on public life, of his final distribution of money to the Roman plebs, and of the forty-years-awaited dedication of the Temple of Mars Ultor and its associated forum (see **29.2**). Note also the exceptional nature of a deputation from the plebs, presumably voted by the popular assembly and headed by the tribunes (shades of the early Republic!). Furthermore, Augustus' initial refusal of the honour could not fail to make his eventual acceptance more striking (cf. his refusal of political power in January 27 B.C.), and may be seen as an almost necessary part of the process by which the formula *Pater Patriae* was converted from a casual term of eulogy to an imperial title. Of subsequent emperors, only Tiberius and apparently Galba, Otho, and Vitellius declined to take it (see *BMC Aug.* ccxv).

ineunti Romae spectacula: another example of the importance of the games as an arena for the demonstration of public opinion; cf. **56.2**.

Valerium Messallam: M. Valerius Messalla Corvinus was an ex-Republican contemporary of Augustus' who had fought with the Liberators at Philippi, but soon left Antony for Augustus, commanded armies for the latter, and received the doubtful honour of holding the consulship of 31 B.C. that was rightly Antony's. Subsequently military success (he triumphed from Aquitania in 27 B.C.), oratorical skill, and literary patronage (of Tibullus, amongst others), together with his ancient and distinguished political lineage, enabled him to pretend to some sort of independence. In 26 B.C. (Jerome's date), or more probably in 25 (Schmitthenner 1962, 81f.), when Augustus was absent in Spain, he laid down the prefecture of the city after holding it for only a few days, claiming that it was inconsistent with the constitution as he understood it (see **37 n. C**). His seniority in the senate, his status as an individual, and his talents as an orator made him the ideal spokesman for the senate on this occasion.

58.2 domuique tuae: the emphasis on Augustus' family is not Republican. The same dynastic note is already present in a state document of 17 B.C. - the prayer offered at the *Ludi Saeculares* (see **31.4** n.). This asks for the blessing of the gods not only on the Roman people and on the college of *Quindecimviri,* as whose spokesman Augustus made the prayer, but on Augustus and his house and family (*mihi domo familiaeque*).

59 Antonius Musa: cf. **81.** Like most doctors, Musa was a Greek freedman. He cured Augustus in 23 B.C. by prescribing cold baths and a diet of lettuce and cold drinks, but failed to save Augustus' nephew Marcellus by the same means later in the year (Dio 53.30.3-4; elder Pliny, *NH* 19.128; cf. Horace, *Epistles* 1.15.3-5).

initium anni: to alter the beginning of the year was not quite so silly as it may seem, since there were numerous different calendars and different starts to the year in the cities of the Mediterranean world; but it was tiresome in Italy, where the Roman calendar was in general use. Cf. the long and eulogistic decree from the province of Asia, probably of 9 B.C., making September 23rd., Augustus' birthday, the start of the year ($E-J^3$ no.98 = *LR* II 64-65).

super templa et aras ludos quoque quinquennales: temples, altars, and games are all the trappings of cult (see **52** n.). *Quinquennales* means every four years, because of inclusive reckoning. This interval was that of the four ancient and famous festivals of Greece, the Olympic, Nemean, Pythian, and Isthmian games. Inter-city rivalry was largely responsible for this multiplication of festivals.

60 Caesareas urbes: Herod the Great's Caesarea on the Judaean coast is the best known of these. It had a temple of Rome and Augustus and quinquennial games; finally dedicated in 10/9 B.C. after twelve years' building, it was a splendid modern Graeco-Roman city and advertised Herod's ability to meet the standards of the rest of the civilised world (Josephus, *Antiquitates Judaicae* 15.331f. and 16.136f.). Others were named, or founded, by Herod's son Philip in Phoenicia, by Juba II in Mauretania, and by Amyntas in Pisidia (see *RE* 3.1 *s.v.* Caesarea).

aedem Iovis Olympii Athenis: this is the great temple some of whose columns still stand to the east of the Acropolis. Begun by Pisistratus in the sixth century B.C., it was not finally completed until the reign of Hadrian.

genio: see **52** nn.

togati: to dress as Romans was to proclaim the kings' subservience to an authority and a civilisation mightier than their own.

61-65 The introductory sentence of 61 marks the beginning of the third and final main division of the work, devoted to Augustus' private life and concluded by his death. The first five chapters are concerned with his family, with which he was notoriously unlucky. The contrast with the climax just reached at the end of the 'public' section is striking and pathetic.

61.2 matrem amisit in primo consulatu: Atia (see **4.1**) died, then, between August 19th and November 27th, 43 B.C. She was honoured by a public funeral (Dio 47.17.6).

sororem Octaviam: Suetonius must mean Augustus' full sister, for whom
see 4.1 n. Dio places her death in 11 B.C. (54.35.4), Suetonius between
September 23rd, 10 B.C. and September 23rd, 9 B.C. Her body lay in state
at the shrine of Divus Julius in the Forum, and Augustus himself
delivered the funeral oration. Her ashes were laid in the Mausoleum of
Augustus beside those of her son Marcellus (see 63.1; Dudley 1967, pl.65).

62   AUGUSTUS' MARRIAGES

(i)   *Servilia* was the daughter of P. Servilius Vatia Isauricus,
who was related by marriage to Brutus, Cassius, and Lepidus,
was a leading senatorial 'moderate' in the events of 44-43
B.C., and had been Caesar's consular colleague in the year of
Pharsalus; her engagement to Augustus was the product of the
political alignment engineered by Cicero in early 43 B.C.
(see 10 n.).

(ii)   The marriage to *Claudia,* as Suetonius explains, took
place for similar reasons of state, late in 43 B.C. Claudia
must have been just twelve, the legal age for marriage (*vixdum
nubilem*). Fulvia's first husband, Cicero's great enemy P.
Clodius Pulcher, was killed in 52, and her second, C. Scribonius
Curio, in 49 B.C. It is not known when she married Antony,
except that it cannot have been later than 46 since their elder
son was old enough to participate in diplomacy and fighting
when Augustus attacked Alexandria in 30 B.C. The 'disagreement'
between Augustus and his mother-in-law arose in 42-41 B.C. (see
14) when his bride was still probably only thirteen.

(iii)   *Scribonia* became Augustus' wife early in 40 B.C., also
for purely political reasons; his object was to forge a hasty
link with Sextus Pompeius in the aftermath of Perusia, when it
was not clear whether Antony would remain a friend (see 17.1-
2 n.). She was sister to Sextus' father-in-law L. Scribonius
Libo. One of her former husbands was a Cornelius Lentulus
Marcellinus, presumably Cn., consul in 56 B.C.; the other was
a Cornelius Scipio, possibly the consul of 35 B.C. (see Groag,
RE 4.1388; *CIL* 6.26033; Propertius 4.11.29-30 and 55-66). The
evidence shows that Scribonia had children by both marriages,
and if Scipio is the man suggested, he reached his consulship
some years after his marriage with Scribonia was over. Augustus
divorced Scribonia in 39 B.C., on the very day of Julia's birth,
if we may believe Dio (48.34.3).

(iv)   The marriage with *Livia Drusilla* (January 17th 38 B.C. -
E-J[3] p.46) is said to have been a love match, but this is not
the whole truth. Note that the divorce with Scribonia (though
it cannot be placed exactly) occurred just when Augustus was
starting to quarrel with Sextus in the latter part of 39 B.C.;
also that Livia's husband Ti. Claudius Nero, a blue-blooded
ex-Republican aristocrat (a type hitherto conspicuously lacking
in the party of Augustus) was at the time he so obligingly
divorced his young, pretty, and pregnant wife, a follower of

Antony, having not so long since abandoned Sextus, to whom he had fled after supporting L. Antonius in the Perusine war (*Tib.* 4). In other words, Augustus was starting to attract to his side some of the Republican nobility (see also Levick 1976, 15). Livia was also of Claudian stock: her father, who fought against the triumvirs at Philippi and committed suicide after the battle, was a Claudius who had been adopted into the family of the Livii Drusi (see Syme 1939, 229). She herself was born in 58 or 57 B.C. (Dio 58.2.1), and bore her sons by Ti. Nero in 42 (Tiberius) and 38 (Drusus).

63.1 Juliam: see (iii) above and 65.
Marcello: C. Claudius Marcellus, Octavia's son by her first husband of the same name (consul 50 B.C.), was born in 42 B.C. (Propertius 3.18.15) and died in the autumn of 23 (cf. 59 n. *Antonius Musa*). Like all Julia's husbands, he was destined by Augustus to succeed to the principate.
M. Agrippae nuptum dedit: for Agrippa, see 16.2 n. The marriage took place in 21 B.C., Augustus himself being absent overseas (Dio 54.6.5). Agrippa's previous match, to the elder of Marcellus' two sisters, had taken place after he had divorced (or lost) his first wife Caecilia, daughter of Cicero's friend Atticus, sometime between 32 and 28 B.C. (Nepos, *Atticus* 21-22; Dio 53.1.2).
exorata sorore, ut sibi generum cederet (genero MSS): it is possible to extract a sense out of the received text, by translating 'he begged his sister to yield to her son-in-law, for his (*sibi*, i.e. Augustus') sake'. But this makes *Agrippa* take the initiative, when the drift of the whole paragraph is what *Augustus* did about Julia's marriages. The correction *generum* gives a simple and precisely appropriate meaning: 'he begged his sister to surrender a son-in-law to him', i.e. he was asking his sister to let *her* son-in-law (by the marriage with Marcella) become *his* (by marrying Julia).

63.2 Tiberium privignum: Tiberius was married to Vipsania Agrippina, Agrippa's daughter by his first marriage to Caecilia (see above), and was deeply attached to her (*Tib.* 7.2-3). Their son Drusus had been born in 14 B.C. Suetonius (*Tib.* 7.2-3) says that the marriage to Julia, which took place in 11 B.C., was satisfactory at first and only degenerated after the death of their baby son, born at Aquileia in 10 or 9 B.C. That Augustus considered a member of the equestrian order as a possible husband for Julia is incredible in the light of his dynastic ruthlessness in arranging her marriages; Tacitus' allusions to the story (*Ann.* 4.39.5 and 40.8) are placed in a context which scarcely confirms its reliability.
M. Antonius scribit ... primum Antonio ... dein Cotisoni: the betrothal of Julia to Antyllus (see 17.5 n.) sealed the compact of Tarentum in 37 B.C., when Julia was about two and young Antonius about eight or nine (Dio 48.54.4). Cotiso in 33 B.C. controlled an area which bordered both on Dalmatia, recently conquered by Augustus, and on Macedonia, the northern flank of Antony's dominions. Both men were anxious to have him as an ally. It may be true that Augustus offered to betroth Julia to him, but he decided to join Antony. The latter wished to publicise the story in order to show Augustus' faithlessness in breaking the earlier engagement and his readiness to contract alliances, just like Antony, with barbarian monarchs.

64.1 nepotes: for Augustus' grandchildren, see the genealogical table II, p. 18.

L. Paullo: on this L. Aemilius Paullus, grandson of Scribonia through her daughter Cornelia's marriage to L. Aemilius Paullus, censor of 22 B.C., see 19 n. vi.

Germanico: Germanicus (born 15 B.C.) was not only Octavia's grandson through the younger Antonia, but also Livia's grandson through her younger son Drusus. Groomed by Augustus as a potential successor to Tiberius, he died in A.D. 19 and it was his 'unsuitable' younger brother Claudius who in fact ended up by becoming emperor.

Gaium et Lucium adoptavit ... per assem et libram: both boys were adopted by Augustus on the birth of Lucius. It was common practice among the Roman aristocracy to adopt (even adults) to prevent a name dying out. Augustus himself owed everything to his adoption by Caesar, and wished to endow his grandsons with similar good fortune. Agrippa's feelings are not recorded, but he too had profited from Augustus' adoption and his own loyalty to the name of Caesar; nor did he cherish his own family name Vipsanius (cf. 16.2 n.). *per assem et libram emptos* describes the routine ritual of a Roman sale; adoption was theoretically the purchase of another man's sons, which by old Roman law were as much his property, to dispose of as he wished, as his oxen; (see Gaius 1.119-122).

ad curam rei publicae: the senate decreed that Gaius and Lucius should participate in the business of the state (*consiliis publicis*) as soon as they had officially come of age and been introduced into public life (see 8.1 n. *quadriennio* and 38.2 n.). We know from Josephus that the first time Gaius attended Augustus' *consilium* (council of state) was when it considered what to do with Judaea on Herod's death (autumn 5 or spring 4 B.C.; Josephus, *Antiquitates Judaicae* 17.229).

consules designatos: much to Augustus' irritation, the people elected Gaius to a consulship in 6 B.C. when he was only fourteen and officially still a child. Both Gaius and Lucius were very popular, and in over-ruling this highly irregular election Augustus had to concede that they could hold the consulship when they were twenty and be officially designated five years before that: so Gaius became consul-designate in 5 B.C. for A.D. 1 and Lucius in 2 B.C. for A.D. 4. Gaius visited the armies in the Balkans and the Danube and took command of the latter in 1 B.C., preparatory to undertaking an expedition in the east which was to lead him to campaign in Arabia in A.D. 1 and ultimately to die at Limyra in Lycia, on February 21st A.D. 4, from a wound received at the siege of Artagira in Armenia (*ILS* 140 = *E-J*[3] no.69; Dio 55.10.17-10a.9). Lucius was sent to visit the Spanish armies, but died at Marseilles on August 20th A.D. 2 (*ILS* 139 = *E-J*3 no.68).

64.2 diurnos commentarios: *GG* translate 'imperial day-book', which is possible, but otherwise unattested, and of obscure function. Suetonius more probably refers to the *acta diurna*, the daily public bulletin of official news, and means that Augustus expected his girls' conduct to be of a standard which would cause no embarrassment if reported in this publication.

L. Vinicio: this eligible and distinguished young man was the son of the consul of 33 B.C. of the same name, and related to M. Vinicius

(consul 19 B.C.), who was a personal friend of Augustus and an exper-
ienced commander of armies. He was of much the same age as Julia.
Baiae, across the bay from Puteoli (Pozzuoli), was thick with the
luxury seaside villas of the wealthy and powerful, and already by
the 50s B.C. had become a byword for luxury, idleness and loose
morals (Cicero, *Pro Caelio* 38; D'Arms 1970, 39-84).

natare: 'swimming': so the MSS but Lipsius' conjecture *notare* 'to write
shorthand' or 'in cipher' is very attractive (cf. **88**).

in imo lecto: at a formal dinner there were three couches, arranged
in an open square, and the least honoured guests were placed on the
'bottom couch'. Adults reclined, but children were expected to sit up.
(The Latin will also bear the interpretation 'they sat on the bottom of
his couch', which is perhaps preferable as it removes the anomaly of the
presence of children at a formal dinner, and the point of Suetonius'
information here is that Augustus kept his grandsons in their place).

65.1 Iulias filiam et neptem: (a) his daughter was relegated by
Augustus to the island of Pandateria (Ventotene) off the Campanian
coast in 2 B.C. She was said to be at the centre of an adultery scandal. Five were implicated, including two ex-consuls: Ti. Sempronius
Gracchus, Cornelius Scipio, Ap. Claudius Pulcher, T.Quinctius Crispinus
Sulpicianus (consul 9 B.C.), and Iullus Antonius (consul 10 B.C.). The
last, Antony's younger son by Fulvia but brought up by Octavia in the
imperial household, was allowed to commit suicide; the others were all
relegated (Velleius Paterculus 2.100.3-5; Dio 55.10.12-16). The number
and nobility of the 'lovers' and the execution of Iullus Antonius (who
was married to the elder Marcella - see **63.1**) point to something more
than a simple sex scandal. It is plausibly conjectured (e.g. by Syme
1939, 427 and Levick 1976, 41) that some treasonable intrigue was
brewing. Adultery there may well have been; but it was not the heart
of the matter.

(b) The younger Julia was relegated in A.D. 8 to the island of
Trimerus off the Apulian coast. Like her mother, she was accused of
adultery, but again there is an oddity in that her lover D. Iunius
Silanus was not exposed to the rigour of the courts but only sent
into informal exile (Tacitus, *Ann.* 3.24.5). In the same year her
brother Agrippa Postumus was relegated to Planasia near Elba and the
poet Ovid, who moved in these circles, to Tomi near the Black Sea. Ovid
is notoriously reticent about the precise nature of the 'error' which
led to his exile, but leaves a reader in no doubt that it was a serious
matter of state. Historians rightly sense a plot, but its nature is
quite mysterious (see Levick 1976, 59f.; Syme 1978, 206f.; and cf. **19**
n.vi).

Gaium et Lucium: see **64.1 n.** *consules designatos.*

Agrippam: Agrippa Postumus, born in 12 B.C. after the death of his
father, was adopted along with Tiberius by Augustus on June 26th A.D. 4.
The *lex curiata* was a law passed by the *comitia curiata,* an assembly which
was an atrophied survival from the period of the kings; it was presided
over by the *pontifex maximus* and the people were represented by thirty
lictors. This assembly performed certain formal acts: conferment of
imperium on magistrates, validation of wills, and installation of priests,
apart from adoptions (*adrogatio*) of persons who, like Agrippa and
Tiberius, were *sui iuris* (fully independent in law) and could not therefore be 'sold' as Gaius and Lucius were (Gellius, *Noctes Atticae* 5.19;

Gaius 1.98ff.).

Since 25 B.C. Augustus' intended successors (Marcellus, Agrippa, Tiberius, Gaius) had all been either his sons-in-law or adopted sons. Tiberius had ceased to be his son-in-law (though remaining his step-son) when Augustus made him divorce Julia after her relegation in 2 B.C. Now that Gaius was dead and Tiberius recalled to public life after ten years' retirement, Augustus wished to mark him out as his heir beyond all doubt; he also gave him tribunician power for ten years, and *imperium* in all the imperial provinces. At the adoption Augustus said 'I do this for the sake of Rome' (Velleius Paterculus 2.104.1), a remark which has been variously interpreted but was surely only meant to deal with the legal point about his automatic acquisition of Tiberius' property (see below).

The adoption of Postumus is not so easily explained. He had done without a father all his life and without a mother since he was ten, and it is hard to avoid the conclusion, in the light of his later truculence, that Augustus wished to control him, as the only surviving male in the emperor's direct line, by bringing him under the control of his own *patria potestas*. A more charitable view would be that he wanted to give him the family name of Iulius, to his future advantage. But there was little question of succession to the purple, as Tiberius not only had a son of his own, Drusus, who was older than Agrippa, but had also by Augustus' express wish adopted Germanicus, who was a year or so older again than Drusus. It seems clear that Augustus intended the succession to pass via Tiberius to Germanicus, or failing him to Drusus. One indisputable legal consequence of Postumus' adoption was that the property which had come to him by his father's death now became Augustus' (an adopter had to swear an oath that his object was not to acquire property, since under Roman law only a person *sui iuris*, that is not in the *patria potestas* of another, could own property - Gellius, *Noctes Atticae* 5.19). Augustus could not handle Postumus, and he first disinherited him and confined him to the imperial villa at Surrentum (A.D. 6 or 7), then (A.D. 7 or 8), finding no improvement, relegated him to Planasia (see below and 19.1 n.vi). The method of disherison practised against Postumus was *abdicatio*, forced emancipation. It was a savage measure, because by restoring Agrippa to the legal status he had possessed before his adoption, that of a free and independent individual, it cut him off from Augustus' family and deprived him not only of his status as Augustus' son but also of all right to the property which had once been his but had passed to Augustus at the time of the adoption (see Levick 1972). No wonder that Augustus found him querulous and intractable (and probably fomenting intrigue) at Surrentum, and left instructions that on his own death the guard commander on Planasia was to kill Postumus (which he did). It is not an accident that Suetonius here uses the word *ferox* to describe Postumus' character (*ingenium*): *ferocia* (unmanageability and liability to be violent) was a recognised ground for *abdicatio* (Quintilian, *Declamationes minores* 269 - 59 Ritter and 279 - 139 Ritter).

65.2 per quaestorem: one of the quaestors was assigned to the emperor as a kind of combined ADC and parliamentary private secretary.

65.3 deprecanti saepe populo Romano: one such demonstration in

favour of Julia is recorded by Dio (55.13.1) under A.D. 3. Before
Gaius' death in A.D. 4 Julia was after all the mother of the heir-
apparent; and after it she and her friends stood for something less
austere and more 'popular' than the ageing Augustus and his grim step-
son Tiberius.

65.4 ex nepte Iulia...infantem: this infant was presumably the
child of Iunius Silanus. On the birth of a child the father or someone acting for him (in this case Augustus, in virtue of *patria potestas*)
formally recognised it, and if he did not it did not count in the family,
regardless of whether it were kept alive.
Agrippam...in insulam: Agrippa was sent to Planasia, S.W. of Elba,
in 7 or 8 A.D.
cavit etiam senatus consulto: why was a decree of the senate
necessary to keep Postumus on his island? Perhaps because unlike his
mother and sister he was guilty of no statutory crime and had therefore
been relegated (like Ovid) by sheer imperial authority. Nor could
Augustus claim to be exercising *patria potestas* once he had inflicted
abdicatio on Postumus. Augustus wished, then, to provide some constitutional backing for his exercise of autocratic power.
αἴθ'ὄφελον...κτλ.: 'I should have lived unwed and childless died'.
Augustus has here altered the reproach of Hector to Paris at *Iliad* 3.40
('You should have been unborn and died unwed') with a pun on ἄγονος =
unborn/childless.

66-67 Suetonius now turns to the other two categories of social
relations: dealings with legal equals ('friends') and with legal
inferiors (freedmen and slaves). Recognition of just deserts
and a disposition to clemency, or at least not to take little
things too seriously, are the characteristics stressed.

66.1 Q.Salvidienus Rufus: older than Agrippa but like him of obscure
and probably Central Italian ancestry (Syme 1939,129), was also at
Apollonia when the news came of Caesar's murder. He accompanied
Augustus to Italy, and became one of the chief generals of Augustus'
party. Instrumental in saving his leader from the Antonian armies in
the war of Perusia, he was rewarded by being designated to the consulship of 39 B.C., though not yet even a senator. But in the months
between the end of the war and the reconciliation of Augustus and
Antony at Brundisium (see 17.1-2 n.) he began to negotiate his desertion from one to the other. If it had come to war between the two
triumvirs, the defection of Salvidienus, who controlled the armies
of Gaul and Spain, must have been decisive. There was no war,
Salvidienus' disloyalty became known, and he was condemned by the
senate and put to death (Dio 48.33.1-2; Velleius Paterculus 2.76.4).
C. Cornelius Gallus: (born ca. 69 B.C.) another non-senator who
rose very high in Augustus' service. He came from Forum Julii
(Fréjus), and is supposed to have been instrumental in exempting the
land of his friend Virgil from the allocations which he was making
to the soldiers of the triumvirs in the Po valley in 42-40 B.C.

He then disappears from the record until 30 B.C., when, having
commanded the army which had advanced through Cyrenaica to Alexandria,
he was installed by Augustus as the first prefect of Egypt (see 18.2 n.).
He offended the emperor by allowing himself to be honoured above his
station (cf. Dio 53.23.5; $E-J^3$ no. 21 = LR II, 45) and suffered
renuntiatio amicitiae ('withdrawal of friendly relations') and banning
from Augustus' provinces. Other enemies then accused him, and the
senate voted that he should be condemned in the courts. He anticipated
a formal verdict by committing suicide. These events occurred at
some time between 28 and 26 B.C. Suetonius' words ob ingratum et
malevolum animum ('on account of his ungrateful and malevolent disposition') do not fit Gallus' alleged misbehaviour in Egypt particularly
well, nor is there anything very damning in Dio's report of his misdeeds,
bearing in mind that (in Strabo's contemporary phrase) the prefect of
Egypt 'has the rank of a king'. Maybe his true crime lay in opposing
Augustus in Rome, and has nothing to do with Egypt. Augustus' action
suggests that Gallus was not formally guilty of breaking any law;
perhaps the accusations of arrogant behaviour in Egypt were trumped
up in the wake of the emperor's displeasure. Gallus was also, at an
earlier stage of his career, a poet much revered by Virgil (Eclogue 10)
and the elegists (Propertius 2.34.91-2; Ovid,Amores 1.15.29-30) for
his amatory verse, addressed to one Lycoris, whose real name was
Volumnia Cytheris; she was an actress who had previously been the
mistress of Antony. A papyrus fragment containing some elegiacs, which
seem likely to be by him but do nothing to explain this reverence, has
recently come to light in a rubbish deposit at Qasr Ibrîm in southern
Egypt. The two complete couplets read (JRS 1979, 140, with spelling
normalised):

> fata mihi, Caesar, tum erunt mea dulcia, quum tu
> maxima Romanae pars eris historiae
> postque tuum reditum multorum templa deorum
> fixa legam spoliis divitiora tuis.

(For a full treatment of Gallus' career and activity, see Boucher 1966).
   A noteworthy aspect of Gallus' fall is the part played by the senate,
which foreshadows its later development as a court (cf. 33 n.ii). It
is clear from Dio that the senate did not itself condemn Gallus, but
passed a motion which amounted to an instruction to the courts; probably
to the effect that Gallus had 'acted against the interests of the state'
(contra rem publicam fecisse - cf. Cicero, ad Quintum fratrem 2.1.2 and
2.3.3). It was nothing new for the senate to indulge in such quasi-
judicial activity: it summoned C. Gracchus and Fulvius Flaccus before it
in 121 B.C. (Appian, Bellum Civile 1.26).

66.3 M. Agrippae patientiam: Agrippa's patience had good cause
to be tested in 25-23 B.C. when Augustus seemed to advancing his
nephew Marcellus to be his successor. Augustus' own blood, young and
untried, was evidently worth more than the immense experience, authority,
ability, and loyal service of Agrippa. However, when it came to the
point during Augustus' critical illness of 23 B.C. it was to Agrippa
and not to Marcellus that he gave his signet-ring (see 50 n.). 'There
were grounds for the opinion that, if Augustus died, Agrippa would
make short work of the Princeps' young nephew' (Syme 1939,344). Subsequently, Agrippa left Rome with a grant of imperium (probably maius,

see Papyrus Coloniensis 4701 = $E-J^3$ no.366; Josephus, *Antiquitates Judaicae* 15.350; Bringmann 1977) over the eastern provinces and made Mitylene his headquarters. As it happened, Marcellus died within two or three months. Suetonius goes further than Dio (53.32.1) in seeing an open rift between Augustus and Marcellus on the one hand and Agrippa on the other; his interpretation, like that of Velleius (2.93.2), must be coloured by his knowledge of Tiberius' (genuine) withdrawal from public life in 6 B.C. when Gaius and Lucius were receiving the same promotion as Marcellus had had. Syme (1939, 341ff.) is surely right to see in these events a victory for Agrippa in the dynastic struggle.

Maecenatis taciturnitatem: for the conspiracy of Murena, Maecenas' brother-in-law, see 19 n.ii. Maecenas is supposed to have told his wife Terentia that the plot had been discovered, and she to have warned her brother. Dio on the other hand says nothing of this when he is speaking of the conspiracy, but reports under 16 B.C. (54.19.3, cf.55.7.5) scandal which connected Terentia with Augustus (and may have been of long standing - cf. 69.2). Whatever the reason, Maecenas is not recorded as being involved in affairs of state between 23 and his death in 8 B.C. (The assertion of Furneaux on Tacitus, *Ann.* 3.30.6 that Maecenas 'retired' in 16 B.C. seems far too precise an inference from Dio.)

C. Maecenas, the wealthy, cultured, self-indulgent, subtle, and effeminate descendant of Etruscan kings, came of a family which had ties with Julius Caesar. He rapidly established himself as chief diplomat and adviser in the revolutionary party of Caesar's heir. He never became a senator or held a consulship, but as regent of Rome in Augustus' absence in 36 and 31-29 B.C. he wielded more power than any consul. His literary accomplishments and above all his patronage of Virgil and Horace have ensured him lasting fame; but like another of Augustus' equestrian friends, Vedius Pollio (see 29.4 n. *Porticus Liviae*; Syme 1961), his tastes and morals consorted ill with the avowed standards of the new age.

66.4 hereditates: it was the custom in a Roman will to recognise one's friends by leaving them legacies or by instituting them second (or third) heirs - in which case they would only inherit if the first (or second) heirs were unable or unwilling to enter, and to be named thus was simply a mark of honour. The reader gains the impression from this passage that Augustus had little interest in the money. In fact his finances depended on it: he received in this way, in the last twenty years of his life, 1,400 million HS (see 101.3), an immense sum. For comparison, his total expenditure on pensions and land for veterans and funding the *aerarium militare* (cf. 49 n.) was 1,430 million HS (*RG* 16-17).

67.1 Licinum et Celadum: Celadus is otherwise unknown, but Dio (54.21.3-8) says Licinus, who had originally been a Gallic captive of Caesar's was made procurator of Gaul by Augustus and enriched both himself and his patron at the expense of his fellow-Gauls.

Diomeden dispensatorem: 'keeper of the purse', 'bursar'. It is not clear from the context whether Diomedes was a slave or a freedman. There survives a funerary inscription ($E-J^3$ 158 = *HRFC* II. 142) of a slave who was *dispensator* under Tiberius of the treasury of Gallia Lugdunensis and had no less than sixteen slaves *of his own* with him when he died on a visit to Rome.

67.2 Thallo a manu ... crura effregit: *a manu* is a general term
for a secretary. The reading *ei fregit* of the better MS seems impossibly
harsh, and *effringere* (properly 'to break open') is used by extension of
bones other than the skull and rib-cage to which it is clearly appropriate.
(Shuckburgh compares 94.7 *prandenti ... ei e manu rapuit*, but *ei*
prandenti is not parallel to *ei Thallo*.)
paedagogum: a boy's tutor was regularly a slave. It is remarkable
that Gaius, a consul of the Roman people, still had a *paedagogus* at the
time of his death. And what, one might ask, were Gaius' entourage of
advisers doing while these slaves were putting on airs? The tale is
difficult to believe, even allowing for the fact that slaves might suffer
recherché punishments unknown to the law of free men.

68-78 These chapters deal with Augustus' pleasures and relax-
ations. In good rhetorical fashion, Suetonius puts the most
discreditable material first and specifically ascribes much of
it to Antony, then palliates the undeniable charges of adultery
(by citing Livia's complicity) and fondness for gambling (by
proving his generosity), before moving on at 72 to calmer
waters where he can pronounce Augustus free of all vice: the
emperor's houses were modest, or at least modestly equipped
(72-73), his dress unremarkable (73), his dinner-parties proper
(74), his liberality witty (75), his taste in food and drink
plebeian and careless (76-77). Finally comes a chapter on
his sleeping habits which is simply descriptive - and
unintentionally revealing, because for once information is
presented which lies outside, and so makes the reader aware
of, the framework of moral approval and disapproval which
structures the whole work and is particularly evident in this
section of it.

68   effeminatum: the charge of homosexual effeminacy was routine in
the political invective of the time - cf. Cicero, *pro Caelio* 6: 'that
sort of slander is very common in the case of any young man of good
looks and handsome appearance'. It was alleged, e.g. against Caesar
(*DJ* 49; Catullus 29 and 57) and Antony (Cicero, *Philippics* 2.44).
in Hispania: in the early summer of 45 B.C. - see 8.1.
gallo matris Deum tympanizante: one of the titles of Cybele was
Mother of the Gods. Her priests were eunuchs and called *galli*. In the
popular mind castration and passive homosexuality were connected, so that
cinaedus was an appropriate in its literal meaning to the *gallus* as to
young Augustus. *orbem temperat* means 'plays the drum' and 'rules the
world'. The theatre audience was quick to pick up such references (cf.
Cicero, *ad Atticum* 2.19.3: the line *nostra miseria tu es magnus* ... was
made an occasion for a demonstration against Pompey in 59 B.C.). The
present episode must belong to the period of the triumvirate, probably
41-39 B.C.

69.1 adulteria: the justification advanced by Augustus' friends for
his proclivities in this direction recalls the explanation of the Perusine
war given at 15.
M. Antonius ... obiecit: for the occasion of Antony's invectives,

see 2.3 n.

festinatas Liviae nuptias ... dimissam Scriboniam: see 62.2,
where Augustus' version of Scribonia's divorce will be found, and 62.2 n.
condiciones: this is the technical word for sexual assignations - cf.
Cicero, *pro Caelio* 36.
denudarent ... tamquam Toranio mangone vendente: this Toranius
is not to be confused with Augustus' guardian at 27.1. Slave-dealers
would be asked to strip slaves naked so that the purchaser could be sure
there were no hidden physical defects.

69.2 Antony's letter:
     The letter from which this passage is an extract can be dated to the
spring of 33 B.C., nine years, by inclusive reckoning, from the first
meeting of Antony and Cleopatra in 41 B.C. It was at the beginning of
33 B.C., after receiving the news of the 'Donations of Alexandria' (by
which Antony the previous autumn had created his children by Cleopatra
monarchs of certain territories within the Roman sphere of influence)
that Augustus first publicly attacked his triumviral colleague. The
letter is a precious piece of evidence for Antony's attitude to Augustus
at this time - pained, basically friendly, and incredulous at the grounds
of attack, which were clearly a case of the pot calling the kettle black.
uxor mea est?: 'Is she my wife?' All editors hitherto have mis-
punctuated the vital words by leaving out the question mark. The line
of Antony's defence is that he has done nothing that Augustus has not,
and between friends what does the odd peccadillo matter anyway? Antony
happened to be married to Augustus' sister, and did not divorce her until
mid-32 B.C. Therefore to state that Cleopatra was his wife, quite apart
from being impossible in Roman law as he could not be married to two
women at once, would be to make complete nonsense of his whole argument.
What is needed, as was pointed out by Kraft (1967c) is a *denial* that
Cleopatra was his wife. The argument requires that she stand in the
same relation to him as Tertulla and the others do to Augustus. These
conditions are perfectly fulfilled by restoring the missing question-
mark - which has the further advantage of producing a satisfactory string
of short, pointed questions, to none of which does the writer need to
supply an answer.
Terentilla: a diminutive of Terentia, very probably Maecenas' wife
(see 66.3 n.). The other women elude identification.

70.1 cena ... secretior: the winter of 39-38 B.C., when there were
difficulties with the corn supply in Rome is a plausible time for this
notorious 'banquet of the twelve gods', but any time before 32 B.C. is
possible. The twelve gods were presumably the twelve Olympians: Juno,
Vesta, Minerva, Ceres, Diana, Venus, Mars, Mercury, Jupiter, Neptune,
Vulcan, and Apollo (so Ennius, *Annales* 63-64V). Antony's intimates
indulged in similar fancy-dress frolics: at one of these Plancus,
naked, covered in blue paint, and equipped with a tail, played the part
of a sea-god (Velleius Paterculus 2.83.2).
     The verses of the lampoon pose difficulties:
     line 1 The problem is the meaning of *mensa*. Heinsius proposed to
read *cum mimum histrorum conduxit mensa choragi* - 'when the table of the
producer had collected a troupe of actors', but this only avoids one
difficulty, the otherwise unexampled use of *mensa* to mean 'guests at
table', by creating two others, that is making the table 'collect' people,

and imposing on *mimum* (itself a conjecture) the extremely strained meaning of 'troupe'. It is better to stay with the traditional interpretation of *mensa* and translate: 'as soon as that table-full of diners had found themselves a producer (i.e. Augustus)'.

    line 2   Mallia remains a mystery. It may go with *mensa* (Mallius' table), but is most plausibly the name either of a house (*Mallia domus*) where such risqué entertainments took place, or of its hostess.

    line 3   mendacia ludit 'plays lies' is a very bold but perfectly intelligible internal accusative. The construction is a favourite one with the poets: an Augustan example of similar boldness is Propertius 1.13.23. *flagrans amor Herculis Heben.* It is incorrect to assert, with Adams, that *mendacium* here means *simulatio* ('imitation'); the lampoonist clearly intends us to understand that Augustus' role-playing traduced the god.

    line 4   cenat adulteria 'dines adulteries' is an astonishing, but in its context still quite comprehensible, example of the same construction as *mendacia ludit* above.

    line 6   thronos is by nearly a hundred years the earliest use of this Greek word for the native Latin *solium*, the next user being the elder Pliny (*NH* 2.178, 35.63). The first of Pliny's references uses the Greek form of the accusative, *thronon,* and the second, like the present passage, speaks of the throne of Jupiter. So there is reason to believe that the word was still felt to be Greek. It thus provides an echo for the Greek term *choragum* in the first line and is completely fitting in verses whose target was vulgarly described by a Greek word. There is no need, then, to question either (with Adams) the triumviral date of the lines or (with Bentley) the soundness of the text of the last line.

70.2 Apollinem ... Tortorem: 'Apollo the Torturer' is not known else-where. The cult may have been in the district of Rome where instruments of punishment and torture, and their operators, were to be obtained; cf. 'Apollo of the Sandalmakers', 57.1.

Corinthiarius: a joke formation after the pattern of nouns denoting occupation - 'a Corinthian-bronzer'. This bronze was an alloy of copper with gold and/or silver, according to Pliny (*NH* 34.6-8). Since Corinth was burnt in 146 B.C. (giving rise to the absurd story that the alloy was produced by the chance of the fire) and since the famous bronze workshops had in any case ceased to produce masterpieces some time previously, genuine Corinthian bronzes, whether dishes or statues, were antiques much sought after by wealthy Roman collectors. Pliny credits Antony with proscribing Verres and Cicero because he coveted their Corinthian bronzes. For the proscriptions see 27.1-4 n., and for Augustus' father as a banker, which Suetonius denies, 3.1.

postquam bis classe ...:   the two fleets were destroyed in 38 B.C. - see 16.1 n. The couplet, in the six-foot iambic line of the dramatic stage, is mock-tragic in tone and may well have been a parody.

71.1 impudicitia: this word refers back to the charges made in 68, while *libidines* below, at the start of the next sentence, refers to 69.

murrinum calicem: 'murrine' vessels were of Eastern origin and inordinately prized at Rome. The identification of *murra* as 'agate' (so *GG*) is not certain, and it may be fluorspar: see Pliny, *NH* 37.18-22 and Eichholz's note on the passage in the Loeb edition.

aleae rumorem: a law against gambling existed at the end of the third
century B.C. (Plautus, *Miles Gloriosus* 164) and an associate of Antony's
was actually condemned under such a law in the late Republic (Cicero,
Philippics 2.56). However, we do not know what its provisions were, and
it is quite clear that public disapproval was minimal by Augustus' day
(cf. Ovid, *Tristia* 2.471ff.; *Claud.* 33.2). Some kind of law continued
to exist under the Empire, directed rather against professionals and
those who made a habit of gaming in public places than against people
who liked a flutter at dinner (*Digest* 11.5; Martial 5.84.3-5 and 14.1.3).
Decembri mense: at the festival of the Saturnalia, which fell on
December 17th-23rd, many of the rules and conventions of every day
behaviour were traditionally ignored or upset.

71.2 Vinicius et Silius pater: these were two stalwarts of the
regime: M. Vinicius, who attained a (suffect) consulship in 19 B.C., was
a new man, son of a local worthy of Cales in Campania, and had a long and
distinguished military career. P. Silius Nerva (consul 20 B.C.), whose
father had attained the praetorship in the 50s B.C., showed similar
military competence in Spain and Illyricum between 19 and 16 B.C. The
sons of both men duly held consulships, in A.D. 2 and A.D. 3 respectively.
geronticos: a transliteration of the Greek adverb 'like old men'.
talis ... canem aut senionem ... Venerem: the sort of dice known
as *tali* had four faces, marked one (*canis,* 'the dog'), three (*ternio*),
four (*quaternio*), and six (*senio*). 'Venus' was the throw (with four
tali) which showed one of each value.

71.3 quinquatrus: this festival, originally of one day, the fifth
after the Ides, had developed by the historical period into a five-day
holiday (March 19th-23rd) in honour of Minerva, patron goddess of craft
workers; see Ovid, *Fasti* 3.809ff.
forum aleatorium: 'the Gambling Exchange': the regular Latin for a
gaming table is *tabula* or *alveus*. Augustus' expression is a joke,
alluding to such terms as *forum holitorium* 'the vegetable market'. (Hence
my preference for the Renaissance emendation of the MS' *aleatorum*).
manus: 'stakes'. The pool was called *aes manuarium* (Gellius, *Noctes
Atticae* 18.13.4).

71.4 par impar ludere: 'to play at odd and even': one player held
some nuts, or similar small objects, in his hand, and the other had to
guess whether there was an odd or even number of them.

72.1 Scalae anulariae: 'the Ring-makers' Steps'. Lugli (*Fontes,*
xix.135) places these at the foot of the Palatine, presumably somewhere
near the northern corner of the hill. There exists no other reference to
them or to Calvus' house.
Calvi oratoris: C. Licinius Calvus, a friend and contemporary of
Catullus, was a poet of distinction (author of the epyllion *Smyrna* or
Myrrha) as well as one of the notable orators of the day (Cicero, *Brutus*
283-5). He died before 46 B.C., while still in his late twenties or early
thirties.
in Palatio ... aedibus modicis Hortensianis: in the late Republic
the Palatine had become the most fashionable residential quarter of Rome.
Q. Hortensius Hortalus (consul 69 B.C.) had been the leading orator in
Rome before the rise of Cicero. He died in 50 B.C., presumably leaving

the property to his son Quintus who fought against the triumvirs at Philippi and was afterwards put to death. Augustus will therefore have acquired the house, now forfeit to the state, in 42 or 41 B.C.

The site lies between the Temple of Apollo (see 29.3) and the *Scalae Caci* on the south-west escarpment of the hill. Recent excavations have recovered the ground-floor rooms of the private wing of the house, two of which contain fine and well-preserved examples of 'second-style' wall-painting, and are in course of revealing a more official suite, whose construction looks to be integral with that of the podium and access ramp of the Temple of Apollo above and behind them. These rooms likewise have yielded wall-paintings of the superb quality one might expect in the First Citizen's residence. The two sets of rooms form a right angle and look on to a peristyle courtyard whose other two sides have not been investigated. The house is large by the standards of other late Republican dwellings on the cramped sites of the Palatine: Suetonius judges it by the scale, not only of the palaces of the later emperors, but of luxury villas of Augustus' own day set in less trammelled surroundings. In fact, Augustus intended to enlarge it considerably, but decided to use all (or most) of the additional property he had bought for this purpose by building instead the temple and libraries of Palatine Apollo (Velleius Paterculus 2.81.3). Thus he forfeited some private luxury and convenience; but all Rome was made aware that the son of one god shared his house with another. Dio (49.15.5) says that the people in return voted a house to him at public expense. Unless this is Hortensius', it appears that he refused it. See Carettoni 1967 and 1978; Coarelli 1974, 141-4; and for a contemporary impression, Ovid, *Tristia* 3.1.33ff.

Albanarum columnarum: columns made of stone from the nearby Alban Hills were in stark contrast with the luxury marbles from Africa and the eastern Mediterranean which were newly fashionable (Pliny, *NH* 36.48ff.).

72.2 Syracusas et technophyon: there are no compelling reasons for altering the MS reading *technophyon* (not found elsewhere) to *technyphion* (not found anywhere). The elements of the word mean 'scheme-generating' and this is precisely what is required; a better form would be *technophyion,* perhaps the true reading. As to 'Syracuse', the reason for the name is a mystery; perhaps the place was effectively an island, like Ortygia, the original heart of Syracuse, or was extremely difficult to penetrate, like the defences of the town in the hands of a Dionysius or an Archimedes. There is no evidence to suggest that it formed part of the house on the Palatine; the verb *transibat* ('went across') might indicate that it was on the Janiculum (across the river) or on the Aventine (across the valley of the Circus Maximus).

ex secessibus: 'country retreats': wealthy Romans were apt to own several of these, because land was the major source of their wealth and the only safe haven for capital. They were, for the most part, productive agricultural estates on which the owner might, or might not, choose to erect a luxury villa. The apparent exceptions are the maritime villas which clustered thickly around the Bay of Naples and extended all along the Tyrrhenian coast, but recent research has shown that these too could generate income by fish-farming and exploitation of the hinterland (D'Arms 1977).

Imperial villas of Augustan date in and around the Bay of Naples are

known on Capreae and Pandateria and at Surrentum, Baiae, Pausilypon
(between Naples and Puteoli), Nola, and Boscotrecase (on all of which,
see D'Arms 1970). Most of these have been located, but the sites of
those in the fashionable hill-towns within easy reach of Rome, Lanuvio,
Palestrina, and Tivoli (to give them their modern names) remain
unidentified.

73   togis neque restrictis nec fusis: Augustus wished to avoid
Caesar's idiosyncratic style; but excessive restriction of the toga, such
as Cato adopted, was as much of an affectation as the over-luxurious
fullness of that of Maecenas (*DJ* 45.3; Seneca, *Epistulae Morales* 92.35
and 114.4).

clavo nec lato nec angusto: the broad stripe on the toga indicated
a senator, the narrow a member of the equestrian order.

74   Valerius Messalla: see 58.1 n.

Mena: the ex-slave Menas (otherwise known as Menodorus) was one of the
admirals of Sextus Pompeius. In 38 B.C. he betrayed to Augustus Corsica
and Sardinia with three legions and the fleet he commanded; in 37 he
rejoined Sextus; and in 36 B.C. he changed sides a third time after
demonstrating his prowess by a brilliant surprise attack on Augustus'
supply-ships. His reward, to be 'deemed of free birth', and the dinner
Suetonius records, surely belong to 38 B.C.

speculator: originally a 'scout', this came to be the term for members
of the imperial bodyguard attached to the praetorian cohorts. There is
no reason to believe that this man was a freedman; the point is that
Augustus was not too superior to dine with the most ordinary people if
the circumstances called for it.

triviales ... ludios: 'street buskers'. *ex circo* does not mean that
such people were part of the official programme at the circus (as *GG*
rather imply), but that the circus area was where they could be found
(cf. Horace, *Satires* 1.6.113 and Cicero, *de Divinatione* 1.132).

aretalogos: hardly 'storytellers' (*GG*), but popular and rather specious
disputers on philosophical topics (Juvenal 15.16 and Acro on Horace,
Satires 1.1.120). The currently popular *suasoriae,* hypothetical speeches
of advice given to historical (or fictional) characters at moments of
crisis, presented with all the gilding of rhetorical artifice, were an
analogous diversion for the educated.

75   Saturnalibus: it was the custom to give small presents especially
at the Saturnalia (see 71.1 n.). Martial, Book XIV is a collection of
riddling couplets describing such things, and no doubt contains exactly
the sort of material which accompanied Augustus' gifts.

nummos ... regios: even if some Romans thought, erroneously, that their
coinage went back to the regal period, there were of course no specimens
for Augustus to distribute. The reference must be to coins of Hellenistic
kings.

per singulos lectos licitatio: 'bidding by couches': the usual
arrangement at a formal dinner was for guests to recline three to a couch.

76   ne Iudaeus quidem: Augustus' mistake in thinking that Jews kept
the Sabbath as a fast proves that he was not on intimate terms with any
of that race.

manducavi: 'I ate'. This, the ordinary word, was avoided in literature, but survived in common speech to become Italian *mangiare*, French *manger*.

77 Cornelius Nepos: a friend and approximate contemporary of Cicero - a literary figure who wrote (apart from the extant 'Short Lives of the Famous') biography, geography, and poetry, and was the dedicatee of Catullus' collection of verse. He died some time after 27 B.C. (elder Pliny, *NH* 9.137).

senos sextantes: a *sextans* was one-sixth of the liquid measure a *sextarius*, which approximated to a pint. It is probable that Augustus' three after-supper drinks in camp were each of a *cyathus* (half a *sextans*), the normal amount for one cup (Horace, *Odes* 3.8.13; Ovid, *Fasti* 3.532).

79-83 Augustus' physical appearance, health, and diversions.

79.2 oculos ... claros et nitidos: it may well be true that Augustus had unusual eyes, though his portraits do not suggest it (see Zanker 1973). The elder Pliny (*NH* 11.143) says that they shone like a horse's and had abnormally large whites, which caused him to be sensitive if people looked intensely into them. Suetonius' mention of the 'divine force' of his gaze takes us into the world of Alexander-imagery (see 50 n.) again. Alexander was famous for his superhuman gaze, while the 'radiance of the sun' was clearly an appropriate attribute for the face of a ruler who had a special relationship with the sun-god Apollo.

Iulius Marathus libertus et a memoria eius: 'his freedman and keeper of records'. Marathus (cf. 94.3) doubtless cashed in on the curiosity of Romans, after Augustus' death, to know this kind of personal detail - and he will not have been alone: Suetonius is extremely unlikely, even in his boyhood, to have met anyone who could have described Augustus from personal recollection. (*et a memoria* is an emendation of Lipsius' for the impossible *etiam memoriam* of the MS: the office *a memoria* is not epigraphically attested until the reign of Hadrian - *CIL* 6.8618 - but is clearly one of the main clerical departments of the imperial household and thus likely to go back in origin to Augustus - see Weaver 1972.)

quinque pedum et dodrantis: five and three-quarter Roman feet works out at about 5'7" since a Roman foot is 1/3" shorter than ours.

80 remedio harenarum et harundinum: this 'remedy of sand and reeds' seems to have been some kind of poultice. Both substances are credited with drawing powers when heated or pounded (Gellius, *Noctes Atticae* 19.8.3; elder Pliny, *NH* 24.87, 31.72). Augustus' infirmity may be connected with the injuries he received in the Dalmatian war (see 20).

digitum salutarem: the forefinger was called the 'greeting finger' because it was extended when the right hand and arm were raised in salutation. The gesture is exactly illustrated in the famous statue of Augustus in armour from Prima Porta, now in the Vatican.

81.1 Antonio Musa: see 59.

81.2 natalem suum: his birthday was September 23rd (see 5)

82.1 Praeneste vel Tibur: normally reckoned to be within an easy day's journey; being 37 and 31.5 km. respectively, by road, distant from the centre of Rome.

82.2 nervorum causa: literally 'on account of his muscles'; this could mean 'rheumatism' (so *GG*), but could equally well describe all sorts of other complaints.

Albulis calidis: supply the noun *aquis*, 'the warm waters of Albula', sulphur springs between Rome and Tibur, the modern Bagni di Tivoli.

83 segestri: the most likely correction for MS *sestertio*. The word means some kind of leather sheet or strip, Varro's etymology from *seges* 'straw' (*de Lingua Latina* 5.166) not being borne out by the other evidence. Here, then, 'a leather cloak'.

84-89 Augustus' literary tastes, accomplishments, and style. These chapters demonstrate Suetonius' familiarity with Augustus' writings, both public and private, also evidenced at *DJ* 55.3-4.

84 non deficeretur: 'he was not failed by', i.e. he was not lacking in, an ability to speak extempore.

85.1 rescripta Bruto de Catone: M. Brutus was the son of Cato's half-sister Servilia, and also his son-in-law. Cato's determination, character, and consciously old-fashioned rectitude made him a leader of the resistance to Caesar, and his suicide at Utica in 46 B.C., in preference to surrender to Caesar, transformed him into a kind of Republican saint and martyr. Panegyrics of him are known to have been composed by Cicero, M. Fabius Gallus, and (L?) Munatius (Plancus?), as well as by Brutus himself, and answers by A. Hirtius and Caesar (Cicero, *ad Atticum* 12.4.2, 12.21.1, 12.40.1 and 13.46.2; *ad Familiares* 7.24.2; Plutarch, *Cato Minor* 37.1). It is a little surprising to find the elderly emperor raking over the ashes of an old (though still relevant) dispute; perhaps the incident indicates some revival, in high places, of sympathy for the ideals of Caesar's opponents.

de Vita Sua: this work was well known to, and used by, both Suetonius and Plutarch. It is likely that the extant portion of Nicolaus of Damascus' *Life* is based on it. Suetonius does not suggest that the work was unfinished, and the Cantabrian War (see 20) made a very suitable point for Augustus to stop writing. It was his final campaign as a front-line commander and immediately preceded his retirement from the highest executive position in the state, which he had held, with the exception of the year 32, continuously from 43 to 23 B.C. After this 'retirement' his public accountability became less, his prestige greater, and his actions stood in little need of justification. The developments in the nature and institutions of the principate which modern historians discern in the rest of Augustus' long reign were not the stuff of which autobiography was made - even if the participants were fully aware of them.

85.2 Epigrammatum: one of Augustus' epigrams, written at the time of the war of Perusia, is preserved by Martial (11.20. 3-8).

Aiacem suum in spongiam incubuisse: in the legend Ajax commits suicide by falling on his sword. A sponge was used by Romans for wholesale erasure of writing in ink (Martial 4.10). According to Macrobius (*Saturnalia* 2.4.2), it was L. Varius, famous as Virgil's literary executor, to whom Augustus made this reply.

86.1 sententiarum ineptis et concinnitate: declamation, the
delivery of an extempore speech of advice or legal argument on a set
topic before an audience, had recently become a fashionable form of
entertainment in literary circles in Rome. The extreme artificiality
of the exercise meant that the superficial stylistic tricks, like
striking phrases or epigrams (*sententiae*) and mellifluous arrangements
of words (*concinnitas*), won applause and counted for more than logical
argument and clear exposition; (see elder Seneca, *Controversiae et
Suasoriae*; younger Seneca, *Epistulae Morales* 114.10-11; Clarke 1953,
especially ch.8: and for discussion and examples, Winterbottom, *Roman
Declamation* (BCP, 1979).
reconditorum verborum fetoribus: *fetor* ('stink') is nowhere else
found as a literary metaphor. Augustus was presumably satirising the
very taste for obscure words and usages which he was criticising.

86.2 cacozelos: a Greek word - 'bad stylists'. Their fault is defined
by Quintilian (8.3.58) as speaking 'otherwise than is natural or right
or sufficient'. Agrippa accused Maecenas of inciting Virgil to invent
a new sort of 'bad style' (Donatus, *Vita Virgilii* 11.180-183).
myrobrechis (=μυροβρεχεῖς) concinnos: 'ringlets wet with perfume',
another sarcastic exaggeration of critical vocabulary along the lines of
the fault criticised. Maecenas was notorious for the luxurious decadence
alike of his morals, his way of life, and his literary style. Cicero
uses the metaphor of 'curling-tongs' (*calamistri*) when discussing style.

86.3 Cimberne Annius an Veranius Flaccus: T. Annius Cimber was
a partisan of Antony in 44-43 B.C. There survives an epigram attributed
to Virgil which attacks him for his conceits of style and alludes to the
charge made by Cicero that he had murdered his brother (Quintilian 8.3.28;
Cicero, *Philippics* 11.14). Nothing is known of Veranius Flaccus unless
he is to be identified with the Veranius who is cited by Festus and
Macrobius as a late Republican writer on legal and religious topics.
Crispus Sallustius: Sallust (C. Sallustius Crispus, 86-34 B.C.),
author of the two extant historical monographs *On the Jugurthine War* and
On the Catilinarian Conspiracy and also of the lost *Histories* (covering
78-67 B.C.), was the first Latin prose author to indulge in conscious
archaism. The elder Cato's *Origines*, an idiosyncratic account of Roman
history, written c. 160 B.C., was the earliest work of Latin prose
literature. To plunder it was therefore to go as far back as possible
in the quest for archaic vocabulary.
Asiaticorum oratorum: Augustus was alluding to a well-known literary
controversy, to which Cicero's stylistic treatise the *Orator* owes its
existence. 'Asiatic' oratory, luxuriant, soft, and highly ornamented,
was contrasted to 'Attic', spare, direct, and unaffected. To the Asian-
ists, Attic style was jejune and boring, to the Atticists, Asian was
long-winded and frigid.

87.1 Kalendas Graecas: 'the Greek Kalends', i.e. never, since the
Greek calendar had no such day. Debts were commonly scheduled to be
repaid on the first of the month.
hoc Catone: commentators cite Macrobius 2.4.18: 'when Strabo, in

flattery of Caesar, condemned Cato, Augustus said "Anyone who does
not want the existing political order changed is a good citizen and
a good man". This does not seem to be relevant to the present passage,
where 'Cato' must stand for some kind of imperfection: the obstruction-
ist, the 'fly in the ointment'. Perhaps the text is corrupt.

87.2 betizare...lachanizare: 'to be (limp as) a beetroot'...'to be
(limp as) a vegetable'. Both verbs show the mixture of Greek and
Latin words and forms which occurred in popular speech in Rome and the
Campanian cities and can be found reproduced in Petronius.
domuos: this is the ancient form of the genitive of the fourth decl-
ension, cf. *senatuos* in the senatorial decree of 186 B.C. on the
Bacchanalian 'conspiracy' (*FIRA* 1. no.30).

89.1 Graecarum disciplinarum: 'Greek learning' included not only
the study of Greek language and literature, but particularly the discipline of philosophy. Greek teachers and philosophers are found in
the entourages of Roman grandees from the second century B.C. and played
an important part in the educational and intellectual life of Rome.
Apollodorus of Pergamum: is known as the author of an influential,
but dry, manual of rhetoric (Quintilian, 3.1.17; Tacitus, *Dialogus* 19.3).
He died at the age of 82, having lived at least long enough after the
trip to Apollonia (see **8.2**) to profit from his association with Augustus
(Strabo 13.4.3).
Areius of Alexandria: seems to have succeeded Apollodorus as Augustus'
teacher. One of the reasons for which Augustus pardoned Alexandria for
its resistance to him in 30 B.C. was that 'his friend Areius' was a
citizen of the place. Areius later served Augustus as imperial procurator in Sicily, and was offered, but declined, an important post
(probably that of *Idios Logos*) in the administration of his native
Egypt (see Bowersock 1965).

comoedia veteri: 'Old Comedy' is that of Athens in the fifth century
B.C., associated above all with the name of Aristophanes.

89.2 Q. Metelli de prole augenda: Q. Caecilius Metellus Macedonicus,
in his capacity as censor in 131 B.C., delivered a speech exhorting all
Romans to take wives - not for pleasure, for which purpose bachelor life
was much better, but to ensure the continuance of the race (*ORF*[3] 107).
The occasion of Augustus' citation must have been the introduction of
his *lex de maritandis ordinibus* (see **34.1** n.)
Rutili de modo aedificiorum: Rutilius will be either P. Rutilius
Lupus (consul 90 B.C.) or, more probably, P. Rutilius Rufus (consul 105
B.C.), who gains a mention as an orator in Cicero's *Brutus* (110 f.) and
wrote an autobiography (Tacitus, *Agricola* 1). The increase in the city
population and the improvements in the techniques of using concrete
which occurred in the second century B.C. produced ever taller buildings
in the centre of Rome. Such structures overshadowed the narrow streets
and were not always soundly built; hence Augustus imposed a height limit
of 70 feet (Vitruvius 2.8.8 and 17; Strabo 5.3.7).
commissionibus: contests of public speaking, at which praise of the

emperor afforded an eminently suitable subject; for such a contest at
Lugdunum, cf. *Caligula* 20.

90-96 By reserving to the end of the 'personal' section of
the work his description of Augustus' attitudes to the super-
natural (90-93), Suetonius prepares the ground for the immediately subsequent account of the signs and prodigies which
marked Augustus out as a man who enjoyed the especial favour
of the gods (94-96). Thus he recapitulates the motif of
Augustus' extraordinary, indeed superhuman, nature, which
concludes the 'public' section. Trivialities dealt with, we
return in these chapters to the underlying greatness of the
man, but presented this time in relation not to the temporal
world, but to the divine.

90 pellem vituli marini: seals were supposed to be immune to
lighting-strike (elder Pliny, *NH* 2.146).
ut praediximus: Augustus' escape from lightning is described at
29.3.

91.1 amici somnio: Augustus' dreaming 'friend' was his doctor
Artorius, according to Velleius (2.70.1).

91.2 Tonanti Iovi: see 29.3n.
tintinnabulis: bells may seem a surprising adornment for a temple
gable, but note Varro's account of the tomb of Porsena of Clusium,
composed of five pyramids, on top of which '...there rests a bronze
disc and cupola, from which hang bells fastened by chains, which
when shaken by the wind can be heard afar' (elder Pliny, *NH* 36.92).
Dio (54.4.4) explains the bell as being that appropriate to a night-
watchman.
stipem quotannis: for this annual 'contribution', cf. 57.1. It
appears to be different from the two there mentioned. Dio (54.35.3) is
sceptical of the story, but to play the beggar for a day might be a way
of averting divine jealousy by showing humility.

92.1 calceus perperam: the detail about wrong shoes comes from
Augustus himself, who retailed a story connecting them with bad luck
(elder Pliny, *NH* 2.24)
palmam: the palm was an emblem of victory
compluvium deorum Penatium: the *di Penates* were the household gods
of the individual family. The Roman state also collectively worshipped
those *Penates* which Aeneas is supposed to have brought from Troy, under
the name of *di Penates Publici*. Augustus built a temple for them on the
Velia, where they were represented by statues of two young men, and it
appears therefore that the cult had to some extent become fused with
that of the Dioscuri (Dionysius of Halicarnassus, 1.68; *RG* 19; see also
Ogilvie's commentary on Livy 1.1.10). The *compluvium* here referred to
should be that of the shrine on the Velia, because Augustus, through the
Iulii, claimed descent from Aeneas. His own *Penates* were therefore none
other than those brought by Aeneas from Troy. (The translation of *GG*,
though technically accurate, gives a misleading impression.)

92.2 Aenaria: modern Ischia. Augustus exchanged it for Capri in 29 B.C. (Dio 52.43.2).
dies quosdam: Kalends, Nones (especially), and Ides were all unlucky, and the days following them worse (Varro, de Lingua Latina 6.29; Ovid, Fasti 1.57-8). Nundinae fell every 'ninth' (to us, eighth) day and were days on which no public business could be done, but do not seem otherwise to have been considered unlucky unless they fell on the first day of the year (Macrobius, Saturnalia 1.13.17).
δυσφημίαν **nominis:** 'the unlucky sound of the word', i.e. non-is = you do not proceed. In this matter of superstition, Augustus affords a clear contrast to Julius Caesar, who was contemptuous of such things (DJ 59).

93 Athenis initiatus: Augustus was admitted as an initiate of the mystery cult of Demeter (the 'Attic Ceres') and Persephone at Eleusis, near Athens, in the autumn of 31 B.C., after his victory at Actium.
Apin: Apis was the sacred bull of Memphis in Egypt, which gave oracles in the name of the god Ptah and at death was embalmed and buried as Osiris-Apis.

94.2 saepius...cum populo Romano belligeraverant: the 'rebellions' (as they are presented in Livy) of Velitrae against Rome belong to the fourth century B.C., when the hold of Rome over Latium was far from secure. Velitrae finally lost her independence in 338 B.C., when Rome broke up the Latin League, and some, if not all, of her citizens had acquired full Roman citizenship before the Hannibalic War (see 2).

94.3 Iulius Marathus: see **79.2** n.
senatus consultum ad aerarium deferretur: decrees of the senate were not valid until they had been deposited at the treasury, in the Temple of Saturn. This was a relic of the concession granted by the Valerio-Horatian laws of 449 B.C., whereby the decisions of the senate (i.e., in effect, the patricians) were made available to the people by being handed over to the plebeian aediles for safe keeping at the Temple of Ceres.

94.4 Asclepiades: from Mendes in the Nile delta, wrote (according to the Suda - s.v. ‘Ηράισκος) a 'harmony' (symphonia) of all religions - presumably the work here referred to by Suetonius.
Atiam: see **4.**; her experience is related also by Dio (45.1.2) who follows it with her dream, and that of Octavius, told in such a way as to make it certain either that Dio was drawing directly on Suetonius or, more probably, that both men took their information from Asclepiades (see Introduction p. 7).

94.5 Catilinae coniuratione: if this report is sound, it is evidence that the senate discussed the conspiracy of Catiline before October 21, the date when Cicero used information about the revolutionary activities of Catiline's partisan C. Manlius in Etruria to persuade the senate to pass the so-called 'last decree' (senatus consultum ultimum), which called upon the consuls to be vigilant and active in defence of the state.
P. Nigidium: P. Nigidius Figulus, senator and friend of Cicero, attained the praetorship in 58 B.C., supported Pompey in the civil war, fought at Pharsalus, and died in exile unreconciled to Caesar in 45/44 B.C.

He was one of the most learned men of his age, versed in philosophical, antiquarian, religious, and astrological matters, and there is still extant, in the Greek translation of John the Lydian, Nigidius' version of an Etruscan calendar dealing with the interpretation of thunder.

94.6 fulmine et sceptro...: apart from the thunderbolt, these are all the attributes of Jupiter Optimus Maximus which were adopted for the day of his triumph by a *triumphator* (see **38.1** n.). The unusual number of twelve white horses may allude to the number of a consul's *fasces*, or of the vultures seen by Romulus at the founding of the city (cf. **95**). C.Drusum: otherwise unknown.

94.8 Q.Catulus post dedicatum Capitolium: Q. Lutatius Catulus (consul 78 B.C.) was placed, after Sulla's death, in charge of the rebuilding of the temple of Jupiter on the Capitol, which had been burnt down in 83 B.C. According to Livy's epitomator (98), he dedicated the temple in 69 or 68 B.C., but the fact that Julius Caesar attempted to deprive Catulus of his post on January 1 62 B.C. (*DJ* 15), must show that the work was still not complete at that date. Even so, Catulus died at the latest in May of 60 B.C. (Cicero, *ad Atticum* 1.20.3), when Augustus was only two and a half, and the story can scarcely be authentic.

94.9 M. Cicero: Cicero himself does not relate this dream, although the *Philippics* would have given him an excellent excuse for so doing. It is certainly apocryphal.

94.10 tunica lati clavi: Augustus assumed the *toga virilis* in 48-47 B.C (see **8.1**). The broad stripe on the tunic was ordinarily reserved for senators. It is possible that Caesar had as a special favour conferred it on the young Augustus, or else that Augustus' 'innovation' of allowing young men who proposed to become senators to assume the broad stripe forthwith was in fact a regularisation of what was already being done (see **38.2**). In Dio's version of the incident (42.2.5) the detail of the stripe is only implied, and it is Augustus himself who is made to interpret the omen.

94.11 apud Mundam: see 8.1 n.

94.12 in secessu Apolloniae: see 8.2 n.
nummum argenteum nota sideris Capricorni: there are several coin issues bearing the type of the Capricorn, all, with the exception of one from the mint of Lugdunum of 12-11 B.C., of the years 22-18 B.C. The statement that Augustus was born under the sign of Capricorn (December-January) seems unlikely to be a mistaken inference by Suetonius from these coins, since Manilius 2.509 gives the same information. Nor can the discrepancy be explained by the tendency of the Roman calendar to get out of step with the sun, since the civil year was shorter than the solar; there would have had to be the intolerable error of nine months to allow the civil date of September 23rd to fall in Capricorn, and in any case Virgil (*Georgics* 1.32-35) and Germanicus Caesar (*Aratea* 558-560) make Augustus' birth-sign Libra, as one would expect for late September. The explanation is that the *moon* was in Capricorn at the hour of Augustus' birth (see Cicero, *de Divinatione* 2.91; and Housman on Manilius 4.776),

and Kraft (1967a) therefore suggests that the message of these coins is that this hour was lucky for the state.

95 **iocinera:** the livers of sacrificial victims were always inspected for portents of good and bad omen. The interpretation of deformities and unusual features of the entrails of animals was the province of the order of priests called *haruspices,* and was a part of the Etruscan religious lore.

96.1 **ad Bononiam:** the negotiations which led to the formation of the triumvirate (see 13.1-2 n.) took place in November 43 B.C. on a small island in the river which flows past Bononia. Dio's notice of this omen (47.1.2-3) gives to Antony and Lepidus equally suitable portents of their future fate.

96.2 **templo, in quod castrorum suorum locum vertit:** see 18.2 n. *templo* here has its fundamental meaning of 'a consecrated area': there was never a temple on the site of Augustus' camp at Actium.

97-101 Suetonius firmly establishes the theme of Augustus' imminent deification with the omen of the eagle (97.1) before launching into the narrative which leads up to Augustus' death (99) and funeral rites (100). He presents Augustus as imbued with a kind of superhuman cheerfulness, in spite of his illness, so that the reader gains the impression of a man drifting inevitably away from this world to a higher order of existence. It is a sympathetic and masterly climax to the work. And finally, Suetonius brings us back to the everyday world with the factual but impressive coda on the emperor's will, which makes plain, once more, Augustus' solicitude for his people.

97.1 **cum lustrum ... conderet:** 'when he was performing the expiatory sacrifice to close the census'. This sacrifice was offered by the censors on behalf of the whole people at the conclusion of their term of office. Augustus and Tiberius, in spite of not taking the title of censor, evidently performed the census of A.D. 14 exactly as though they were censors. For the 'censorships' of Augustus, see 27.5 n. (*lustrum* comes to mean 'a period of five years' because in the Republic a census was customarily held every five years: there is no suggestion in the present passage either that Augustus and Tiberius had held office for five years or that such a sacrifice was performed every five years. *GG*'s translation is thus a little misleading.)
vicinam aedem super nomen Agrippae: Agrippa built much on the Campus Martius (see 29.5 n.), but we only know of one temple, namely his Pantheon.

97.3 **interpellatores ... in iure dicendo detinerent:** for Augustus' powers of civil jurisdiction, see 33 n. vii. This passage is valuable evidence for the eagerness of litigants to obtain an imperial decision, and the willingness (in principle) of Augustus to take cases.

98.2 **nautaeque ... candidati coronatique et tura libantes:** these sailors were dressed as though to perform a religious rite, and the language in which they speak of Augustus is that appropriate to a prayer of thanksgiving to a god. Emperor-worship suddenly becomes, at this point in Suetonius' narrative, a real and significant thing. (Contrast 52).

98.3 togas ... ac pallia: the *pallium* was the outer garment characteristic of Greeks, as the toga was of Romans. Naples remained an identifiably Greek city until well into the Empire, and Capri, being Neapolitan territory until 29 B.C. (see 92.2), must have had a substantial Greek element in its population.

ephebos: 'ephebes' were the members of an institution found in the Greek world from the fourth century B.C.; originally they were young men in their late teens, not yet full citizens, who underwent a period of military training followed by garrison or frontier service, but later the military aspect became less important and they received instruction in intellectual disciplines such as philosophy and rhetoric as well as physical sports and athletics. They, or their families, paid for this themselves, and the result was that the ephebate became a kind of upper-class educational club and 'finishing establishment', with admission controlled by the existing members, although it still remained an official institution of the state. At Alexandria in the Roman period boys became qualified to be ephebes at about fourteen.

98.4 vicinam Capreis insulam Apragopolim: the view of Shuckburgh, followed by *GG,* that this phrase means 'he used to call the neighbouring island Capri *Donothington*' involves (a) taking *Capreis* as a locative in apposition to an accusative, and (b) having to understand some place not mentioned in the text as that to which Capri is near. This forcing of the Latin arises from the mistaken idea that there are no islands off Capri. There is in fact a tiny islet near the south-east corner which would perfectly fit Suetonius' story about Masgabas, and allows us to preserve the plain meaning of the Latin: 'he used to call an island off Capri *Donothington*'.

κτίστου ...: 'I see the founder's tomb agleam with fire'.

Thrasyllus: a Greek astrologer (*mathematicus*) whom Tiberius had met during his years of exile and brought back with him from Rhodes (*Tib.* 14.4).

Ὁρᾷς ...: 'seest thou the torches honouring Masgabas?'

98.5 revocatum ex itinere Tiberium: according to Tacitus (*Ann.* 1.5.3) Tiberius had reached Illyricum and was summoned back by Livia, who may have suppressed the news of Augustus' death until her son was safely on the spot. There is no reason to believe Tacitus against Suetonius, especially as Tiberius' position was so strong that the motive Tacitus provides for Livia's devious behaviour, to ensure his succession, is quite implausible. It is possible that Suetonius is deliberately correcting the recently published work of Tacitus.

99.1 clausula: the formal closing lines of a play, often, as here, asking for applause. The lines themselves are very corrupt in the MS, and their authorship unknown.

Drusi filia aegra: Livia Julia or, Livilla, Livia's granddaughter, sister of Germanicus and Claudius, and wife of Tiberius' son Drusus

after being widowed at about sixteen by the death of Gaius Caesar in
A.D. 4.

100.4 Mausoleo: Augustus' Mausoleum was a stepped circular tumulus
87m. in diameter and originally 44m. high, faced with marble, planted
with cypresses, and topped by a statue of the emperor (Strabo 5.3.8).
Much of the earth and concrete core of the mound remains (and concerts
have occasionally been given there). Suetonius' date (28 B.C.) refers
to its completion: its conception must belong to about 32 B.C. at the
height of the propaganda battle with Antony. Antony in his will,
forcibly opened by Augustus in that year, expressed a wish to be buried
in Alexandria. Augustus' Mausoleum is to be seen as his counter-statement,
making clear his intention to remain a Roman in death as in life.
Furthermore, the form of the monument (which is almost certainly earlier
than any of the other famous circular tombs like that of Munatius Plancus
at Gaeta - see 7.2 n. - or of Caecilia Metella on the Appian Way) is
best explained, not as a historically uncomfortable reminiscence of the
tombs of Etruscan dynasts, which do indeed afford a kind of parallel,
but as a recreation of the tumuli in which the princes of Troy, from whom
the Iulii claimed descent, and the Greek heroes of the Homeric age were
supposed to be buried (Strabo 13.1.34; Virgil, *Aeneid* 3.22, 3.304 and
6.232); see Holloway 1966 and Kraft 1967b.

101.1 Virgines Vestales: it was not unusual for important private
documents to be deposited with the Vestals, e.g. the wills of Caesar
and Antony (*DJ* 83.1; Plutarch, *Antony* 58.3) and the 'treaty' of
Misenum of 39 B.C. (Appian, *Bellum Civile* 5.73).

101.2 heredes instituit primos: the 'first heirs' are the true ones.
The 'seconds' would only succeed if the 'firsts' either refused the
inheritance or (if they were minors) died before coming of age. Here
the 'seconds' are anyway the natural heirs of the 'firsts', but often it
was no more than a mark of friendship, or honour, to be so named; and
this is patently the case with the 'third heirs'.
quos et ferre nomen suum iussit: it was only Livia whose name was
changed (to Iulia Augusta) as a result of Augustus' will. Tiberius
had borne Augustus' name (i.e. Iulius Caesar) since his adoption in
A.D. 4, and he initially refused to assume the special and unique cognomen
Augustus.
Germanicum liberosque eius tres: the three sons of Germanicus were
Nero, Drusus, and Gaius, of whom the two former died as a result of
Sejanus' machinations before his fall in A.D. 31, while Gaius ('Caligula')
eventually became emperor.
**legavit populo Romano quadringenties, tribubus tricies quin-
quies:**   what is the difference between the 'Roman people' and 'the
tribes', given that every Roman citizen belonged to a tribe? The fact
that there were 35 tribes and the sum left to them was 3.5 million HS
must surely dispose of Shuckburgh's interpretation (followed by *GG*) of
the tribes as Augustus' own two tribes (Fabia and Scaptia, see 40.2).
Tacitus (*Ann.* 1.8.2) adds the two sums together, saying that Augustus
left 43.5 million HS to 'the people and plebs of Rome'. Thus *plebs*
in Tacitus appears to be equated with 'tribes' in Suetonius, and if
Tacitus' usage is that of Augustus (a dangerous assumption), *plebs* will
mean the *plebs frumentaria*, the free inhabitants of Rome who received

the corn dole (*RG* 15); we may therefore conclude that Augustus left 40 million HS to all Roman citizens, wherever they might be, and 3.5. million HS to the urban populace. This seems not unjust. But there were practically 5 million citizens in A.D. 14 (*RG* 8.4) and even if only one in four of these was an adult male eligible for the bequest each could have received only 32 HS or 8 *denarii* - which is absurd. If, on the other hand, by the 'Roman people' Suetonius means the *plebs frumentaria* (numbering *ca.* 200,000), each will have received 200 HS or 50 *denarii*, which is in line with the 300 HS per head left by Julius Caesar's will and the range of 240-400 HS for Augustus' own largesses in his lifetime (*RG* 15). The conclusion seems inescapable that Augustus left 40 million HS to the urban populace. What then of 'the tribes'? We know that they did have some kind of administrative structure and corporate identity, and were capable, for example, of erecting a gilded equestrian statue in honour of Antony's brother Lucius in 44 B.C. This presupposes financial resources, so perhaps we should understand that Augustus intended each tribe's central funds to receive 100,000 HS. This will have been the only part of the legacy which in any way directly benefited Roman citizens who were neither soldiers nor inhabitants of the capital.

praetorianis militibus ...: the scale of legacies to the three categories of soldiers is in proportion to their pay (see **49** n.A).

Iulias: see **65.**1 n.

101.4 indicem rerum a se gestarum: our knowledge of the *Res Gestae* comes chiefly from the copy cut on the walls of the temple of Rome and Augustus at Ancyra (*Monumentum Ancyranum*): its preamble states that the original was 'cut on two bronze pillars, which are at Rome'.

fiscis: not 'the privy purse' (*GG*), but the local treasuries of each province. The use of *fiscus* in the singular to denote monies under imperial management (and, in practice, never accounted for to the senate) is later (see Millar 1963). Augustus had published regular statements of the imperial accounts - a practice discontinued by Tiberius but reinstituted by Gaius (*Caligula* 16.1).

INDEX TO TEXT AND NOTES

All references are to sections of the Text (T) or to
the correspondingly numbered Notes (N).

The index is in three parts. Index 1 contains proper
names and subjects. Proper names which appear in the
Latin text are in capitals; those referring to the
notes alone, are in lower case. Subjects, e.g. *Aerarium*,
whether in text or notes, are in italics. If there
is a Text entry (T), the corresponding Note (N) has
not been listed but should always be consulted. Some
names which appear in their adjectival form in the
Latin have been entered in the index under the
appropriate nominal form. Not indexed are Roma, Italia,
Augustus (except as a *cognomen*), some persons mentioned
en passant in the notes, and people whose names are in
reality dates.

Index II lists the references in the notes to passages
of Dio Cassius, Tacitus, Velleius Paterculus, and
Suetonius' other imperial biographies.

Index III is intended to be a complete epigraphic
index to the notes, and it is here that Augustus'
Res Gestae is to be found.

I   INDEX OF NAMES AND SUBJECTS

A

II   INDEX OF PASSAGES CITED FROM
DIO, SUETONIUS, TACITUS, AND VELLEIUS

DIO CASSIUS

DIO CASSIUS	NOTE
55.9.1	56.2
9.4	27.5
10.7	43.1
10.12-16	65.1
10.17-	
10a.9	64.1
12.4-5	57.2
13.1	27.5,
	65.3
13.3	37D(i)
22.3	52
22.4	44.1
22.5	31.3
24.7	49A
25.5	49A
26.1-2	42.3
26.2	37B
26.3	41.2
26.4-5	30
27.1-3	40.2,
	55
27.2	19(v)
28.1	47A
29 f	21.1
31.4	37B
34.1	33
34.2	40.2,
	56.1
56.1.2	34.1
7.2	34 1
18-21	21.1
25.4	37D(ii)
25.7-8	43.3
27.5	29.4
28.1	27.5
28.2-3	35.3-4
30.4	28.3
41.5	53.2
57.14.8	37A(iv)
23.2	5.1
24	35.2
58.2.1	62(iv)

SUETONIUS

Divus Julius	NOTE
6	8.1
15	94.8
20.1	5.1
20.3	4.1
27.1	4.1
39.1-2	43.3

Divus Julius	NOTE
39.2	43.2
41.3	8.2
43.2	34
45.3	73
49	68
52	17.5
55.3-4	84-89
59	92.2
67.2	23.2,
	25.1
76.1	58.1
76.1-2	57.1
76.2-3	26,
	57.1
78.1	53.2.
	57.1
80.2	35.1-2
83.1	101.1
83.2	7.2,
	8.2,
	27.1
85	58.1

Tiberius	NOTE
4	62(iv)
6.3	27.4
7.2-3	63.1
8	24.1,
	32.1
9	21.1
9.3	27.5
14.4	98.4
37.1	32.1
73	5.1

Gaius	NOTE
7	7.1
16.1	101.4
42	57.1

Claudius	NOTE
4	45.1
26.1	19(iv)
33.2	7.1

Nero	NOTE
7.1	43.2

Domitian	NOTE
1.1	5.1
14.3	57.1
34	57.1

TACITUS

Annals	NOTE
1.5.3	98.5
7	37B
8.2	101.2
10.1	11
15.1	40.2
17.3	49.1
24	49.1
36.4	24.2
44.2-5	24.2
60-61	21.1
72.4	33, 51.1,
	55, 56.3
75.5	41.1
76.3	37A(iv)
77	45.4
78	49A
2.37.2	41.1
3.24.5	65.1
30.6	66.3
54	34.1
4.5	49A
21	56.3
34-35	35.2
37	52
39.5	63.2
40.8	63.2
6.11.3	49A
11.4-6	37C
44	56.1
11.25.3	2.1
12.23.3	31.4
13.23.3-4	32.2
29	36
15.20	34.1

VELLEIUS PATERCULUS

VELLEIUS PATERCULUS	NOTE
1.11	29.4
2.59.2	3.1
70.1	91.1
76.1	7.2
76.4	66.1

VELLEIUS PATERCULUS	NOTE
2.81.3	29.3, 72.1
83.1	7.2
83.2	70.1
86.3	43.2
87.3	4.2
88	19(i)
89.3-4	28.1-2
91.2	19(iv)
93.2	66.3
97.1	23.1
100.3-5	65.1
104.1	65.1
108.1	21.1
110 f.	21.1
111.1	25.2
113.1	49A
117-119	21.1
130.2	24.1

III INDEX OF COINS AND INSCRIPTIONS CITED

A *INSCRIPTIONS*

[Ehrenberg & Jones
  (continued)]

NO.	NOTE	NO.	NOTE
224	46	301	40.3-4
235	56.3	302	40.3-4
241	see ILS	307	47B
	847	311	33(vi),
274	49A		33.3,
276	49A		35.3-4
278	32.3,	312	33(iii)
	37A(i)	323	26, 27.5
281	37A(i)	366	66.3
282	28.1-2,	371	40.1
	46	379	29.3,
286	30.1		47B
287	37A(ii)		
295	37A(iv)		

Fontes Iuris Romani Anteiustiniani ed. S. Riccobono (= **FIRA**)

Vol I no 7	32.3
no 30	87.2
no 44	32.2

Inscriptiones Italiae (= **Inscr. It.**)

XIII. 1. 58 and	
134	8.2
502 ff.	26

Inscriptiones Latinae Liberae Rei Publicae ed. A. Degrassi
  (= ILLRP)

no. 407-410	58.1
409	2.1
1046	2.3

Inscriptiones Latinae Selectae, ed. H. Dessau (= **ILS**)

no. 47	3.1
84	30.1
96	58.1
98	37A(i)
104	46
112	see EJ[3] no.100A
139	see EJ[3] no. 68
140	see EJ[3] no. 69
154	see EJ[3] no. 101
842	43.4

[*Inscriptiones Latinae Selectae*
  (continued)]

NO.	NOTE	NO.	NOTE
847	49A	5026	19(vi)
877	37B	5050	31.3 and 4
886	see EJ^3 no. 187	5743	28.1-2, 46
887	37B	5923d	37A(iv)
907	37B	5924	37A(iv)
911	38.2	6123	see EJ^3 no. 323
915	37A(ii)	6755	58.1
932	37A(iii)	6774/5	see EJ^3 no. 111
1514	67.1	8783	4.1
2676	see EJ^3 no. 235	8963	4.1
2819	see EJ^3 no. 274	8995	see EJ^3 no. 21
2822	see EJ^3 no. 276	9007	46
3612	31.4	9483	37D(ii)
4966	32.1	9495	see EJ^3 no. 106

Journal of Roman Studies (= JRS)

Vol 66 (1976) p. 106   49B

Olympia

Vol 5, 53   49

B   COINS

The Coins of the Roman Empire in the British Museum, vol I
  (= BMC Aug)

NO.	NOTE
79 ff	37A(ii)
91	28.1-2
362 ff	29.3
397 ff	58.1